THE
ESSENTIAL
HEALTH
PLAYBOOK

A Holistic Method to Beat Fatigue, Boost Strength, & Heal Your Gut

For more information, email info@lazarusmethod.com

ISBN: 979-8-89109-853-4 - paperback
ISBN: 979-8-89109-854-1 - ebook
ISBN: 979-8-89109-855-8 - hardcover

THE ESSENTIAL HEALTH PLAYBOOK

A Holistic Method to Beat Fatigue, Boost Strength, & Heal Your Gut

Dr. Ryan Lazarus DC, MSc, CNS, IFMCP

Dedication

I dedicate this book to my family, my patients, and my mentors. I have had the honor of working with incredible patients who trusted me with their health, and we witnessed remarkable transformations together. I'm forever grateful for the personal mentors and spiritual teachers who offered valuable guidance and timeless wisdom.

Thank you to my parents for their loving guidance and patience throughout my early quest to forge my own unique path. A heartfelt thank you to my children, Cienna, and Easton, for patiently entertaining my endless ideas on our family adventures, long road trips and during our dinner chats.

Thank you to my wife, best friend, and soulmate, Natalia, for her constant support during our hikes, quick getaways, and early morning coffee conversations. This book reflects our shared journey, the invaluable contributions of many, and my love and sincere gratitude for all the amazing people in my life.

Unlock Your Exclusive Health Toolkit!

The "Essential Health Toolkit" is a collection of valuable resources meticulously crafted to enhance and support your experience with this book. It is the perfect companion to "The Essential Health Playbook," providing you with implementation strategies to use right away and start seeing results immediately.

Hear What Others Are Saying

"This book introduced so many original health concepts, and the Essential Health Toolkit tied it all together for me. I highly recommend it if you want the simple nutrition steps to get started." - Amelia

"Integrating the Essential Health Toolkit was huge for my health journey. The additional resources provided me with exactly what I needed to lean up and get fit." - Kevin

"These tools are amazing! Thank you so much for providing them." 🙏 - Cassie

Get Started Now:

Scan to Unlock Your Complimentary Essential Health Toolkit!

It's easy, quick, and the first step towards unlocking your health potential.

TABLE OF CONTENTS

CONTENTS

Foreword

In the middle of the Atlantic Ocean, 700 miles off the coast of West Africa, I watched as an emergency boat saved our two other teammates and sailed off into the horizon. They were on their way to the Verde Islands, the closest location to a hospital.

I was in the middle of what many believe to be the toughest race in the world, a 3,000-mile rowing race across the Atlantic Ocean from Africa to America, with hopes of not just winning this race against 25 other teams from around the world but breaking the then 13-year world record for the fastest team to ever make the crossing.

But now it all seemed impossible. Our focus and attention pivoted to the remaining 2,400 miles, and a single but brutal question remained: Could we actually complete the crossing, or were we merely postponing an inevitable rescue, whether it be in days, weeks, or even months?

Fifty-one treacherous days after our journey began, we finally crossed the finish line in Antigua, completely exhausted, depleted, and far from setting a world record. Despite this being a victory against overwhelming odds, genuine happiness eluded me. Amidst the unfolding celebrations at the harbor, surrounded by cheering crowds, I found myself simulating joy and excitement that I didn't truly feel. This lack of fulfillment cast a shadow of inexplicable shame over me, and I couldn't explain why.

I returned home to recuperate, regain the weight I had lost, and reintegrate into my everyday life. In this familiar setting, I shared tales of my adventure with friends and the broader community. Everyone wanted to know what it was like out there. Everyone asked the same questions. How hard was it? What were the nights like? Weren't you scared?

And through this redundancy, I found myself mindlessly giving the same surface-level answers to the same surface-level questions. But it wasn't these thoughtless questions that bothered me the most. What irritated me was the underlying sense of pity I heard in their voices. The more conversations I had, the more I came to realize that people saw my crossing as a failure. A failure that I endured. Their praise wasn't in the accomplishment of the crossing, it was in the surviving of a disaster.

One month after arriving home, I made the tough decision to make the crossing again the very next year. That meant that I had 9 months to build and train a new team and lead them across 3,000 miles of what I now knew, not suspected, would be the most grueling thing any mind and body could put itself through.

And it was this very week that I met Dr. Ryan Lazarus. We both live in the same small town in the Bay Area. We had seen each other around, exchanging those customary nods of recognition that fellow runners and gym-goers often share in passing. But one morning, he approached me at a coffee shop, ready to talk. He mentioned he was aware of my recent endeavor and my plans to take on the challenge once more. As we talked, I was struck by the refreshing and unfamiliar tone of our conversation. He didn't know me and only had a vague notion of what I had just completed, but he didn't pity me - he celebrated me.

He also asked new questions. Deep and relevant health questions. Questions that took me off autopilot and made me think. How many days did it take you to clear your seasickness? How many minutes of deep sleep were you getting per day? How did you rally from your darkest hours? What was your hydration strategy, and what was your calorie consumption? Why was this important to you?

Dr. Ryan proposed questions, concepts, and tactics to potentially enhance my strength and speed for a more successful second crossing. He ran labs for each team member and customized a performance plan for each person. He talked excitedly yet clearly about ways he believed I could improve recovery on the ocean, improve sleep, reduce seasickness, maintain strength, and how we could supplement our diets to counteract our poor nourishment.

He asked and suggested but never assumed he knew what I went through. He posed scenarios and possibilities but never made me feel stupid for not considering it for my first crossing. Through our entire conversation, I could tell he believed in it all. He believed in the combination of his expertise and my ability. For the first time, I saw the world record as not only possible but within reach. He gave me hope.

Maybe it was his demeanor, or maybe it was my desperation, but for the next 7 months, my team and I gave all of ourselves to Dr. Ryan and his program, and he did the same for himself.

He didn't tell us what to do, he taught us why we should do it. He didn't tell us what to eat, he outlined what was absolutely essential. He didn't tell us to meditate. He showed us the benefits of mental fitness and breathwork and how it improved our physiology.

He introduced all his health concepts as reasons, not rules. This allowed us to understand the benefits of these changes before deciding to commit to them. Soon it was December, and our team made its way to the start line halfway across the world. His work was done.

As we pushed off from the starting line, I felt fully prepared to finish what I had begun. Armed with the knowledge and tools provided by Dr. Ryan, I was truly ready to attack the race, not simply survive it. With his guidance fueling my confidence, I approached the race not just as a challenge to endure but as an opportunity to excel, reminding every one of us that with the right support, we can all surpass our own expectations.

And 35 days, 14 hours, and 3 minutes after pushing off that second time, our team came into English Harbor of Antigua, having broken the world record as the fastest four to ever row across the Atlantic Ocean.

Since that crossing, our adventure racing team has trekked unassisted across the Namib Desert in 2018 - the oldest desert in the world. We've rowed across the Pacific Ocean, breaking that world record in 30 days in 2021. We even put out an all-women team who rowed across the Pacific, breaking the all-women world record in 2022.

Within our relentless pursuit of world records and challenges, a profound revelation has emerged: the capabilities of the human body are not just remarkable; they are awe-inspiring, pushing the boundaries of what we believe possible.

And behind each team was Dr. Ryan Lazarus. Today he is a constant within every team that races. Athletes cycle in and out, but no matter what man or woman stands on the edge of the next great adventure, Dr. Ryan is right behind them. He is the man behind the athlete.

We are all on a personal journey, and that journey is there to define us. But the irony in the journey is that although they are personal, they are never completed alone. Whether it is rowing across an ocean, beating addiction, running a marathon, or losing that stubborn weight, we need not and cannot do it alone. Through his expertise, process, and mentorship, I was able to unlock the potential I never knew I had or even needed.

This book is an essential playbook for health, and the game plan provided in it will change your life. The action steps he recommends in this book are essential for health. His guidance was my vessel, and his health tools were my oars. I still had to take the strokes, but I can assure you that the content in this book is the key to unlocking the potential in you, and I'm excited about your journey. Because in the end it's not one 3,000-mile race, but 3,000 1-mile races, and that first race starts today.

Jason Caldwell
2-Time World Record Holder
Founder, Lat 35 Leadership

CHAPTER 1

RISING FROM PAIN TO POWER

Here's the real pandemic. Waking up each morning, not to the refreshing excitement of a new day but to a relentless feeling of fatigue. Your body, weighed down by extra pounds, moves sluggishly as you drag yourself out of bed. Throughout the day, your energy doesn't improve, and you often find yourself searching for quick energy fixes. It's as if you're trying to navigate through a dense fog, your mind and body never fully awakening.

Each task feels monumental, overshadowed by the disappointment of unfulfilled potential and a body that refuses to cooperate. Digestive issues turn eating into a source of frustration rather than nourishment and pleasure. Life seems to pass by in a blur, each day rolling into the next.

I know this experience all too well; it was once my reality. Fatigue, metabolic issues, brain fog, and digestive imbalances were my daily life.

If you feel like you're going through the motions and not reaching your potential, this book is written for you. If any of these health struggles resonate with you, then consider this playbook as a dedicated guide meant specifically for you. Allow me to elaborate.

I thought I was going to die.

In high school, athletics was my number one focus. Being a performer on the field fueled essentially every facet of my teenage existence. But sports weren't just my obsession. I thought they were the key to my entire future.

During my senior year, I was on top of the world. I had never played better, and I had the college recruitment to prove it. The one and only life I'd ever pictured for myself was humming along perfectly. Everything was perfect. I started to feel that maybe I was perfect. And to be honest, I think I needed to feel that way at the time.

Sometimes change is subtle. It can sneak up on you slowly and make its modifications so carefully that it can become impossible to detect. And if you're lucky, when the change is finally complete, you yourself are ready to face it. But sometimes, change puts down the paintbrush and picks up a jackhammer.

Tragedy

It was supposed to be a routine game, and I'd run this play hundreds of times. This one would be just like all the rest. Except it wasn't. To this day, I'm still not entirely sure what happened. Maybe I took my eye off my own trajectory to scout the field. Maybe I missed the spacing without realizing it. Maybe a higher power pushed me. All I know is that I crashed into the low wall of the indoor soccer field with enough force to crush my organs. A pain beyond words.

It was a freak accident. In a bizarre twist of fate, it wasn't the usual knee or shoulder injury; astonishingly, I had somehow managed to crush my pancreas. I'll spare you the horrific details, but I was rushed to the emergency room for surgery to save my life. I really don't remember much prior to the surgery. All I know is that I wasn't there. My body was lying there, being prepped for emergency surgery, but my mind was in another dimension.

What dimension my mind was in is subject to interpretation. Some call it an NDE (near-death experience), some describe it as seeing the light, and neuroscientists have defined it as "disturbed multisensory integration" that occurs during life-threatening events. Whatever you call it, it was a profound sudden peace and relief from pain that has caused a ripple effect in my life ever since.

The surgeon ended up removing the crushed region of my pancreas along with my entire spleen. I have an impressive scar from my chest to my belly button that I used to be self-conscious about. Now that scar represents so much and reminds me every day of my journey.

Most people don't realize just how important a pancreas is. I certainly had no idea. But, I received a crash course (pun intended). I always thought it was like the appendix—just some organ that was somewhere in my body but nothing too important. Well, it turns out that the pancreas is an essential internal organ. That's great news for the pancreas. For me? Not so much.

The pancreas is essential because it produces insulin, which regulates blood sugar and releases digestive enzymes that are required to digest food. You can survive with a partial, damaged one. The spleen plays a very important role in regard to red blood cells and the immune system. But you can live without one.

Partial pancreas and no spleen? Good luck, kid. I now had type 1 diabetes and exocrine pancreatic insufficiency. I could no longer control my blood sugar or successfully digest about half of what the average person eats on a weekly basis. That's not to mention the legion of downstream digestive disorders such as SIBO (small intestine bacterial overgrowth), pancreatitis, gastroparesis, and dysbiosis playing havoc with my mental and emotional selves as well.

Strategy

After my accident, I immediately changed everything about my life. I mastered the perfect diet, exercised for ninety minutes each day, prioritized sleep, took all my essential medications, and never missed any dose. I started meditating every single day and began therapy to deal with the emotional trauma. I even took a course at Johns Hopkins just to better understand what was really happening to me.

Thank God I don't need a pancreas to lie.

I didn't do any of that. What I did instead was get angry and play the victim role. And stay angry. But the worst part was that I focused the consequences of that anger on the absolute worst person—the person I was truly the most upset with. Myself.

I had no drunk driver to shake my fist at. There was no group of muggers or some unexpected natural disaster to absorb all of my rage. At the end of the day, this was a horrible accident. But it was also a mistake. *My* mistake. If I had just turned quicker, run some other direction, or paid a bit more attention, I would still be okay. I would still be that excited person I used to be.

But instead...I was sick. I was irreversibly, unchangeably, unstoppably sick. There were no reasonable procedures to fix me. And so, armed with very little information and sporting one extremely large chip on my shoulder, I left the hospital restored to some form of working order, eager to rejoin my life in progress. But it wasn't there anymore.

I wasn't the dynamic athlete at school or at home anymore. I was just a broken, furious, really sick kid who needed to be fed through an IV just to get enough strength for his dad to bathe him. I had no interest in adapting or changing. And honestly, sometimes it felt good to feel that bad. When you're curled up on your bathroom floor for hours, you have a real understanding of why this particular situation isn't exactly a delight.

After years of ignoring my problems and following the diet of a typical twenty-three-year-old, I was admitted to hospitals multiple times for digestive failure. But I didn't care. I refused to let this "thing" slow me down. It wasn't fair. No single mistake should cost this much. I was the one who'd been hurt. So why was I also the one being punished?

For years, I'd been seeing specialists and working with nurses and therapists. All of them were kind and sympathetic. They wanted to do what reasonable people do when they see a fellow human being in pain: give comfort. They wanted to help me feel better. They could see how far I'd fallen, and it broke their hearts as it did mine. Of course, they wanted to help fix what was broken. That's their job, right?

They meant well, but fixing a broken body with missing organs was not in their textbook protocols. They were able to write prescriptions for the essential medicines I now require, such as Humalog, Lantus, Glucagon, and Creon.

These essential medications helped me survive but didn't provide the essential medicine I needed.

I was offered Prozac, Zofran, naproxen, benzodiazepines, Ambien, Lomotil, Actos, and vaccines to manage the symptoms. I was told to go see a pain specialist, gastroenterologist, endocrinologist, psychologist, and immunologist. If that didn't work, I was to find another specialist that ended with -ist.

It was during this time there came a moment of clarity. A moment when I received something almost better than a new pancreas. I received the single greatest thing that any chronically or perpetually ill person can ever receive: the truth.

It was the doctor who shot a quick look at my chart, looked me dead in the eyes, and said, "Your body doesn't work correctly any longer, so you need to come to terms with it. If you continue like you have been, you are going to be dead in ten years. You need to make a decision. What would you like to do?"

Period. Full stop. He didn't even apologize or offer any sort of condolence. He just looked at me, waiting for a response as if he were a waiter asking if Pepsi would be all right instead. And that's when it clicked.

I'll never forget that conversation. Those words planted a terrible seed in my head. A seed that I wasn't going to have a normal life or be able to digest properly again. I was going to have to inject myself with insulin, I was going to have a device stuck to me for the rest of my life, and I was going to get sick all the time. I wasn't going to be "normal" or be able to do the things I wanted to do. I call it a seed, but others have called it a curse. Whatever you call it, it was a moment where I realized I needed to make a decision.

I didn't die the day of the accident, but a certain version of me did. And I think those self-destructive years were my way of mourning what I'd lost. But looking at that doctor as he awaited my reply, I realized something else.

No matter how much I liked the person I was before, that wasn't my reality anymore. And reality doesn't care very much about what's fair. It's not good or bad, right or wrong. It's just like this doctor. It tells it like it is and waits for us to make the next move. The greatest thing about being human is that as long as we are alive, we have the ability to make decisions. Our consciousness evens the playing field with reality. If we're still here, we still get to decide. Reality isn't just something that happens to us. It's something we get to participate in. One decision at a time.

All I had to do was make one vital decision: persist on the path of illness or seek a healthier route.

In that single life-changing moment of post-disaster clarity, I finally saw the path that had been lying open before me. I'd spent so much time staring at where I couldn't go anymore, I never stopped to think about where I could. And so, I smiled with more genuine joy and clarity than I'd felt in a long time. I finally understood the bigger picture and my calling.

I became obsessed with healing and optimal health. My healing journey became my career and my medicine. I've slowly crawled out of the deep, dark hole, and I'm staring into the light. I write to you not from a pedestal but from the trenches, still in the midst of my journey.

The crucial knowledge and wisdom I've gathered are not my personal pearls; they occurred, so they can be shared. I'm eager and honored to share them with you as part of our collective path toward health and vitality.

Advocacy

In an effort to help myself, I began a relentless mission to understand everything I could about how the body works. I attended Cal Poly in San Luis Obispo, California, and graduated with an undergraduate degree in pre-med/exercise science. I continued my education at Palmer West to become a holistic Doctor of Chiropractic. I established my own private practice, Lazarus Wellness in Napa, and helped heal thousands of patients. But I was still yearning for more knowledge.

I went back to graduate school and received a master's degree in human nutrition and then became a board-certified practitioner in functional medicine with the IFM (Institute for Functional Medicine). Needing more, I became a board-certified nutrition specialist and was recruited to become faculty at the University of Western States, where I trained graduate students about metabolism science and lectured to physicians from all over the world.

I have spent the last twenty years in private practice teaching patients what was not taught to me. I helped patients the way I wanted to be helped. I challenged the conventional approach and used a new functional framework for health.

Physician, Heal Thyself

It's often said that the darkest hours can lead to the most illuminating moments. In a path filled with challenges and heartaches, the journey to where I stand today has been anything but smooth. I navigated through a maze of illness, confusion, setbacks, and despair, often questioning the purpose and meaning behind the suffering. Yet, it was precisely this burden of hardship that molded my resilience, shaped my methods, and fueled my passion for helping others.

Tragedy, in its rawest form, has a mysterious way of laying bare the vulnerabilities and complexities of life. It cracks open the façade of normality and forces an examination of the underlying issues that might otherwise go unnoticed. When I was at my lowest, I was compelled to find strategies to not just survive, but to thrive. It was an urgent form of problem-solving, a way to salvage hope from what seemed like a relentless downward spiral.

This is where my strategy emerged. By dissecting my own experiences and the shortcomings in traditional healthcare approaches, I pieced together a more holistic view of well-being—considering not just physical symptoms but the emotional, mental, and even spiritual aspects.

Through trial and error, research into various healing paradigms, and relentless determination, I gradually crafted a system that worked for me. As I began to employ this tailored system with each of my patients, I was astounded by its replicable success across a diverse range of cases. This became the genesis of the Lazarus Method Program, an essential holistic playbook for health.

As my strategies proved successful, I felt a newfound sense of responsibility to share these insights, leading to my role as an advocate. Advocacy is more than merely speaking up; it's a commitment to imparting knowledge and transforming lives. I transitioned from a solitary traveler on a difficult path to a guide for serving others using a functional method.

I served thousands of patients, and over that time, I have witnessed what works and doesn't work for health. With humility and confidence, I present this playbook as a holistic method that has been beneficial for my patients, and it has the power to do the same for you.

Dysfunctional Medicine

I do want to be clear that emergency medicine saved my life. The skilled surgeon and the exceptional emergency medical team who attended to me were nothing short of remarkable. They stand as genuine heroes, conducting lifesaving procedures daily across the globe. In the field of acute trauma and emergency care, the United States ranks among the finest, boasting one of the most advanced emergency medical systems in the world. My gratitude for what they accomplished on my behalf is boundless, leaving an enduring mark of appreciation that I will carry with me always.

On the other hand, our conventional medical model is inherently flawed, functioning as a reactive system that relies on pharmaceutical or surgical interventions to alleviate symptoms. Despite the presence of many compassionate and brilliant medical doctors, they find themselves constrained by a model that is both outdated and dysfunctional.

Our current medical system is intertwined with financial motives, including the influence of pharmaceutical corporations, insurance companies dictating patient care, and medical associations that advocate pharmaceutical-centered approaches. The integrity of research within this model is further compromised by much of the funding originating from the very drug companies whose products are being studied. These days, there is a pill for every ill.

Have you ever made an appointment to see your primary care physician for nagging symptoms such as fatigue, pain, weight gain, digestive issues, persistent cough, high cholesterol, or maybe even acid reflux?

If so, I'm willing to bet you likely left with nothing but a prescription.

This frustrating approach is something I've encountered frequently. The same is true for most of my patients, and chances are, you've experienced it too.

Kelly's Turning Point

Let me introduce you to Kelly. On vacation in Hawaii, Kelly was excited about the pool life and the dazzling beaches but more so about the opportunity to relax and take her mind off her own struggles. But as she scrolled through vacation photos on her phone from the previous day, she was startled by the person she saw. It wasn't the Kelly she remembered. It wasn't the Kelly who had once been full of life, who had once brimmed with energy and optimism. The picture showed an exhausted woman overshadowed by frustration.

One photo shocked her to her core, taken by her husband as she'd been walking toward the hotel pool. She was watching her seven- and nine-year-old running, each one holding a pool toy, their faces beaming with youthful expectation. She had a large, striped pool bag slung over one shoulder, weighed down with sunscreens, towels, and snacks. In her other hand, she held a large double espresso iced coffee, her crutch to keep her fatigue at bay.

The surroundings were beautiful—palm trees, the pool's water sparkling under the Hawaiian sun, and people laughing at the pool bar. Yet, all this fun and beauty was completely absent as she closely examined her picture. It seemed that years of neglect had turned her physique into something she didn't recognize.

The once firm muscles on her arms and legs had surrendered to a soft layer of fat. The cellulite on her thighs, once only a mild annoyance, had multiplied. Her waist had expanded over her bikini bottoms. She lifted her glasses and zoomed in with dread. It brought her to tears. She felt a sadness so profound it turned into a physical ache.

Kelly had been so consumed with her daily responsibilities, with her family's needs that she had completely forgotten about herself. She knew to stay away from fast food and sodas and made some effort to go for walks when she had time. She'd learned to ignore the bloating after every meal, to suppress the crushing fatigue with endless cups of coffee. But this photo, this stark representation of her reality, was something she couldn't ignore any longer.

That moment was her turning point. She couldn't bear the thought of the person in that photo being her future. It planted a seed to finally make a decision to change her path. It wasn't about vanity, but about reclaiming her health, her energy, her life.

Everyone's journey is different, and the promise of progress and the courage to move forward varies from person to person. Corey, the life of the party, the joker, the sports enthusiast, is the perfect example.

Corey's Soccer Trophy

You can't forget Corey. He's unforgettable. He was a forty-one-year-old man with high spirits, characterized by his hearty laughter and engaging personality. His charm was infectious, and his wide grin could light up even the gloomiest of rooms. He was a people person, starting conversations with everyone in front of him. He maintained connections with all his friends from his high school and college days, sharing old memories over rounds of beers or watching a 49ers game on the big screen at the local sports bar. His love for the San Francisco Giants was legendary in his circle, and his sporty camaraderie earned him frequent invites to games and fun-filled business events.

Yet, beneath his ever-smiling exterior was the tough reality of the stress of a high-pressure career in finance. The few stolen moments of joy for him were his weekend golf trips with his buddies, where he could temporarily shed the weight of his responsibilities and relish the freedom on the greens.

Unfortunately, years of stress, irregular meals, quick fixes of fast food and drinks, along with little physical activity had taken a toll on Corey's health. The once fit and athletic Corey had gradually been replaced with an overweight figure that his friends jokingly referred to as the "Captain Dad Bod." He would laugh along, downplaying his discomfort with a dismissive wave of his hand and a joke.

As time wore on, he started noticing worrying signs. His favorite jeans were suddenly too tight around his waist, climbing stairs felt like climbing a mountain, and he often woke up feeling like he hadn't slept at all. Despite his doctor prescribing medications to manage his blood pressure, blood sugar, and sleep issues, Corey stubbornly resisted admitting to himself the severity of his health problems. The mirror became a painful reminder of the man he once was and the man he had become.

The moment of harsh reality came unexpectedly during one of his oldest kids' weekend soccer games. He was cheering from the sidelines when a ball went astray. He quickly sprang into action to retrieve it. As he ran after the ball, his breath grew shallow, his heart pounded fiercely against his rib cage, and beads of sweat trickled down his forehead. When he finally returned the ball to the field, he stood bent over, hands on knees, panting as if he had run a marathon. He could feel the eyes on him, their silent judgment loud in his ears.

His friends, his peers, and the people he shared jokes and drinks with were exchanging glances, some laughing behind their hands, others looking away awkwardly. Even his kids were making fun of him. That was the moment he realized how far he had allowed his health to slip. The whispers and laughter echoed in his mind that night as he tossed and turned in bed, wrestling with insomnia, and finally decided to make a change.

Have you ever felt confused, frustrated, or uncertain about your symptoms?

Have you ever felt like you need to make a decision about your health?

If you're like Kelly, Corey, and myself, you're definitely not alone. In fact, you're like millions of people who are at a crossroads in their health and interested in a holistic method. Enter functional medicine.

Functional Medicine

I often say emergency medicine saved my life, conventional medicine compromised it, and functional medicine restored it. Functional medicine is the new medical model being used around the globe to heal patients, prevent disease, and optimize performance. It healed me, and it will help you.

It's a personalized, science-based approach that empowers you to identify and address the underlying causes of your symptoms. Rather than focusing solely on treating the symptoms of a specific disease, functional medicine seeks to understand the root cause of health problems by considering all of the biological, psychological, and lifestyle factors that influence your health.

This often involves a detailed understanding of your unique story, physiology, blood chemistry, genetics, and lifestyle factors and leveraging that data to direct personalized treatment plans. By addressing the root cause rather than symptoms, functional medicine aims to restore balance and promote optimal functioning in the body.

Now, let's say you visited a functional medicine practitioner for those same nagging symptoms listed in the previous section, such as pain, fatigue, weight gain, or digestive issues. Instead of another prescription, you'd leave with the proper tests that would have identified the underlying imbalances that were causing each one of those symptoms. You'd be provided with a holistic method, nutraceutical medicine, personalized nutritional guidelines, fitness prescriptions, and preventive measures.

This is the new operating system for health around the globe. An increasing number of individuals are now recognizing the inadequacies of our existing health system and are in search of a modern functional approach. They're searching for an approach that offers a holistic strategy for pinpointing the root causes of symptoms and effectively reversing them.

This playbook will introduce you to this new operating system. It provides an extraordinary journey through the intricacies of human metabolism, the complexities of our physical body, and the profound depths of our minds. It's more than just a playbook; it's an adventure that offers a transformative experience and a portal to the potential that lies within.

Welcome to The Essential Health Playbook, the new paradigm of healing, health, and human potential.

CHAPTER 2

THE WINNING GAMEPLAN

In the swirling game of life, we're all playing for the same top trophies—health and happiness. From books to podcasts, retreats and seminars, and from Instagram handles to Netflix documentaries, there's a flood of formulas and cheat codes promising us a shot at the win. This quest is universal, and we're all searching for it whether we realize it or not.

So, what is the mysterious successful playbook everyone's searching for? We are all waiting eagerly, ready to learn, our hearts filled with anticipation for the secret play we've all been seeking. So, brace yourself for this revelation...

The winning gameplan is...*you.*

I know what you may be thinking. Oh great...here comes yet another health book, full of pep talks, preaching the gospel of self-love, spoon-feeding me on a diet of greens, yoga, and meditation. Before I know it, I'll be prancing through meadows, drunk on sheer joy.

Wrong. I'm not going to feed you any nonsense about how to cash in your golden ticket and live happily ever after. This isn't a fairy tale; it's real life, and there are many challenges we all face daily. What I promise you, though, is an innovative playbook with a winning game plan that will empower *you* to take control of your health.

The Wrong Playbook

Before I introduce the essential health playbook, it's important to reflect and question: what happened, and how did we arrive at this point? No, not just Corey and Kelly. To some degree, each of us, including you and me, is shaped by the cultural influences of the modern day. It's a long story that takes place over the last century, so I'll summarize it for you with some simple explanations.

Our current culture has witnessed an era of human devolution for the reasons stated below. A significant discrepancy now exists between our current way of living and the manner in which we were naturally intended to live. This discrepancy has resulted in a large population of people executing the incorrect game plan from the wrong playbook.

Characteristics of Human Devolution

Human Nourishment

Dilemma: Many have replaced nutrient-dense plants, meat, and fat with processed, artificial, sugar-filled junk. It is now inconvenient to eat healthy food and convenient to eat crap. Food is the most powerful medicine or slowest form of poison.

Solution: In the Nourish Chapter, you will develop your own logical and practical nutritional guidelines.

Human Movement

Dilemma: Many have replaced outdoor games, recreation, and exploring with fake indoor, virtual, digital environments. We evolved to move constantly, not sit in front of a screen and make up for it on a treadmill. Our body is the most priceless possession; our top priority is to take care of it.

Solution: In the Move Chapter, you will learn the Three Pillars of Movement, which include a diversity of fun activities, play, and recreation.

Human Rest

Dilemma: Many have sacrificed their most crucial recovery period and get the least amount of sleep possible to be able to maximize their overscheduled, busy days. Winding down and relaxing has often been replaced with prioritizing evening work schedules and late-night screen time.

Solution: In the Rest Chapter, you will learn how to make small tweaks to your daily routine for optimal sleep and recovery.

Human Connection

Dilemma: Many have replaced eye-to-eye connection in respectful, reciprocal conversations with online trolling, keyboard drama, and mobile scrolling. We were meant to spend time in nature, have moments of stillness, and connect with our family and community. What we have now is a failure to communicate and connect.

Solution: In the Connect Chapter, you will develop an effective framework to identify and reconnect with what is truly important in your life.

Human Experience

Dilemma: Many have replaced authenticity, meaning, and truth with appearance, pettiness, and social media fantasy. Learning new health concepts and having new experiences allows us to question the popular narrative and challenge conventional wisdom.

Solution: In the Learn Chapter, your new perspective will facilitate a flow state and expand your cognitive capabilities.

Human Challenges

Dilemma: Many have relied on technology and modern conveniences for an easy life and limit their challenges for fear of failure instead of challenging their limitations to grasp their potential.

Solution: In the Challenge Chapter, you will learn how to set micro and macro challenges for yourself, which facilitates daily motivation and inspiration. Get comfortable with being uncomfortable.

Human Spark

Dilemma: Many have prioritized a life full of materialistic things and completely neglected the spark within them. Instead of cultivating their soul's mission, many people work jobs they hate, buy things they don't need, and try to impress people they don't like.

Solution: In the Spark Chapter, you will identify the light inside you and cultivate it to become a raging fire.

Vertical Illness

Instead of updating the game plan and adjusting our playbook, our current healthcare system has focused on symptom management. This has led to a reactive approach to health, often neglecting the underlying causes of illness.

What do you think about when you hear the word illness? The typical perception of illness often involves a hospital setting where patients are "horizontally ill," confined to beds and grappling with acute conditions that demand immediate medical attention. This form of illness is palpable, often involving diagnostics, procedures, and acute interventions.

On the other hand, there exists a large group of "vertically ill" individuals—those who are well enough to go about their daily responsibilities but are burdened by a persistent, underlying sickness. These individuals do not require hospitalization and are going about their daily routine, but they frequently experience symptoms like brain fog, fatigue, weight issues, and digestive problems. While they may appear functional and even "healthy" on the surface, their quality of life is compromised.

The vertically ill navigate a silent struggle, often resorting to coping mechanisms rather than finding true resolutions for their health challenges. Thus, while the horizontally ill face acute, immediate health crises, the vertically ill deal with chronic, subtler forms of sickness that nonetheless have a profound impact on their health and overall happiness. I was vertically ill for years, and you might also feel as though you're vertically ill at times.

This state of vertical illness leads people to head to their primary care doctor for answers to issues such as fatigue, weight gain, gut issues, and depression. They're provided with the appropriate diagnosis that label these symptoms. Diagnoses are ways for healthcare practitioners to identify and categorize health conditions based on symptoms, medical history, and test results, enabling practitioners to develop effective treatment plans.

You're Not a Diagnosis

While diagnosing health conditions is a critical aspect of medical care, this process can sometimes lead to less productive outcomes, particularly when it results in excessive labeling or misinterpretation of symptoms. Labeling theory, which is supported by a considerable body of research and evidence, suggests that a single medical diagnosis can profoundly impact an individual's self-identity.

When a person receives a diagnosis for any condition, it may become a dominant identity in their life, leading them to see themselves primarily through the lens of their condition. In other words, people can literally become their symptom, diagnosis, condition, or even disease.

This theory also includes individuals who self-diagnose from descriptions on the internet. When individuals read about symptoms and conditions online, they may start identifying with these descriptions, leading them to self-diagnose. This innocent self-diagnosis can create a self-fulfilling prophecy where individuals start to exhibit behaviors and attitudes that align with the condition they believe they have. This can result in changes in behavior where the person might consciously or unconsciously act in ways that align with their diagnosis, effectively creating a self-fulfilling prophecy. This process of identifying with a diagnosis can even exacerbate symptoms of the condition itself. The diagnosis can become a central plot point in the individual's narrative identity.

For example, a person with chronic fatigue might attribute any instance of tiredness or low energy directly to their condition, overlooking other potential causes like poor nutrition, sedentary lifestyle, stress, or sleep issues. This tendency to attribute everyday symptoms to their condition further cements their identity as being defined by their diagnosis, affecting how they perceive their health.

The labeling phenomenon occurs often, and it occurred to me. I was told I was an insulin-dependent diabetic with digestive insufficiency and was going to struggle to manage my blood sugar and digestion for the rest of my life. This harmless label felt like a curse, and I subconsciously began to manifest it. I began to blame everyday symptoms on my disease, and this label began to define me and influence all my decisions.

Do you ever feel like you're vertically ill?

Have you ever placed a label on yourself?

If you do, you're not alone. Nagging symptoms and even health labels impaired the quality of life for Corey, Kelly, and millions of other people. This state of vertical illness emphasizes the need for a holistic method, addressing the root causes of Corey's and Kelly's and maybe even your symptoms.

Playbook For Success

Both Kelly and Corey recognized they were not thriving, and they were ready to take control of their health but didn't know where to get help. Kelly started searching on her phone and navigating through social media advertisements. She knew the mainstream health model couldn't help her and felt like she was wandering through a maze. The advice was contradictory and confusing, making her feel even more frustrated, stuck on a path that led nowhere.

She was unhappy, unhealthy, and confused. She wasn't interested in more prescriptions that she knew would only mask her symptoms and make her worse. I was quite sympathetic because I've been there as well and remember being confused and unsure of what to do.

Corey also made a decision that would alter the course of his life. He wanted to reclaim his health, not just for himself, but for his kids too. He wanted to be an active part of their lives, not a panting, tired sideline observer. And with that thought fueling his determination, he was ready to find a solution.

The internet was riddled with professionals promising quick-fix solutions and overnight transformations, but none resonated with him. They all seemed to offer the same regimen—strict diets, rigid exercise routines, and sacrifices he wasn't ready to make. He needed a realistic and practical method that could fit into his lifestyle.

Kelly's and Corey's health journeys are truly remarkable, and you'll be amazed at how their journeys unfold. They were so different, but they had one characteristic in common. *They were fed up with being tired, overweight, and unhealthy.* They were truly ready to get their lives back. They didn't need magic wands; they just needed a holistic playbook and a personalized game plan.

The method sketched out in the chapters that follow is meant to guide you step by step using your own game plan. It's a collection of medical facts, reality checks, captivating stories, mystical wisdom, and essential health elements to inspire and sustain a healthy change despite the tough obstacles you may encounter.

Consider The Lazarus Method as your personal playbook, strategically designed to guide you to correct your chronic symptoms. It's not the only game plan, but it offers a diverse array of choices and strategies, each leading toward your peak potential.

It's not a pre-ordained, inflexible game plan. I've tried fixed formulas, and they don't work. I propose a flexible formula that accommodates your unique personality and helps you find your spark and fuel its flames using proven strategies.

To benefit the most from this book, I strongly encourage you to pause, reflect, and consider which essential health element resonates most with you. If you're up for the challenge, assess yourself by giving yourself a grade for each element and note which recommendations could be most beneficial for your health journey.

Red or Blue?

That was the choice "Mr. Anderson," aka "Neo," had to make at the very beginning of *The Matrix*. A simple choice, really. Just two options: a red pill and a blue pill. One would return him to his bed safe and sound, the other would open his eyes. And although I may struggle to this day to remember which color does which, the weight of that moment has permanently tattooed the scene into my brain.

Because as tempting as the promise of truth, adventure, and enlightenment may have been, both Mr. Anderson and those in the audience knew it wasn't that simple. No matter what revelations or rewards this "reality" might be able to offer, this would be a one-way trip. Once his eyes were open, there would be no closing them again. You and I are about to take a journey together. Just like Morpheus in the movie, I'm about to offer you a choice.

The more I've learned about the human body and its optimal functioning over the last two decades of research, education, and practice, the more the gravity around me seemed to increase. What began as a journey to improve my own health evolved slowly into the sobering reality that only a minority of people are implementing the strategies and solutions I was learning so much about.

And the worst part is we've convinced ourselves it's normal.

This book is, in many ways, my attempt to correct that central misunderstanding. The misunderstanding that it is normal to be exhausted, overweight, bloated and burned out. These symptoms don't indicate a state of health; they are characteristics of someone who is merely surviving, not truly thriving. The upcoming chapters will reveal why this has occurred and how to correct it.

You can, if you feel so inclined, place this book back on the shelf and never give it another thought. Doing so may not do much for your health, but there's something to be said for waiting to learn until you're fully ready to implement. The last thing I want to do is to try to convince you to read the next ten chapters if you're not ready to be challenged. Ignorance really can be bliss sometimes. The book will still be here when you're ready (I hope).

However, if you're ready and feel prepared to absorb fascinating—but challenging—information, then I suggest you brace yourself accordingly. The concepts outlined in the upcoming chapters will provide a proven game plan to upgrade your health. It will show you how to elevate your energy, boost strength, fix your gut, and master the game of life.

Just like Neo, once you know what you're about to read, there won't be any going back. You are always one decision away from a totally different existence. Read that again and let that sink in. Choose wisely.

Are you going to take the red pill, use the reactive, conventional approach, take a pill for every ill, and just get by to survive?

or

Are you going to take the blue pill, use the Lazarus Method in the Essential Health Playbook, reach your full potential, and strive to thrive?

CHAPTER 3

THE LAZARUS METHOD

In life's strategic game, imagine reviewing your current personal playbook. Based on the average life expectancy of 77 years, if you're 50 years old, you've completed about 65% of your life's journey, whereas at 35, you've crossed the 45% mark. Each stage is a distinct chapter in the playbook of existence, offering unique challenges and triumphs as you navigate through the phases of your life.

This analogy serves as a reflective pause, an opportunity to consider whether you've previously opted for the metaphorical red pill or blue pill in your life's choices. It also allows you to strategize and anticipate the plays ahead, understanding where you stand in the timeline of your life. Whatever the percentages, whatever the numbers, you are at an exact spot on your life's timeline as you read this, and it's precisely where you should be.

All the countless choices, both significant and seemingly inconsequential, have guided you to this unique moment in time. And all the decisions you will make from here on out will shape your path, steering you toward the destinations you desire.

In the grand timeline of existence, our lives may seem like a fleeting moment, a mere speck in the continuum of time and space. Yet, the time period you and I inhabit, 2024 (at the time this book was published), is a unique and wondrous intersection between ancestral living and rapid innovation. It's a confluence where the echoes of ancient health wisdom meet the pulsing rhythm of modern medical technology, and it's one of the most unique aspects of our time.

Historic Holistic Paradigms

Historically, there have been many primitive and ancient medicine paradigms. These concepts have significantly influenced views on health, encouraging a shift from merely addressing symptoms to understanding the underlying psychological and emotional factors that contribute to health.

Energy Healing

From the shamanic practices of indigenous tribes to the chakra system that identifies seven energy centers to the meridians in Chinese medicine, pathways where the vital energy or "qi" flows. These methodologies have been foundational in achieving optimal health for millions of people since the beginning of time. They were born of a profound connection to nature, a deep understanding of the human body and soul. Each offers a unique approach to healing through the alignment and balance of internal energies.

Powerful Philosophies

Add the wisdom of ancient philosophies such as Stoicism and Taoism that have long provided a foundational framework for understanding the world and our place within it. Stoicism, originating from

Ancient Greece, focuses on the cultivation of virtue and wisdom, particularly in the face of life's challenges. Taoism emphasizes living in harmony with the natural order of the Tao, or "the Way."

Both philosophies promote a balanced approach to life, recognizing the interconnectedness of all things and the importance of aligning oneself with nature's rhythms. They offer not just intellectual insights but practical guidance, serving as both a moral compass and spiritual grounding for healing. In our current world, which is often charged with complexity, these timeless teachings continue to inspire a path toward simplicity, integrity, and inner peace.

Mystic Mindsets

Now add a series of plays of historic psychology with Carl Jung's and Stan Grof's emphasis on the non-ordinary states of consciousness and individuation, recognizing the interconnection between shared cultural experiences and personal growth. Similarly, Maslow's hierarchy of needs introduced a layered understanding of human well-being, identifying a progression of physical, emotional, and self-fulfillment needs.

Historically, these concepts have significantly influenced views on health, encouraging a shift from merely addressing symptoms to understanding the underlying psychological and emotional factors that contribute to health.

Modern Medicine

Fast-forward to today, and we find ourselves in an age where technology has reached unprecedented heights. Sophisticated instruments and studies can peer into the very fabric of our being, evaluating our bodies with a precision that was once unimaginable. A single lab panel or test can provide an immediate and comprehensive analysis of our current health status. Recent advancements in epigenetics and functional medicine are not just tools but gateways that open up new vistas of understanding and treatment.

Epigenetics: You Write Your Own Destiny

Epigenetics sounds like something from a long time ago in a galaxy far, far away, but it's actually a newly revitalized area of scientific research for health. You see, for generations— centuries even—biological science viewed our bodies' responses to their own genetic code as a fixed process. The consensus was that DNA is written in pen, not pencil—and what the DNA says goes. This was wrong.

Your genetic hardware was locked at conception, but the software interpreting it is not. This is incredibly hopeful news for you and all of humanity. It's a whisper of hope to anyone feeling repressed, rather than supported, by the DNA they were born with. No, you can't make yourself six-foot-nine and NBA-ready just through sheer discipline. But you absolutely can foster a digestive system that purrs so smoothly it would make Enzo Ferrari blush.

Methylation is a key epigenetic mechanism occurring every second of your life which involves adding methyl groups to DNA, influencing gene activity and regulation. Methylation is like having a playbook in sports; while the playbook (DNA) contains the strategies, methylation creates the specific game plan, deciding which plays to use in a game.

Epigenetics is the story of how your body has responded to the lifestyle you offer it. This includes what you consume, how you move, your sleep, your connections, and your mindset. It all matters. It all connects.

Each and every system that creates us has the potential to be improved by our own choices and every action. Bad decisions equal symptoms, sickness, and disease, and good decisions equal health, performance, and disease prevention. It's not the cards you're dealt, it's how you play those cards.

Everyone is aware of their chronological age. However, this figure doesn't always provide an accurate reflection of one's health status. This discrepancy has given rise to the concept of biological age, a more nuanced measure that assesses health and vitality. Biological age offers a better assessment of a person's functional health and aging. The introduction of epigenetic age measurements has provided a more effective tool for evaluating this.

Are you curious to find out your true biological age?

There are simple and reliable tests that can reveal your pace of aging based on epigenetic data analysis. They measure the methylation status of 900,000 points in your DNA to determine your biological age and health risk. This reveals how you're actually playing your cards and how to improve it.

The Perfect Health Fusion

However you may be playing your cards, there's one thing that is certain. The fusion of ancestral wisdom and modern medical technology creates a symbiotic relationship. This integration offers precision and rapidity in addressing health issues, achieving a level of efficiency that would have been unimaginable to ancient healers.

My method emerged decades ago from the synthesis of these ancient healing paradigms and the innovative opportunities of modern science. Drawing inspiration from ancient healing paradigms, I began to see beyond the symptoms of illness and recognize the individual as an integrated system with a profound interconnection between mind, body, and spirit. With this newfound insight, I devised a method that was applied to every patient, yielding remarkable outcomes.

Symptoms were alleviated, diseases were prevented, and individuals seemed to be on the brink of attaining unprecedented levels of transcendence and self-actualization. It was as though I had discovered a secret genius within myself. However, I soon confronted a sobering truth.

The scenario painted above was more an aspiration than a reality.

While I did witness success among many of my patients, there was a notable gap in my approach, ingredients that I had overlooked but were crucial to help them all. The missing ingredients were personalization, simplicity, and gamification.

A process, however comprehensive and refined it may be, needs to resonate with the individual it is intended for. As I explained in the previous chapter, the winning game plan for health lies within *you*.

I sat in the trenches with my patients day after day for years, loaded with healing ammo, and witnessed what was working and what wasn't working. What I gathered through this necessary learning experience was that you truly need an approach that is clear, uncomplicated, engaging, and enjoyable. This blend is not merely a combination; it is magical medicine, one that has the power to rejuvenate, heal, and inspire.

The Lazarus Method

The Lazarus Method offers an integrated, personalized approach to health. It stands apart in its all-encompassing framework that recognizes the unique health requirements of each individual, ensuring that no aspect—be it nutritional, physical, emotional, or physiological—is neglected.

Rather than merely serving as a health and performance optimization program, it embodies a holistic lifestyle philosophy. It empowers individuals to take definitive control over their own health journey, setting the stage for them to flourish into the best versions of themselves.

Evaluating patients through this unique lens enables the development of personalized treatment plans that target root causes instead of merely treating symptoms. This approach encourages a more holistic understanding of health, recognizing the complex interactions and dependencies within the body's systems.

THE LAZARUS METHOD SYSTEMS INCLUDE:

Digestion: This imbalance focuses on the gut and digestive system, examining how nutrients are assimilated into the body.	**Related Conditions and Symptoms:** Irritable bowel syndrome (IBS), celiac/colitis disease, food sensitivities, bloating, gas, diarrhea, constipation, heartburn, and abdominal pain.
Energy: This category examines cellular energy production and metabolic functions. It focuses on how effectively the body is utilizing energy.	**Related Conditions and Symptoms:** Chronic fatigue syndrome, metabolic syndrome, diabetes, weight gain, brain fog, mood swings, frequent hunger.
Immunity: This looks at how the body's immune system is functioning. An imbalance here can lead to conditions that involve heightened or weakened immune response.	**Related Conditions and Symptoms:** Autoimmune diseases, allergies, chronic inflammation, fatigue, frequent infections, allergic reactions, skin rashes, and joint pain.
Hormones: This focuses on the endocrine system, neurotransmitters, and other hormonal pathways that facilitate internal communication within the body.	**Related Conditions and Symptoms:** PMS, depression, fatigue, sleep issues, mood changes, brain fog, decreased libido.

THE LAZARUS METHOD SYSTEMS INCLUDE:

Detoxification: This concerns the body's detoxification processes and how well toxins and waste products are being eliminated.	**Related Conditions and Symptoms:** Liver disease, hormonal imbalances, heavy metal toxicity, persistent fatigue, hormonal fluctuations, headaches, bad breath, and body odor.
Structure: This considers the physical structure of the body, including muscles, bones, joints, and tissues.	**Related Conditions and Symptoms:** Osteoporosis, arthritis, musculoskeletal pain, joint pain, limited range of motion, weakness, muscle cramps.
Transport: This relates to the circulatory and lymph systems, examining how nutrients and oxygen are transported to cells and waste is removed.	**Related Conditions and Symptoms:** Cardiovascular diseases, lymphedema, shortness of breath, swelling in limbs, chest pain, varicose veins, cold hands and feet.

Have you ever had any of these symptoms?

Do you struggle with any of these conditions?

If you do, you're definitely not alone. These are common issues for patients. The Lazarus Method Program has evidence-based protocols that address each one of these imbalances using a holistic playbook that will help address them naturally. To make it easy for you, these imbalances are integrated into the essential health elements:

The Essential Health Elements

NOURISH *is your nutrition and hydration strategy.*

MOVE *is the diversity of fun activities, exercise, or recreation.*

REST *is your sleep quality and relaxation time.*

CONNECT *is your connection with nature, yourself, tribe, and community.*

LEARN *is expanding your mind and perspective.*

CHALLENGE *is your personal intentions, which facilitate inspiration and motivation.*

SPARK *is your purpose, your mission, your soul.*

What happens when you apply and prioritize these essential health elements?

Actually, something quite extraordinary will occur.

The magic unfolds when you direct your energy to each health component, not treating them as separate entities but as interconnected elements that fuel every aspect of your life. This unified approach leads you to boost energy, gain strength, lose weight, fix your digestion, upgrade your mental state, and a sense of inner confidence will begin to permeate your being.

The Essential Holistic Playbook

Imagine an old, worn-out playbook used in a crucial game. This playbook, filled with outdated strategies and moves, has been the team's guide for decades. However, as the game evolves, the players find themselves repeatedly outcoached, unable to score or defend effectively. The playbook, once a source of success, now leads to repeated failures and frustrations on the field. The team culture is toxic, morale is low, and you are losing.

This scenario mirrors the traditional approach in healthcare, where doctors rely on medications and outdated treatments. Like the outdated plays, these methods sometimes result in temporary relief or small victories, but often, they are insufficient to tackle the complex health challenges faced by patients.

Contrast this with the introduction of a revolutionary, updated holistic playbook. This new guide is not only about making smart, strategic plays on the field but also about understanding the game's dynamics and preemptively planning to prevent losses. It involves examining the entire field, understanding the opposing team's tactics, and training players with effective techniques and plays. The team culture is confident, morale is high, and you are winning.

This modern approach symbolizes the Lazarus Method. Instead of solely reacting to the symptoms (or the opponent's moves), it evolves into understanding the underlying causes (understanding the game) and offers a comprehensive strategy for health.

This essential holistic playbook represents a shift from short-term fixes to a complete, sustainable approach to health, like transforming a struggling team into champions through insightful, innovative strategies.

The ripple effect of this newfound equilibrium is truly incredible, extending into every aspect of your existence. It may carry over into your personal relationships, your professional life, and even your relationship with yourself, casting a positive influence that resonates well beyond the boundaries of health. It's not merely a method; it's a lifestyle transformation, a therapeutic alignment with oneself that paves the way for a fulfilled and balanced life.

~~Sick and Tired,~~ Excited and Energetic

Remember Kelly and Corey, who were so desperate for a change? Kelly was vertically ill, confused, experiencing gut problems, extreme fatigue, and a sense of despair. Corey was overweight, burned out, and lacking the strength and confidence he once had.

They were using an outdated playbook and were searching for a holistic health method to help them take control of their lives. They both needed help to uncover which health elements were lacking and needed a clear plan to improve them.

Just when Kelly felt lost, her close friend recommended that she check out the Lazarus Method. Her friends who faced similar challenges had success with this approach. Kelly didn't know that I had similar health issues, experiencing gut problems, extreme fatigue, and a sense of despair.

She read all about the method and was surprised at how straightforward it was. It was different than anything she'd ever heard about. The strategy and suggestions made perfect sense to her, and she recognized it was the solution she was looking for. The individual health elements revealed how and why she was feeling that way.

Sometimes, our symptoms are so overwhelming you don't know where or how to even start. She sobbed with joy and replied, "I can't believe you just captured my entire story, and there's actually a way to reverse it!" For the first time in years, she was confident that her life was going to change.

When Corey found the Lazarus Method website and reached out, our team directed him to some of the complimentary quizzes and resources to get a sense of the method. As a sports fan, he loved the concept and simplicity of the playbook, but he was hesitant to start because he was worried about his demanding schedule. However, when he realized the flexibility of the method, he was confident this approach would work for him, and he was super stoked to start.

The essential health elements revealed not only their imbalances but also their vulnerabilities. Their personalized playbook was strategically designed, providing clear and specific strategies to tackle their health issues effectively. The method used in their playbook is the very framework that I am about to introduce to you.

Your Essential Holistic Playbook

You may be familiar with the challenges of making healthy choices, addressing fatigue, metabolic issues, and gut problems. I've been there, I struggled with my health for decades. It's a journey many have walked, including others just like you.

Standing alongside numerous individuals, observing their universal struggles, has led to the development of a method that transforms the journey to health into a memorable, engaging adventure. This method is designed to be shared, aiming to make your path to health less of an uphill battle.

Throughout this journey, you'll discover a wealth of unique concepts, strategies, clever tips, secret hacks, and cheat codes. These elements are what make the Lazarus Method stand out. Together, let's explore each element in the next seven chapters, helping you gain a comprehensive understanding and empowering you on your path to health.

Choose Your Own Health Adventure

But before you turn the page, in the spirit of this book and your health, I want to present you with another choice. No, it's not another red or blue pill...this choice is your very own health adventure, empowering you to select the plays and call the shots.

Who doesn't want new adventures? We've evolved to seek out unfamiliar information and experiences. This book is an adventure, your opportunity to choose the path that speaks to you as you read it.

I didn't like to read as a child and had a difficult time getting into books, until I was introduced to the Choose Your Own Adventure series. I was able to choose the way I wanted the story to unfold. I was in control. If I selected the wrong trail, trusted the shady stranger, or selected the curious rusty door that ended my journey early, it was completely my choice.

To be honest, I would select these options knowing they'd lead me to an inevitable demise. I was curious what would happen when the journey ended. It was interesting but not rewarding. So, after a few deliberate wrong turns and bad decisions, I decided I was going to use my intuition and see where the adventure would lead me.

I remember reading for hours into the late night, under the covers, waiting to find out my ultimate fate. Every intersection, confusing conversation, and inevitable dilemma was an opportunity for me to choose my destiny. Ladies and gentlemen, that's the game of life.

Research has indicated that you make roughly 35,000 decisions daily. The sum of all your daily decisions reveals your ultimate health and happiness. You choose your own life, and now is the perfect time to start your health adventure.

The next seven chapters review each health element in detail. Listen to your intuition, follow your curiosity, and select which chapter calls you. Each health element is essential, and none should be neglected. Are you ready to start your health adventure?

HEALTH IS A SUM OF YOUR CHOICES
CHOOSE WISELY

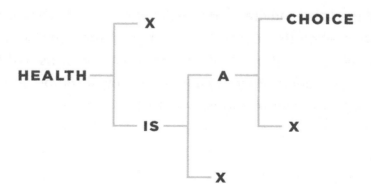

Echoing the philosophy of Friedrich Nietzsche, **"You have your way. I have my way. As for the right way, the correct way, and the only way, it does not exist."**

As you read on, you're reminded that each way is unique, and each choice is a personal journey. Will you select the way that feels inherently right for you, embracing its individuality and the lessons it holds? Or will you explore a way that diverges from your norm, understanding that in the realm of choices, there is no single correct path?

Every direction you consider is an opportunity to learn and improve your health in your own way.

"Choose Your Own Health Adventure"

If you're drawn to **Identify Your Inner Voice and True Purpose**, *let your intuition guide you to page 149 in the Spark Chapter.* This section offers a glimpse of self-discovery, offering methods for identifying your life scorecard and an introduction to your avatar. It also introduces spark igniters, tools designed to stimulate personal growth and self-awareness.

If you're looking to **Elevate your Motivation and Inspiration**, *I dare you to turn to page 287 in the Challenge Chapter.* This section explores unique concepts like the universe test and your quantum coach, providing innovative perspectives on personal growth. You'll also learn about setting realistic challenges that involve establishing floors and ceilings to define and achieve your goals effectively.

If your primary goal is to **Lose Weight and Optimize your Digestion**, *turn to page 55 in the Nourish Chapter.* The recommendations provided in this chapter will help you improve your body composition and jumpstart your metabolism. The concepts that will help you are the Nourish Target, Metabolic Flexibility, Intuitive Eating, EAT Protocol, and the 80/20 Eating Principle.

If you can't wait to **Enhance Brain Function and Mental Clarity**, *navigate to page 255 in the Learn Chapter.* This section is dedicated to helping you diminish brain fog, enter your personal flow zone, and offer insight into achieving a mental makeover. It introduces the principles of neuroplasticity, providing you with tools to sharpen your cognitive abilities and enhance mental acuity.

If you want to learn how to **Increase Strength and Improve your Metabolism**, *run to page 219 in the Move Chapter.* Here, you'll explore the effective 2nd Gear Strategy, delve into the three foundational pillars of movement, review compound and functional movements, and discover the importance of incorporating play into your routine.

For those seeking to **Boost Energy Levels and Overcome Fatigue**, *chill out and go to page 119 in the Rest Chapter.* This section will introduce you to the concept of your chronotype and circadian rhythm for optimal sleep. It provides detailed guidance on the RESTED Protocol, designed to optimize your rest and energy and two-minute timeouts, a strategy to rejuvenate and maintain sustained energy throughout your day.

If you want to prioritize **Being Present, Awareness, and Clarity**, *please focus on page 171 in the Connect Chapter.* This section is specifically tailored to enhance your mental fitness and sharpen your focus flashlight, a technique for cultivating mindfulness. You will also explore the happiness gap for true happiness and find your "thrive tribe" to achieve a heightened state of community and support.

CHAPTER 4

NOURISH

In the heart of our existence lies a simple, potent term: nourish. It's a word that goes beyond the act of merely feeding oneself; it's a promise of growth, strength, repair, conscious replenishment, and profound healing. This critical chapter unfolds the secrets of the Nourish element, breaking it down into three life-altering components: food, hydration, and supplements.

First, we'll review the function of food, your primary source of sustenance and repair. But it's more than just fuel for your body. Each compound you consume has the potential to either enhance your health or harm it. Choosing a balanced diet rich in nutrients is your first step toward proper nourishment. It's not about restrictive diets or fleeting food fads; it's about a wholesome, sustainable approach to eating that strengthens, repairs, and builds your body.

Next, we'll plunge into the essence of life itself: water. Adequate hydration plays a silent yet powerful role in our overall health. From boosting cognitive functions to maintaining body chemistry balance to ensuring optimal organ function, water is a non-negotiable aspect of nourishment. Here, I demystify the truth behind how much water we genuinely need and the best ways to hydrate yourself effectively.

Finally, let's explore the world of supplements, the necessary compounds that bridge the nutritional gap. Though they're not a replacement for a balanced diet, they necessitate valuable additions to ensure your body is not deficient in any crucial nutrients and has the ability to heal underlying imbalances. This section navigates through the often confusing and controversial world of supplements, providing you with the necessary guidance to make informed choices.

Nutrition Warning

This enlightening chapter is a full twelve-course meal. There's a lot of great information to digest, and you may be full by the fourth course. If that's the case, I recommend you take a break, choose another health adventure, and explore another essential element. You can always come back when you're hungry for more. Bon appetite!

Part I: Food

For as long as we have existed, humans have been obsessed with food.

Through generation upon generation of constant study and disciplined investigation, we have created a body of work analyzing what and how we should eat that is greater than any other subject in history. More than questions related to how we should live or what happens after we die, homo sapiens want to know one thing above all else: What the hell am I supposed to eat?

At first, we just wanted to find food in hunter/gatherer societies. Then, we began to control it through agriculture and experimentation. Today, you might be led to believe that our species has arrived at a complete understanding of "perfect" food.

Everywhere you look, there's someone telling you exactly which foods are "good" and which are "bad." They tell you often and with full confidence exactly how to eat to become healthy, wealthy, and immortal. But whether this was told to you through a pyramid in school or some expert on a Netflix special, I've got news for you: There is only one absolute law of food. Everything else is subjective, debatable, still under review, or unique to your own individual genetic potential.

I have spent my entire adult life trying to understand food.

Facing personal battles with nutrition as an insulin-dependent diabetic and living with the challenges of digestive failure because of the removal of digestive organs, I came to understand firsthand the confusion and frustration that can develop. These daily struggles shaped a journey that has inspired the nourish aspects of the Lazarus Method. It has not only transformed my relationship with food but can do the same for you. This approach is not just a theoretical concept; it is a distillation of lessons learned over years of struggle and triumph.

I also have advanced degrees that I earned by doing nothing but reading nutrition science journals. I have functional nutrition practices where I've helped patients understand optimal nutrition. But before that, I spent time and effort thinking I would be able to "master" something this primal and essential. But all that effort didn't bring me to a place of confident enlightenment. I did not find that single dietary philosophy powerful enough to save sick people like me and my patients.

But I did find something.

The one thing that I and other experts agree on—the one thing that humans in all of our searching have been able to conclude is definitively true— the one simple, absolute law of food. And here it is:

There is no absolute perfect diet.

I'm sorry to disappoint you if you picked up this book for the magic diet potion. There is no such thing. There are, however, Ten Universal Truths, which are fundamental parameters you should know.

- The food you eat can be a powerful form of medicine...or the slowest form of poison.
- Optimal nutrition should be personalized based on your unique blood chemistry, genetics, medical history, symptoms, fitness, and body comp goals.
- Processed food and fast food are as addicting as drugs.
- Fermented foods and a diversity of colors from real food protect and heal your body.
- Proper protein and fat repair your body, slow down digestion (which helps manage sugar levels), improve satiation, and are a cleaner fuel than simple carbohydrates.
- You have two brains, and the brain in your gut significantly affects the brain between your ears.
- Your gut needs time to rest. Help it rest by eating at specific intervals during the day.
- Food is bonding. Cooking at home is ideal for your family, budget, and your health.
- Focus on consistency and enjoy your food, not being a diet robot.
- Long-term nutritional success is built on a sustainable food plan, not a diet.

Practical Food Plan

There is no single "perfect diet" that applies to all of us. We have different physiologies, genetics, microbiomes, preferences, body types, philosophies, and lives. There's now an entire industry that provides nutritional solutions to your uniqueness.

There's a handful of clever programs and apps where you can enter your data and goals, and the AI can spit out what will work best for you. There are thousands of social media gurus who will provide you with the missing secret to your nutritional success for a perfect life. Many are grounded in the latest research, offer sensible approaches, and work very well. I've suggested to many of my patients to give them a try.

So, how's my message any different? I'm going to provide you with a game plan based on nutrition research, evolutionary logic, and thousands of hours working with patients as a nutrition expert. I know what works and what doesn't. Most importantly, I'm going to offer a game plan that allows for flexibility and enjoyment.

This approach promotes a realistic and enjoyable way of eating, blending the pleasure of food with essential nourishment to bolster, strengthen, and repair. By emphasizing wholesome foods, this method supports your body's metabolic functions, enhances energy levels, and helps mitigate life's inevitable stressors.

Healthy eating becomes an everyday pleasure rather than a daunting task, thus integrating seamlessly into any lifestyle. This method appreciates that we all are on defense intermittently and that a perfect diet isn't always feasible. Instead of pushing for dietary perfection and self-criticism, it nurtures a healthier relationship with food. It allows room for indulgence, removing guilt and stress associated with occasional slip-ups, and promotes flexibility when life circumstances limit our food choices.

If you want to discover *exactly how you should eat*, I recommend consulting with a certified nutrition expert and looking into your body chemistry, microbiome, genetic metabolic machinery, and body composition, all in conjunction with your goals. The Lazarus Method is a great coaching platform for personalization, and optimal nutrition can be applied even if you don't have the information for personalization.

~~Diet~~ Food Plan

Let's talk about the "D" word.

I hate the word "diet." Diet is just a four-letter word that starts with "die." Instead, I refer to my nutrition recommendations to patients as "food plans." And this seems to create a much more appropriate relationship with these new suggestions.

It may seem like a simple nuance, but nuance can change a lot. Diet equals tedious food rules and restrictions. A diet sounds like a temporary curse. I've witnessed this torment ruin people's daily existence. We're wired to eat, and setting narrow constraints to this necessity is not healthy.

A food plan is an opportunity to solve a problem through commitment and intelligence. The goal of a diet is to achieve a thinner waistline. The goal of a food plan is to maintain an enjoyable, consistent relationship with food as a lifestyle.

Many people, maybe even yourself, often approach their nutrition by wondering, *Will this diet work for me? What sort of predetermined diet is "working" right now, and should I try it?* Many rarely consider their unique biology and circumstances. We see the goal as creating some new body rather than learning to take proper care of the one we were already blessed with.

From vegan to carnivore and everything in between, there are popular diets that often promise substantial results for all people in all circumstances. And many of these diets do. You will absolutely improve your health if you upgrade your nutrition from the standard American diet to any of the aforementioned diets. They work for millions of people, but they're not personalized. There is no diet that will do what healthy eating does. Skip the diet. Just eat healthy. Let's discuss how.

Nourish Nuggets

In the vast sea of nutrition research that's come to light in the past decade, four game-changing topics have emerged, promising to radically transform our understanding of health. I've named these concepts the "Nourish Nuggets," and these areas of study delve deep into the molecular mechanisms of nutrition, providing unprecedented insights into how what we eat affects us right down to our genes and cells.

> *Microbiome* investigates the complex world of trillions of microbes living in our guts, showcasing the profound impact they have on our overall health.
>
> *Nutrigenomics* takes nutrition to the cellular level, exploring how different nutrients are specific information that influences how our genes work.

Metabolic Flexibility is a concept revolving around our body's ability to use and adapt to varying mealtimes and energy sources.

Macronutrients are the different percentages of carbs, proteins, and fats that you can alter to ensure proper satiety and body composition.

Each of these topics doesn't merely introduce new facts about nutrition. They entirely shift the paradigm, paving the way for a more personalized and effective approach to your health. You will have a basic understanding of them and be able to apply them to your routine.

Microbiome

If you've been following any of the latest health research, the term "microbiome" has been on your radar, given its recent surge in popularity within the wellness sphere. It has become a buzzword in the health space these days. And for a good reason.

A microbiome is the community of bacteria or microbes, often referred to as "flora" or "microbiota," that reside in your gut. The microbiome, particularly the gut microbiome, comprises a vast community of commensal, symbiotic, and pathogenic microorganisms, including bacteria, archaea, viruses, fungi, prions, protozoa, and algae. These organisms interact with each other as well as your immune system and your brain. Your microbiome develops at birth and continues to change throughout your life, influenced by your lifestyle and the food you feed it.

A balanced and diverse gut microbiome plays a multifaceted role in overall health. It aids in efficient digestion and nutrient absorption by breaking down complex foods. The microbiome is also intrinsically linked to immune function, as it helps regulate immune cells and contributes to enhanced disease resistance.

It supports mental well-being through the gut-brain axis, potentially reducing the risk of mood disorders like depression and anxiety. It also influences weight management by affecting fat storage, glucose balance, and hunger hormones. Lastly, a healthy gut microbiome may serve as a preventive measure against chronic diseases such as type 2 diabetes, heart disease, and certain cancers.

Your Unique Rainforest

Picture your microbiome as a vibrant, active Amazon rainforest within your own body. In this complex ecosystem of ten trillion microorganisms, each entity plays a crucial role, much like the diverse species coexisting harmoniously within the vastness of the rainforest. A rainforest contains thousands of plant species intermingling from the wet soil, creeks with millions of fungi, towering trees, ferns within the shadows, and countless bushes bearing flowers that add dashes of unexpected color and sustenance to this dynamic ecosystem. Just as the rainforest's health hinges on its biodiversity, so too does your body rely on the rich variety of these microscopic bacterial organisms.

It's crucial to realize that the real, natural foods our bodies need are vastly different from the unhealthy modern diet most people eat today. Just as deforestation or a massive wildfire can severely disrupt the delicate balance of a rainforest, an imbalance in your body's internal ecosystem will lead to symptoms like fatigue, digestive issues, weight gain, mood swings, and poor skin health. Nourishing your internal rainforest—your microbiome—through a balanced, diverse food plan is vital for your gut, immune system, and brain.

Nutrigenomics

Nutrigenomics is a cutting-edge field at the intersection of genomics and nutrition, exploring how dietary nutrients interact with your genes. Central to this field is the concept of diet-gene interactions, where the nutrients consumed can significantly influence gene expression and function.

This includes the impact of micronutrients—vitamins and minerals—on our body. These essential dietary elements are crucial for immune system support, energy production, bone health, cellular growth, and even mood and brain function. Additionally, phytonutrients, bioactive compounds found in plants, play a role in health through their antioxidant and anti-inflammatory properties.

Nutrigenomics also delves into individual genetic variations, known as SNPs (single nucleotide polymorphisms), which influence your unique metabolic responses to specific foods. These genetic differences can lead to varied nutrient requirements and diet-related symptoms such as fatigue and brain fog.

Food is Information

Here's a simple way for you to understand nutrigenomics. Food is information. The food you eat is a language. Your body either recognizes this information and understands this language, or it doesn't. Food can be medicine if you speak the correct language. Each food, like a word, carries its own nutritional meaning, and your meals are like sentences. Your body is confused if you don't communicate properly. Your body will nourish, strengthen, heal, and repair itself if you feed it the correct language.

However, just as miscommunication can lead to confusion and problems in a conversation, feeding your body a language it struggles to understand will result in a host of health complications. A diet heavily laden with fast food, additives and preservatives, toxic fats, seed oils, and sugars will distort the dialogue between your food and your body, causing a major misunderstanding.

This misunderstanding may manifest as gut dysbiosis, weight gain, systemic inflammation, persistent fatigue, cognitive difficulties such as brain fog, and a wide array of other health concerns. So, the language of food we choose to "speak" to our bodies, influenced by our genetic makeup, is fundamental to our health.

LAZARUS METHOD FOODPLAN	MODERN DIETS
Maximized Nutrients	Minimized Nutrients
Foods from Fertile Soil	Foods from Depleted Soil
Organ Meats & Muscle Meats	Few to No Organ Meats
Virgin, Cold Pressed Oils	Processed Vegetable Oils
Animals on Pasture	Animals in Confinement
Raw Dairy Products	Pastuerized Dairy Products
Bone Broths	MSG, Artificial Flavorings
Unrefined Sweeteners	Artificial Sweeteners
Fermented Vegetables	Frozen, GMO Veggies
Fermented Beverages	Modern Soft Drinks
Himalayan/Sea Salt	Refined Salt
Natural Vitamins Occurring in Foods	Synthetic Vitamins Added to Foods
Traditional Cooking	Microwave, Irradiation
Traditional Seeds, Open Pollination	Hybrid Seeds, GMO Seeds

Macronutrients

"Macros," short for macronutrients, is a term commonly used in the fields of fitness and nutrition, referring to the practice of monitoring and adjusting one's intake of proteins, carbohydrates, and fats with precision. This practice, known as "macro counting" or "macro hacking," is a dietary strategy designed to optimize body composition, energy levels, and overall health. Rather than focusing on calorie count alone, the emphasis is on the composition of those calories—how many of them come from each macronutrient group.

Macronutrients are the classes of foods that you consume in the largest quantities and provide the bulk of energy. These are proteins, carbohydrates, and fats. Proteins, composed of amino acids, are essential for the growth and repair of body tissues and play vital roles in enzymatic and hormonal processes. Carbohydrates, including sugars and starches, serve as the fastest energy source and include dietary fiber, which is important for maintaining your microbiome. Fats, or lipids, also a crucial energy source, are indispensable for hormone production, absorption of fat-soluble vitamins, and insulation of the body.

The exact ratios will depend on various factors such as an individual's age, gender, activity level, body composition, microbiome, blood chemistry, genetics, and specific health or fitness goals. For example, someone trying to gain muscle mass will require a higher proportion of proteins, while an endurance athlete might need a diet rich in carbohydrates.

By carefully manipulating these ratios, individuals can exert finer control over their body composition. Macro counting has gained popularity among athletes and fitness enthusiasts, but it is also used in clinical settings to help reverse metabolic and digestive symptoms. Let's review the different macronutrients.

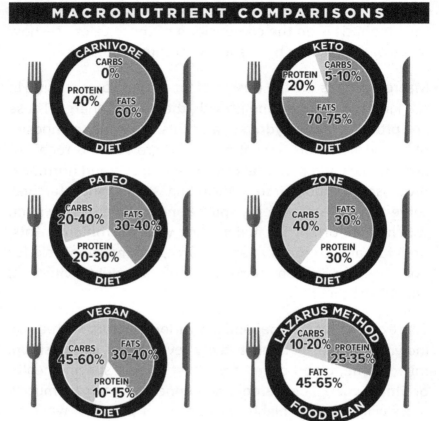

Protein Threshold

Protein is more than just a buzzword in the health and fitness industry. Protein metabolism is a complex biochemical process involving the synthesis, breakdown, and conversion of proteins and amino acids, regulated by the body's enzymatic activity and hormonal control. It can get technical, so I've broken it down to the essential information you should know.

Protein drives several vital functions, from building and repairing tissues to creating enzymes and hormones. It is your body's MVP macronutrient for muscle recovery and growth, especially after exercise. Protein is your trusty sidekick in your journey towards improving your body composition with muscle gain or fat loss.

Now, let's introduce MPS, which is short for massive protein shakes. Just kidding, it stands for muscle protein synthesis. This is the body's way of creating new muscle fibers from amino acids, involving the intracellular anabolic mechanism where polypeptide chains are constructed, facilitating muscle repair and growth.

Look at it this way: it's your body's construction crew that manufactures new proteins to repair and build muscle tissue. It's like sending in the builders to start new projects after a workout has demolished the old structures. The amount of protein required varies significantly from person to person, but there is a general range.

> **The range is to aim for 0.5 grams to 1 gram per pound of body weight.**
>
> *Example: A 150-pound individual should consume 75 to 150 grams in divided amounts daily.*

For each protein serving, you should clock in at least 0.2 grams per pound of lean body weight – this is your key to unlocking the leucine threshold for muscle growth. This equates to 25-40 grams per serving of high-quality protein. For my vegan and plant-based friends, you may need a specific strategy to meet your amino acid requirements.

However, there's a catch: if your intake falls short of the minimum per serving, you won't reach the MPS threshold.

It's like trying to save $100 by only depositing pennies – it'll take forever, right?

Think of hitting your MPS goal like a piggy bank. Frequent, consistent deposits are key; more servings (3 to 5) support lean and muscular body composition.

Protein Tips:

- Consuming all your protein in a single meal won't speed up your gains.

- If your serving doesn't hit the 0.2 gram per pound lean body weight mark, it won't trigger MPS, but it'll still count towards your daily total.

- Science is constantly evolving, but the consensus suggests MPS deposits should be spaced 3-5 hours apart due to the refractory period (which is a period that doesn't respond as effectively to additional protein.)

- It's important to know your kidney function and drink plenty of water if you exceed 1 gram per pound of body weight.

- Minimizing muscle loss for longevity is more important than the hypothetical risk of eating more protein. A balanced approach would be to build muscle for a period of time, then transition to maintenance with my Nourish Target, EAT Plan, and intuitive eating approach, ensuring sufficient protein but fewer MPS hits.

- To optimize muscle recovery and growth after a workout, consume 20 to 40 grams of protein, rich in leucine, within 30 minutes to 2 hours post-exercise.

Quality Protein

Amino acids, the building blocks of proteins, are categorized as essential, non-essential, and conditionally essential, with their importance varying based on dietary needs and health goals. There are methods that are used to evaluate and compare protein quality based on amino acid profiles and digestibility, such as biological value and net protein utilization.

These assessments are important to ensure a complete amino acid profile, especially in vegetarian or vegan diets. However, for most people with varied diets, meticulous comparison of protein sources is usually unnecessary. Analyzing protein contributes to more paralysis by analysis.

Clean Protein

My definition of "quality protein" emphasizes the source. I highly recommend being selective about where you get your meat, eggs, and dairy. Conventional meat and egg production often involves the use of antibiotics, growth hormones, pesticides, and chemical residues in food. These have been proven to cause antibiotic resistance, hormonal imbalances, immune dysfunction, and altered gut microbiome.

Most dairy is highly processed through pasteurization and homogenization, which may lead to reduced levels of certain beneficial nutrients and altered milk proteins, which could impact digestion and potentially increase the likelihood of allergic reactions.

Most people are not raising their own livestock and controlling the feed and environment, so it's important to purchase protein sources that are free of any antibiotics and obtained from organic sources. Organic protein sources are those that are grown or raised without the use of synthetic fertilizers, pesticides, or genetically modified organisms (GMOs).

For healthier and more sustainable meat and egg choices, opt for organic, local, free-range, or pasture-raised products, which can be sourced from farmers' markets, local butchers, health food stores, co-ops, or online sustainable meat suppliers. Consider using raw dairy from reliable sources. These sources typically offer products with higher animal welfare standards and less exposure to synthetic chemicals, though they may come at a higher cost.

The Skinny on Fats

Over the past 50 years, there has been an explosion of research on the significance of fats in health and disease. There is considerable evidence that links certain toxic fats with many of the most common forms of illness. However, realizing that not all fats are created equal is fundamental. Simply put, there are essential good fats and toxic bad fats, and you should know the difference.

There's a lot to know about all the fats using the different nomenclature of oils, fatty acids, and saturated, monounsaturated, or polyunsaturated omega classifications, but I have not included that information here. The technical nature of the topic tends to elicit a confused look from my patients when I try to explain it. To make it more palatable, we're going to keep things straightforward.

Dietary fats serve many functions in the body. Perhaps the most important is structural -- they are the major constituent of every cell membrane in the body. A cell's membrane, or outer lining, determines what goes into and out of that cell -- like a gatekeeper. As such, fats are critical in the proper functioning of the cell.

They're also an efficient energy source during periods of low carbohydrate intake or prolonged physical activity. This energy is released in a slower, more sustained manner compared to carbohydrates, making fats an essential fuel source for longer-lasting activities and for maintaining energy levels when food intake is not immediate or frequent.

Monounsaturated fats, such as those in olive oil, avocados, along with polyunsaturated fats like nuts and seeds, including omega-3 found in cold water fish and omega-6 fatty acids found in flaxseeds and walnuts, are essential for a balanced diet.

Additionally, incorporating medium-chain triglycerides (MCTs), primarily found in coconut oil and known for their rapid metabolism into energy, as well as healthy saturated fats from sources like grass-fed butter and ghee, is beneficial. These fats not only support cellular health by maintaining the integrity of cell membranes but also provide a stable source of energy, contribute to the absorption of fat-soluble vitamins, and play a role in the synthesis and regulation of important hormones.

Carbs

Carbohydrates are categorized into simple carbohydrates (like sugars) and complex carbohydrates (such as starches and fiber). Simple carbohydrates provide quick energy, while complex carbohydrates offer sustained energy and are often rich in fiber, aiding in digestion and providing a sense of fullness. Carbohydrates are found in a variety of foods, including fruits, vegetables, and grains.

Carbohydrates are not "essential," meaning that unlike essential fatty acids and essential amino acids, the body can survive without them. This is because the body can produce glucose – the primary fuel for most cells – through a process called gluconeogenesis, using sources other than carbohydrates such as proteins and fats.

They do offer several benefits, the most immediate of which is the provision of quick energy, making them a valuable fast fuel source, especially for the brain and for high-intensity physical activities. Additionally, they are high in prebiotic fibers, which are crucial for supporting a healthy gut microbiome.

For individuals engaged in regular, high-intensity physical activities, carbohydrates become particularly valuable as they are the primary source for replenishing glycogen – the stored form of glucose in muscles and the liver, essential for sustained energy during prolonged or intense exercise.

No Carb Left Behind

The typical consumption levels of carbohydrates in the standard American diet far exceed what most people need. Excessive intake of refined and processed carbohydrates is linked to a handful of health issues, including weight gain, metabolic disorders, brain fog, and an increased risk of type 2 and type 3 diabetes.

Yes, you read that correctly: Type 3 Diabetes. Although it's not an official diagnosis, Type 3 diabetes is a term that has been proposed in recent years to describe a condition where excessive sugar and insulin resistance occur in the brain, leading to symptoms similar to Alzheimer's disease.

Therefore, while carbohydrates play a role in quick energy provision and may support your microbiome, their intake should be balanced and aligned with individual energy needs, activity levels, and overall health goals, with a focus on whole, unprocessed sources for optimal metabolic and digestive health.

My top carb recommendations are nuts, seeds, low glycemic fruits and starches such as vegetables, root vegetables such as sweet potatoes, yams, and squash varieties, like butternut, acorn, and spaghetti squash. Tubers like Jerusalem artichokes and cassava also make my list for their unique health benefits, including prebiotic fiber, rounding out a selection of starches that contribute to a diverse microbiome. The Nourish Target identifies the carbs to emphasize and minimize. The Essential Health Toolkit also has a list of the top prebiotic carbs.

GFAF

Gluten Free as F*ck. There's countless jokes, puns, and memes regarding gluten these days. Over the last few decades, there's been a widespread movement towards gluten awareness that many people know of, yet quite a few still don't understand what exactly gluten is. Gluten is a group of prolamin and glutelin proteins, primarily gliadin and glutenin, found in certain grains like wheat, barley, and rye, and it gives dough its elasticity and bread its fluffy texture.

For many individuals, gluten can cause health issues, such as in those with celiac disease, where it triggers an immune response that damages the small intestine, or in cases of non-celiac gluten sensitivity, where it causes symptoms like bloating, gas, abdominal pain, brain fog, and attention issues.

Removing gluten from the diet for a period of time is a useful strategy to assess your reaction to it. This elimination helps to determine if symptoms improve or disappear without gluten, indicating a possible sensitivity. It is a valuable diagnostic tool, especially for those experiencing unexplained digestive issues, fatigue, or other symptoms that could be linked to dietary factors. There are also blood tests that can reveal your immune reaction to it. Over the last two decades in my practice, I have witnessed dramatic improvements in patients who have removed it.

Building Your Campfire

Imagine yourself seated next to a crackling campfire, your hands full of different types of wood to use on the fire. You begin with twigs and leaves, which are like high-glycemic carbohydrates like white bread, pasta, pastries, cereal, crackers, chips, juices, and sweet drinks. They ignite quickly, flaring up with a brief but intense blaze that mirrors the quick energy burst these foods offer. Each snap and pop of the burning twigs echoes the metabolic combustion within the mitochondria, your body's cellular engines of metabolism.

However, the flames subside rapidly, leaving behind a thick plume of smoke. This smoke is an analogy for reactive oxygen species (ROS), harmful byproducts of metabolic activity linked to cellular aging. Just as the smoke can cloud your campsite, these ROS can cause damage within your cells. When it comes to high-glycemic carbohydrates, the breakdown process can lead to an overproduction of smoke, contributing to cellular damage and aging.

Next, you select the bigger branches and large logs lying next to you, representing proteins and high-quality fats found in foods like olives, olive oil, fatty fish, avocados and avocado oil, coconut oil, nut butter, eggs, ghee, and butter. They take longer to ignite, but once ablaze, they burn slowly and steadily, mirroring the enduring energy these nutrients provide. As they burn, the snaps and pops lessen, and the smoke clears up, representing a cleaner metabolic fuel that puts less stress on your body's metabolic machinery and leads to less cellular stress.

As the fire burns into the night, the lesson becomes clear. Managing your inner metabolic fire and cellular stress is similar to tending this campfire—offsetting the quick, smoke-filled burst of the twigs with the slow, steady, cleaner burn of the logs. It's not just about keeping the fire going but also about how you fuel it and manage the "smoke," or ROS, promoting cellular strength and resilience.

Building the Perfect Campfire

"Macro hacking" has become a popular discussion point in the realm of nutrition recently. Essentially, this involves deliberately choosing to eat specific foods that align with a precise balance of macronutrients. For example:

- **Carnivore Diet:** This diet is based on animal products, so it's predominantly proteins and fats, with virtually no carbohydrates. Protein intake can range from 20 to 35 percent, fats from 65 to 80 percent, and carbs are virtually 0 percent.

- **Keto Diet:** The typical macronutrient ratio for a ketogenic diet is around 70 to 75 percent fats, 20 percent proteins, and 5 to 10 percent carbohydrates.

- **Paleo Diet:** The Paleo Diet does not have a set macronutrient breakdown and varies greatly depending on individual choices within the food groups. However, a common distribution might be around 30 to 40 percent fat, 20 to 30 percent protein, and 30 to 40 percent carbs, mostly from fruits and vegetables.

- **Zone Diet:** The Zone Diet is typically split into a 40/30/30 ratio. That means about 40 percent of your daily calories come from carbohydrates, 30 percent from proteins, and 30 percent from fats.

- **Vegan Diet:** Similar to Paleo, there's no set macronutrient breakdown for a vegan diet, as it depends on the individual's choice of plant-based foods. On average, it might be around 10 to 15 percent protein, 30 to 40 percent fat (mainly from nuts, seeds, and avocados), and 45 to 60 percent carbohydrates.

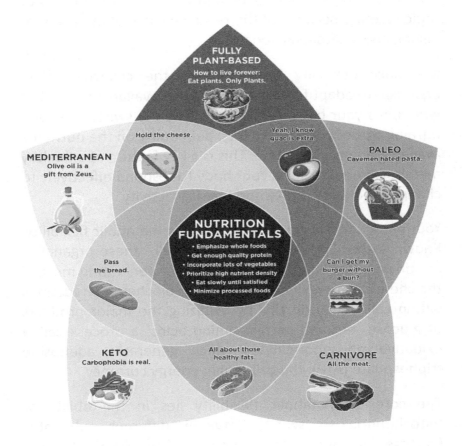

All of these diets, when followed for short durations, may be considered healthy, provided they prioritize nutrient-rich foods and exclude harmful ones. However, the most beneficial food plan is the one you can consistently adhere to.

Metabolic Flexibility

This concept has been a passion of mine for over a decade, and it was the focus of my master's thesis. I've been interviewed on the importance of it and have taught graduate students the underlying physiology behind it. It has become a hot topic recently because of the recent science of intermittent fasting and a ketogenic food plan.

Metabolic flexibility is defined as the capacity of an organism to adapt fuel oxidation to fuel availability. In other words, it's your body's ability to efficiently switch between burning carbohydrates and fats, depending on the nutrients available at any given time. This is a key feature of a healthy metabolism, as it allows your body to respond effectively to changes in dietary intake and physical activity.

Your mitochondria play a pivotal role in metabolic flexibility. Known as the "powerhouses of the cell," these organelles are tiny engines that are responsible for generating most of the chemical energy needed to power biochemical reactions within cells. They do this by oxidizing the major products of glucose, fat, and certain amino acids, a process called oxidative phosphorylation, which generates adenosine triphosphate (ATP), the cell's main energy currency.

The core of metabolic flexibility lies in the ability of mitochondria to switch between different substrates (glucose, fats, and certain amino acids) for ATP production, depending on their availability and the energy needs of the cell.

Metabolic flexibility allows your body the ability to switch between burning fat or sugar, thereby promoting sustained energy, better blood sugar control, reduced cravings, and improved fat burning. When your body is metabolically flexible, it can efficiently use the energy from the food you consume, store any excess energy for later use, and tap into fat stores when needed. If you're looking to burn fat and reduce fatigue, tapping into this primal process will kickstart your metabolic activity.

Your Hybrid Metabolism

Imagine your body as a hybrid car that can run on both gas and electricity. Your car has an intelligent system that knows when to switch between these two energy sources based on the driving conditions. When you're cruising at high speeds on the highway, your car uses gas because it provides quick and substantial power. But when you're driving around town with frequent stops and starts, your car seamlessly switches to electricity because it's more efficient and saves gas for when it's really needed.

What happens when your car's fuel management system malfunctions and it can't efficiently switch between gas and electricity? This would cause problems—your car might run out of gas faster on the highway or inefficiently use gas around town when it could be using electricity. Similarly, when our bodies lose metabolic flexibility, they may not use the right fuel at the right time, leading to problems like higher levels of blood sugar and fats and contributing to weight gain and other health issues.

When you're metabolically flexible (like the well-functioning hybrid car), your body can effortlessly switch between carbs and fats as fuel sources, depending on what's available. After a carbohydrate-rich meal like pasta, pancakes, or venti Starbucks Frappuccino, your body can efficiently use those carbs for energy and store the rest as glycogen in your muscles.

During periods of fasting or in the absence of carbs (like when following a keto diet), your body can tap into its stored fat or dietary fat for energy. This system prevents you from experiencing sharp highs and lows in your energy levels, thus reducing cravings and keeping you satisfied for longer.

So, just as the hybrid car doesn't need to be constantly refueled, a metabolically flexible body doesn't need to be constantly fed. It can maintain energy levels and keep hunger at bay by switching between different fuel sources, resulting in overall better metabolic health.

Measuring Metabolic Fitness

Imagine setting a goal to complete a one-mile uphill run in your neighborhood as fast as possible. Your first attempt will not be a full-mile sprint, and if it is, you'll be in a world of hurt. Instead, you'll probably maintain a moderate pace with intermittent stops to regain your breath. But with each successive run, gradually extending your distance and pace, you'll start to experience noticeable progress.

You can even monitor your progress by using a wearable device or a fitness app. Fitbit, Apple Watch, Oura ring, and Whoop measure your caloric stats, and you can track your time with the Strava app to record your time splits. This adds an element of competition and fulfillment as you witness measurable improvement.

Improving your metabolic flexibility is no different. Consistently making the proper macronutrient choices that favor metabolic flexibility allows you to cultivate an enhanced level of metabolic fitness. Your cellular powerhouse, the mitochondria, becomes more efficient at converting carbs and fats into energy, leading to an elevated resting metabolic rate. That's great news for you if you want to burn fat while you're sitting down reading this chapter.

There are now devices that can monitor your metabolic fitness just as you do with physical fitness. Glucose, the principal energy substrate in metabolism, can be continuously monitored using a device known as a continuous glucose monitor (CGM). There's another innovative tool that measures your body's metabolism by analyzing the carbon dioxide concentration in your breath. Essentially, it determines whether you are primarily burning carbohydrates or fats for energy. This process involves inhaling a fixed volume of air through the device, holding it for a brief period, and then exhaling.

Just as your Fitbit or Apple Watch provides valuable exercise metrics, these devices can provide invaluable insights into your metabolic status. This technology helps you understand how your diet, exercise, sleep, and stress levels are impacting your metabolic health, enabling you to make informed choices.

Have you ever faced an aggravating situation where, despite your relentless efforts in the gym or restricting calories, you find yourself unexpectedly gaining weight?

The information from these devices can profoundly influence your diet and exercise choices, allowing for tailored nutrition plans and optimized exercise routines. By adjusting your diet and physical activity based on whether you're burning carbs or fats, you can effectively manage your weight, enhance energy levels, and achieve specific health goals, ultimately leading to improved metabolic health.

As a type 1 diabetic, I have firsthand experience with these technologies, as I used it for twelve years to track my blood sugar levels. I was a participant in a CGM beta program and witnessed the vital data these devices provide. They're now accessible to everyone, and I highly recommend using one to evaluate your metabolic flexibility. I've incorporated these devices into our health programs and have observed significant positive outcomes among participants.

Driving Your Hybrid Vehicle

You can enhance metabolic flexibility with strategic eating patterns as well. Intermittent fasting is a popular topic these days—and for good reason. Intermittent fasting is a practice that involves alternating cycles of eating and fasting. It does not specify which foods to eat but rather when to eat.

Intermittent fasting aligns with our ancestral eating patterns and has physiological benefits for our bodies. Our hunter-gatherer ancestors did not have the luxury of regular meals; they ate when they found food, which could often involve extended periods of fasting. Our bodies have evolved to adapt to this pattern of eating and fasting.

Common methods include:

12/12 (Overnight Fast): The simplest form of intermittent fasting, where you fast for twelve hours overnight. It's a great starting point if you're new to this practice. Just make sure not to snack between dinner and breakfast.

16/8: This schedule requires you to eat all your daily calories within an eight-hour window. You don't need to restrict your calories but rather consciously feast to get sufficient nutrients. It's compatible with fat loss and muscle maintenance.

OMAD (One Meal a Day): As the name suggests, you eat only one meal per day with all your calories in it. However, it may cause unintentional calorie restriction and should be done carefully, especially by athletes and people with certain medical conditions like diabetes.

5:2: With this weekly fasting method, you eat between 0 and 25 percent of your normal caloric intake on two non-consecutive days per week. It helps with weight loss and may suit some athletes.

ADF (Alternate-Day Fasting): This is an aggressive intermittent fasting schedule where you consume 0 to 25 percent of your usual calories every other day. It's often used for therapeutic purposes but is not for everyone because of its demanding nature.

Autophagy

Fasting also initiates cellular repair processes, including autophagy, where cells clean and remove old and dysfunctional proteins that build up inside cells. It plays a crucial role in maintaining cellular homeostasis, responding to stress, and preventing diseases such as cancer, neurodegeneration, and infections. Dysregulation of autophagy has been implicated in a variety of diseases, making it a significant focus of biomedical research. In fact, the 2016 Nobel Prize in Physiology or Medicine was awarded to Yoshinori Ohsumi for his groundbreaking work on the mechanisms of autophagy.

Autophagy is like doing a full maintenance service on your hybrid car. The process of changing the oil is like getting rid of damaged cell parts, and the oil filter cleans out the impurities just like the lysosome breaks down the unwanted materials. Checking the tires and ensuring they're in good condition is like the cell's process of recycling components for reuse. Lastly, updating the car's software to improve its functions is akin to the cell using these recycled materials to create new, functional cell parts. All of these maintenance steps ensure your hybrid car (the cell) runs smoothly and efficiently.

~~Intermittent fasting~~ Intuitive Eating

The word fasting often rings alarm bells of deprivation and agony. I've found myself tiptoeing around the term these days, given the knee-jerk panic it can spark in my patients who haven't dabbled in it before. It's similar to words like "diet," "exercise," and "meditation." Despite being cornerstones of health and performance, these words often trigger mental images of restriction and torture. For this very reason, I've taken to calling it "intuitive eating"—it sounds more like an inviting brunch date with your body rather than a daunting food-free marathon!

The concept of "intuitive eating" refers to a flexible and adaptable approach to eating.

Intuitive eating stands out from other fasting types, as it is designed to be neither hard nor restrictive; it isn't about depriving yourself of food. Instead, it's about establishing basic communication with your body.

To enhance your intuition and effectively listen to the subtle signals from your body, I encourage you to develop your metabolic flexibility. I've found intuitive eating to be an excellent method to achieve this and have witnessed great results with patients who utilize a flexible eating schedule. Consider it metabolic yoga—we're expanding and reducing fasting and eating periods to attain metabolic adaptability over time.

The idea of adhering to rigid fasting schedules can be intimidating, especially if you are new to this practice. It's important to start with a basic structure for your daily eating routine. I recommend beginning with a 16:8 fasting-to-eating ratio. This means you confine your eating within an eight-hour window, for instance, between 10 am and 6 pm.

As you become more comfortable with this routine, you can progressively narrow down your eating window to six or four hours or even one meal per day. The essence of intuitive eating is to have a foundational structure but adjust it as necessary based on your body's signals or intuition. For instance, if you find yourself starving by 10 a.m., eat something! Conversely, if it's noon, traditionally lunchtime, but you're not hungry, simply wait until your body signals hunger before eating.

I've personally been using this approach and guiding patients through it for decades. Once you get the hang of it, the rewards are truly impressive. Not only does it contribute to physical health through metabolic flexibility, but it also nurtures a more in-depth understanding of your body's needs, promoting a profound and empowering connection with your body. It's about giving your body what it needs when it needs it, which is the true spirit of intuitive eating.

At the start of this chapter, I highlighted the universal question: "What the hell am I supposed eat?" Chances are, you might be pondering the same thing at this very moment. Enter the Lazarus Method food plan.

This food plan is based on emphasizing the foods that support a healthy microbiome, micronutrients, phytonutrients, and proper macronutrients for cellular health and metabolic flexibility. It's also about enjoying the pleasure of food, whether it's family traditions, experimenting with new recipes, eating at a party, or dining out with family or friends. This approach values food as energy, connection, information, and medicine.

Flexibility and sticking to realistic and practical parameters, not tight constraints, is the formula for success in the long term. The efficacy of this method is demonstrated by those who have embraced it, who report fat loss, increased energy, and improved digestion. Ultimately, this nutritional strategy aims to create not just a healthy diet but a fun, adaptable lifestyle that considers the food you consume, the quantity of your meals, and the timing of your eating.

Now that you understand the most crucial nutritional concepts, the food plan I'm about to share with you will naturally align with your new knowledge. Let me assure you one of the greatest aspects of this plan is its practicality and realism—it offers guidance rather than imposing restrictions. You'll soon discover that incorporating this method into your daily life is remarkably straightforward and seamlessly fits into your existing routine.

The foods to focus on support the most important nourishing components.

Boosting your Personal Rainforest: *Feeding your microbiome with probiotic and prebiotic foods.*

Downloading the Correct Information: *Emphasizing essential micronutrients and phytonutrients.*

Driving your Hybrid Vehicle: *Enhancing metabolic flexibility with strategic eating patterns.*

Building the Perfect Campfire: *Eating within a practical macronutrient range.*

Here's an easy way to remember this. Simply imagine hopping into your hybrid car, setting the GPS to download the exact directions to a local wilderness area, and, as soon as you arrive, gathering the appropriate wood to start the perfect campfire.

This simple story represents four decades of extensive and often complex nutritional science research. By recalling this narrative, you'll understand the logic behind choosing specific foods. You now have reasons to eat well rather than harsh rules. Once you put this technique into practice, you'll appreciate how tasty and simple it can be.

Nourish Target

Optimal nutrition isn't always black and white. There's a ton of grey areas. The Nourish Target is an important part of the nourish playbook designed to encourage a balanced and flexible approach to eating, particularly focusing on the consumption of healthy, nutrient-rich "green" foods. At its core, this concept visualizes food choices as a target or bullseye, with the most nutritious foods positioned at the center. The green foods have the proper macronutrients, micronutrients, and phytonutrients to aim for.

The magic of the Nourish Target lies in its recognition that perfection in food is unrealistic and unnecessary for most people. Instead of rigidly adhering to only the healthiest food options, this approach allows for flexibility and variety. It acknowledges that sometimes, one may not always hit the bullseye with every meal or snack and need to select yellow foods.

This imagery of the target is effective because it visually communicates the idea of aiming for the best nutritional choices while also permitting deviations without guilt or stress. It's a departure from strict dieting mentalities, promoting a more sustainable and psychologically healthy way of thinking about food.

NOURISH TARGET

(Please note that the target in the book doesn't include all foods.
For a printable version, please refer to the Essential Health Toolkit)

Plate Size Matters (Bigger Isn't Always Better)

We've all experienced it, and for some of us, it's a common occurrence. The tempting pull of delicious food often leads us to intentionally ignore our body's signals of fullness. This can happen when we're faced with an array of mouthwatering dishes at a barbecue, holiday event, or even during casual hangouts with friends where the food is simply irresistible. This is my personal challenge with food.

Most of my patients also have a difficult time modifying the amount they eat. I often have them improve when and what to eat first. Controlling how much you eat can be complicated because of a handful of biological, emotional, hormonal, and social factors.

Our bodies' top priority is survival, and that often pushes us to eat more. We're hardwired to eat. Stress can also lead us to use food as a coping mechanism to distract us from issues we're processing. Restaurants with large portion sizes and food-centric social events definitely contribute to overeating. A lack of mindful eating, often exacerbated by distractions during meals, makes us overlook our body's satiety signals, making it even more challenging to control how much we eat.

Satiety is the normal feeling of satisfaction during or after eating that suppresses the urge to eat. It's different from being full or "stuffed." Stuffed refers to a sensation of being overly full, often to the point of discomfort, after consuming a large quantity of food. It's a physical sensation where the stomach is stretched beyond its comfortable limit. This state is beyond simply being full, and it often includes feelings of bloating and fatigue.

The actual mechanism of satiety is quite interesting. The signals are based on different gut hormones that can be grouped into two primary types:

Those that spark hunger (orexigenic)

vs.

Those that stop hunger (anorexigenic)

Just like a traffic light regulates the flow of cars, these hormones regulate our need for food. Working together, these hormones guide our body's food intake like a traffic light system manages vehicle movement, maintaining a cycle of hunger (green light) and fullness (red light).

Ghrelin and neuropeptide Y (NPY) are like the green light in our traffic light system. They tell your body that it's time to eat. Ghrelin is like a dinner bell ringing; it tells your stomach to get ready for food and reaches its highest level right before you eat, but it drops once you start eating. It decreases when you sleep and increases when you're stressed. Protein can lower it the most. NPY is another hormone that encourages eating and conserves energy, which can cause weight gain if there's too much of it.

Leptin, GLP and cholecystokinin (CCK) act like red lights. Leptin is made by your body's fat cells and also your stomach during a meal. Its job is to tell your brain that you've had enough to eat. It reduces hunger and helps you feel satisfied. CCK, which is produced in response to eating fats and proteins, helps in digestion and also suppresses the hunger signal from ghrelin while boosting other fullness hormones.

These hormones are a team of traffic controllers managing your body's hunger and fullness, making sure your body's "cars" (energy and food intake) move in the right direction and at the right speed.

Have you heard about the new weight loss wonder drug? There's a recent surge in popularity for Semaglutide, a medication originally designed for Type 2 Diabetes management. Known as a GLP-1 agonist, this injectable treatment works by slowing the pace at which food exits the stomach. As a result of this slowed gastric emptying, food stays in the stomach longer, thereby extending the sensation of fullness post-meal.

It's essentially a drug that bypasses your body's normal traffic light system and keeps you sitting at a red light for hours or even days. People lose wight because they don't eat, or their caloric intake is so low because they experience constant or frequent nausea. After reading this chapter, you'll have the knowledge and tools to be able to decide for yourself if this approach is sustainable and healthy.

Traffic Light Failure

I touched on the point earlier that overeating is a complex issue influenced by various emotional elements. The psychological aspects of eating are an essential area of focus for nutritionists. Based on my experience with patients, I believe it's crucial for you to discern between physiological and psychological hunger.

Physiological hunger arises from your body's genuine need for nourishment, often signaled by physical cues like a growling stomach or low energy levels, especially after moving all day or skipping a meal or two. These cues override many other functions and tell you to find food now.

In contrast, psychological hunger is emotionally driven, manifesting in situations like stress, boredom, or emotional processing, and often leads to the consumption of high-reward snacky foods that may not satisfy true hunger or nutritional needs. In my experience, patients who recognize the difference between these two types of hunger can slowly improve their relationship with food, making it easier to make proper choices and prevent overeating.

However, there are several substances and factors that can disrupt the delicate balance of the hunger and fullness signals, just as a faulty traffic light can lead to traffic chaos. If you frequently overeat, you should be aware of these reasons. These include:

Processed foods: High in sugar and fat, these can trick the brain into ignoring the leptin signal, causing us to overeat.

Alcohol: It can stimulate ghrelin production, leading to increased hunger and potential overeating. It also tends to lower inhibitions, leading to poor food choices.

Artificial sweeteners: They can confuse the body's natural ability to manage calories based on tasting something sweet.

Lack of sleep: It can interfere with the body's leptin and ghrelin balance, leading to increased hunger and decreased feelings of fullness.

Stress: Chronic stress can trigger the release of hormones like cortisol, which can disrupt the balance of hunger and satiety hormones.

Fullness Formula

If you, similar to myself and numerous patients I work with, struggle with overeating, the following method might prove beneficial. The fullness formula is a simple approach that will help you understand and recognize your body's satiety signals. It's designed to help you find the perfect balance in your meals, where you feel comfortably satiated without feeling full.

Set an Intention:

Before eating, set a simple intention not to overeat. Simple mantras like "eat, pause, reflect," or "chew, savor, assess."

Use Smaller Portions:

Begin with smaller amounts of food on your plate. It's easier to add more if you're still hungry rather than dealing with overeating.

Eat Slowly and Mindfully:

Take your time with each bite, savoring the flavors and textures, to better recognize when you are approaching fullness.

Pause Mid-Meal:

Halfway through your meal, take a brief break to assess your hunger and fullness levels.

Avoid Distractions:

Eat without engaging in other activities, like watching TV or using your phone, to maintain focus on your eating experience and fullness cues.

Although these steps may sound silly, they actually work quite well. If you apply these steps consistently, you can recalibrate your traffic light failure, reset your hunger hormones, and take control of your eating. This will improve your energy levels, help you lose weight, and improve your digestion.

The 80/20 Nourish Principle

My 80/20 Nourish Principle advocates a balanced, flexible approach to healthy eating. Instead of striving for the often-unattainable goal of eating "perfectly" 100 percent of the time, the principle proposes that it's appropriate and productive to make optimal choices 80 percent of the time. That's the average you may aim for.

The Lazarus Method 80/20 Nourish Principle is an innovative, adaptable approach to eating that takes into account the ebbs and flows of motivation, health, and inevitable life circumstances. At its core, this principle is about maintaining a balance and ensuring consistency, acknowledging that your nutritional habits can flex depending on your current situation and mental state.

There will be periods when you're on the offense, propelled by high motivation to consume the power foods I outlined. During these times, you might fully embrace intuitive eating strategies and align completely with your macro targets. This high-energy phase could last a week, a month, or even longer, often fueled by a specific goal or challenge you or I have set.

Conversely, there are times when you'll find yourself on the defense. These periods may be characterized by stress, fatigue, burnout, or illness, and it's during these times that the aim is to meet your floor goals. In other words, you strive for the minimum standard of nutrition needed to maintain your health without the pressure to reach perfection. You can allow yourself to enjoy the pleasure of food without the guilt. The power of this approach lies in acknowledging these momentum shifts and using them to inform your approach to eating.

The ultimate objective of my 80/20 Nourish Principle is to establish a sensible and sustainable strategy. By setting a realistic range for your eating habits rather than a fixed formula, you can ensure consistent nutrition regardless of the circumstances. This approach allows for flexibility and forgiveness, supporting a healthy relationship with food that can be sustained over the long term.

80/20 RULE

WEEKLY: 80% NUTRIENT DENSE FOODS & 20% TREATS

Day						%
MON						100%
TUES						80%
WED						80%
THUR						100%
FRI						60%
SAT						60%
SUN						80%

What, When, and How Much

There are many different ways to integrate my recommendations and improve how you eat. It's one of the main reasons why people have had success over the years. Most people focus on modifying *what* they eat, often removing certain obvious bad foods, which usually only last a few weeks or months.

There's another approach that you may want to consider that allows you more flexibility if you've had difficulty maintaining consistency. It puts the power of modification in your hands. This simple process has been so effective over the years I wanted to create a way for my patients to remember it. So, after countless hours of brainstorming, focus groups, and, believe it or not, consulting with a team of linguistic scholars, I've arrived at a name for this process. My process is not just exciting but also breathtakingly original.

I've called this culinary masterpiece of a process the... EAT plan.

Simply select when you're eating, what you're eating, and/ or how much you're eating. If you know the patterns that make eating healthy a struggle, select what will be easiest for you to start. If you don't want to eat less, eat right. If you don't want to eat right, eat less. If you don't want to do either, start by eating at strategic times.

People thrive when they're in control and have some basic structure to their daily eating routines in terms of what they eat, how much they eat, or when they eat. So that's where I start. *You get to decide. Choose what works best for you.*

AMOUNT Modify How Much You Eat

NUTRITION GOALS

ALWAYS (100%) - APPLY 1

OFTEN (75%) - APPLY 2

SOMETIMES (25%) - APPLY 3

ESSENTIALS Modify What You Eat

TIMING Modify When You Eat

"Bored" Meetings and Buffets

Take Corey as a case in point. Before diving into the Nourish Target and EAT Plan, his eating habits were rather chaotic. "I basically eat when I'm bored, even if I'm not hungry," he confessed during one of our sessions. "Especially at our boring lunch or dinner meetings. That damn buffet is such a trap! I just eat it because it's there, and it looks good."

To introduce some structure, we settled on a unique strategy tailored for him. "How about we try this: you can eat what you want until you're 80 percent full, but only between 12 p.m. and 6 p.m.," I suggested.

He looked skeptical but intrigued. I said, "Is that an ideal plan? No, but it could be a start. Just try it and let me know how it goes."

We both knew it wasn't a perfect solution, but it was a starting point that worked for Corey. Within a couple of weeks, he'd not only adhered to this eating strategy and eating window but also started making other improvements in what he was eating. "I can't believe how much better my digestion feels," he reported enthusiastically.

Made confident by these quick wins, I coached him on how to apply the momentum he'd gained to other variables. He avoided all the red foods in the Nourish Target and was aiming for all green foods. As he continued to make strides, we decided to introduce him to my 80/20 Nourish Principle, which accounts for the natural ups and downs of life, including fluctuating motivation levels and varying health conditions.

"Think of it this way," I explained to Corey, "80 percent of the time, consume the foods I've outlined for you. The remaining 20 percent allows for flexibility—perhaps a dinner date, a family gathering, or those moments when you just need comfort food."

Corey's eyes lit up at the suggestion. "So, I can still have a ballpark hot dog at the game without guilt?"

"Exactly," I affirmed. "It's about balance and consistency, not deprivation. Your eating habits can adapt to your current life circumstances and emotional state. There are just basic parameters to keep in mind. This flexibility is what makes the food plan sustainable."

Incorporating the 80/20 Nourish Principle into his lifestyle was like unlocking a new level for Corey. He found it easier to maintain good eating habits. The principle meshed seamlessly with his other improvements, making the entire process feel realistic and well-rounded.

By recognizing the ebb and flow of life and the complexities of human behavior, the 80/20 Rule, Nourish Target and Intuitive Eating principles offered Corey a realistic and sustainable path to better nutrition. Corey didn't recognize at first that he was accumulating invaluable knowledge and building confidence, setting the stage for future modifications to the EAT Plan where he could aim for 90 to 100 percent compliance. Making drastic changes right away simply wasn't reasonable for him.

I've developed a real understanding of the pace that suits each individual best. I knew that immediate, drastic changes wouldn't be realistic for Corey. As expected, the tailored approach worked precisely as planned. The transformation he experienced was successful, but it's not what you may think happened. Stay tuned.

***

Part II: Hydration & Supplements

Food is fuel and energy. Water is a fundamental necessity for life, and yet its importance is frequently underestimated. Second only to oxygen in its necessity, it's an essential component for all living beings. Recognizing the significance of proper hydration is crucial for proper metabolism, energy, and digestion.

Approximately 50 to 75 percent of our bodies are water. This liquid asset supports a constellation of essential processes, from physical performance, cognitive function, and thermoregulation to nutrient transport and waste removal—even maintaining the structure of our cells.

But before you decide to drink a gallon of water a day as many experts recommend, understand this: Chugging water indiscriminately, no matter your age, lifestyle, or diet, is not the magical elixir for health and longevity we've been led to believe. More isn't always better. A delicate balance is required.

Yes, it wards off dehydration, but on the flip side, it may tip the scales toward overhydration—an undesirable bargain. Rather, the goal is to strike the perfect balance in your hydration, which I've named your "fluid equilibrium."

Fluid Equilibrium

So, how do you find and navigate your fluid equilibrium? By turning to a time-tested, primitive, built-in body mechanism: *thirst.* When parched, grab a drink. If not, forcing down more H2O than you actually need may not do you any favors.

So, what's the winning water bottle for achieving optimal hydration? Well, it isn't a one-size-fits-all scenario. Hydration needs can vary based on age, gender, weight, activity level, climate, and body comp goals. My recommendation for optimal hydration is to drink at least eight eight-ounce glasses of water a day, which equals about sixty-four ounces or approximately two liters. This is often referred to as the "eight-by-eight rule" and is easy to remember.

Electrolytes: The Salty Truth About Sodium

Water isn't the only player in the hydration game. Electrolytes, such as sodium, potassium, and magnesium, are essential for fluid balance and nerve and muscle function. These come in handy, especially during workouts or in hot weather, when sweat takes electrolytes along with it.

Sodium—the little mineral that could—is not only a vital part of our existence but often an underestimated one. For several reasons, many of us need more sodium than we might realize. Think of athletes glistening in a hot climate. Now, that's not just sweat but also up to seven grams of sodium dripping away daily. Athletes can actually experience a staggering ten-gram sodium loss during intense training sessions or matches.

Foods and Hydration

The foods you eat also play a pivotal role in managing your body's sodium equilibrium and hydration status. You see, what you munch on throughout the day can influence your sodium levels in one of two ways—it can either restrict your sodium intake or speed up its exodus from your body. Let's break it down.

If your food plan leans toward natural, whole foods, you're likely taking in less sodium compared to those feasting on processed goodies. That's because about 70 percent of a typical American's sodium intake comes from processed and pre-packaged foods, which aren't on the menu in a whole-food diet.

On the other hand, if you're on a low-carb or ketogenic diet, your insulin levels are kept low. This is important because insulin plays a role in helping your kidneys decide how much sodium to retain or release. Lower insulin levels tell your kidneys to show sodium the exit, which leads to a faster elimination.

Fasting, or what I often refer to as "intuitive eating," follows a similar playbook. During the fasting period, your insulin is kept low, which can ramp up sodium's departure, while at the same time, your sodium intake is naturally cut. So, whether you're a fan of fasting, a devotee of the paleo lifestyle, or a keto enthusiast, your food plan can have a significant impact on how your body manages its sodium balance.

I have my patients aim for a daily sodium intake of four to six grams.

What about salt's notorious reputation for wreaking havoc on the heart? Well, it's not quite as black and white as it's been painted. My four-to-six-gram target draws from research, which discovered that a daily intake of four to six grams of sodium hits the bull's eye for minimizing the risks of heart attack and stroke. But remember, this is just a launch pad.

If you're considering adhering to the aforementioned diets or lifestyle factors, you may need to add a bit more salt to your nourish routine. On the other hand, if your health condition necessitates a reduced sodium diet, consulting with a clinical nutritionist is advisable to determine the most suitable approach for your needs.

Pairing this salty wisdom with our previous discussion on hydration, we see how essential sodium is, not just for flavor but also for hydration harmony. So next time you reach for your water, remember it's not just about the H2O but also about keeping your electrolytes, especially sodium, in perfect balance.

Fluid Equilibrium Hacks

Struggling to hit these hydration and electrolyte goals? No sweat! There's a whole bunch of clever tricks out there to get your fluid intake up. So, let's explore some fun and easy ways to make sure you're getting the proper amount of H2O and electrolytes each day.

HYDRATION STRATEGY	DESCRIPTION
1. HYDRATE FIRST	Start your day with a glass of water. Even before your coffee. It's a simple way to jump-start your hydration.
2. SET A TIMER	Schedule your hydration breaks just like your meetings or workouts. A reminder every hour could greatly boost your water intake.
3. UPGRADED WATER	Boost your hydration with functional beverages like hydration powders, herbal teas, flavored waters, or bone broths. You can also add fresh fruit, cucumber, jalapeno, or salt to your water for a spicy and tasty twist.
4. WATER PAIRING	Integrate water into your daily activities. Drink a hydration beverage during your morning routine, water during your commute, or a Wellness Warrior hydration drink post-workout.
5. BOTTLE SERVICE	Get a water bottle that you really like. Treat it as a must-have accessory, and you'll be surprised how much more you'll drink.

***

Part III: Nutraceuticals and Supplements

Nutraceuticals, as intriguing as they sound, are quite simple. They're natural biological compounds, a necessary fusion of nature and science, offering more than just nutrition. They've got an effective little side hustle as cellular medicine and protectors against common symptoms such as fatigue, metabolism issues, and digestive disorders.

But isn't that just supplements? Well, yes and no. For many, the term "supplements" conjures up bodybuilding pills and protein powders, like those sold online or in shopping malls. Through my clinical nutrition training and master's program, where I researched hundreds of clinical studies, I gained insights into the real effectiveness of these nutritional components. Working with patients over the years has given me the opportunity to observe firsthand how effective nutraceuticals and supplements can be.

Here's the dose. Nutraceuticals and supplements are not just overenthusiastic multivitamins on a power trip. Oh no, they're precisely what their name suggests: supplementary additions to your food plan that act as underlying insurance policies.

The Three-Tiered Parachute

The world of supplements and nutraceuticals can be seen as a three-tiered parachute system. Each tier serves a unique purpose, and they all work together to create a comprehensive approach to achieving optimal health and performance.

Essentials

The first tier, known as the essentials, forms the foundation of health and performance. It's similar to the canopy of the parachute, the part that catches the air and slows your descent. Just as the parachute canopy provides you with essential protection during your jump, the essential supplements provide your body with the fundamental nutrients it needs for overall well-being.

These foundational supplements often include a broad spectrum of vitamins and minerals, along with omega fatty acids, probiotics, and Vitamin D3/K2. They serve as a cellular foundation, supporting a range of functions from energy production and immune function to maintaining the health of our skin and brain.

Support/Repair

The second tier is the support and repair stage. It addresses specific imbalances in your body's biochemistry, much like adjusting the steering lines on your parachute to guide your direction and keep you on course. This tier includes supplements that treat any specific deficiencies or excesses detected in your blood chemistry, and it helps address your specific health goals.

If you're dealing with chronic inflammation, for example, you might need a higher dose of turmeric or bromelain. If your gut is imbalanced, you may benefit from DGL, berberine, or L-glutamine. Or if your stress level has been high, you may need adaptogenic compounds like ashwagandha or rhodiola. This is where the beauty of functional medicine comes into play. The second tier is highly personalized and will vary greatly from person to person.

Prevention

Finally, the third tier is about prevention. It's like the reserve parachute you pack for emergencies, ready to deploy based on any potential challenges you might face due to family history or genetics. This tier includes supplements that are selected with a focus on preventing diseases to which you may be predisposed because of your genetic makeup or family medical history.

For example, if heart disease runs in your family, certain supplements, like coenzyme Q10 or magnesium, may be recommended as part of your prevention strategy. Likewise, if your genetic profile suggests a higher risk for age-related cognitive decline, certain nootropic supplements might be part of your third tier.

The essence of successfully traversing these tiers of health is deeply rooted in the personalized approach of functional medicine. Utilizing cutting-edge testing, we gain valuable insights into your body's specific needs across all three levels, leading to the creation of a tailored supplement regimen. This regimen acts like a personalized health parachute, meticulously crafted to guide you safely and effectively on your health journey.

TIER	STRATEGY	LAZARUS METHOD SUPPLEMENT STRATEGY
1	ESSENTIALS	The Foundations for Health & Performance
2	SUPPORT	Addresses Symptoms or Specific Goals
3	PREVENTION	Based on Family History and Genetics

Peptides

These powerful compounds motivate and energize people towards achieving their goals, overcoming challenges, or improving performance. Actually, those are pep talks, and interestingly, their impact is quite similar to the effects of peptides.

Peptides are short chains of amino acids that are linked together by peptide bonds. Amino acids are the building blocks of proteins, and peptides are essentially smaller versions of proteins, typically containing between two and fifty amino acids. They are found naturally in the body and play various vital roles in biological processes.

In the body, peptides function as signaling molecules, telling cells how to respond to different stimuli. They can act as hormones, neurotransmitters, and growth factors and have other functions as well. Their relatively small size and specific structure allow them to interact with target cells in precise ways, triggering specific biological responses.

Think of peptides as personal keys that fit into your unique locks (receptors) on cell surfaces. When the key fits the lock, it triggers a reaction inside the cell, like unlocking a door. This natural connection can be utilized for various therapeutic purposes, allowing you to unlock specific reactions within the body to heal and regenerate.

NAD

NAD stands for "Nutrition and Diet," squeezed into a tiny pill. Just pop one, and you'll instantly become unstoppable. Pop two, and you'll be bulletproof. Not true, but these little energy batteries have great potential if you're feeling fatigued.

NAD is actually Vitamin B3, which is a form of niacin called nicotinamide adenine dinucleotide, and it's a vital enzyme that's needed by all human cells to function. By age fifty, only half of NAD is left, which leads to reduced cellular function and unrepaired DNA damage. These cellular failures are the root causes of aging.

NAD boosters, such as NMN or NR, support cellular communication and energy production. Incorporating a NAD booster into your routine enhances NAD levels, aiding in the restoration of cells' youthful function. They have been demonstrated to support DNA health, support brain and heart function, and enhance energy levels. Many of my patients who have incorporated an NAD booster into their daily regimen reported noticeable improvements in energy, mental clarity, and mood within just a few weeks.

Personalized Nutraceutical Prescriptions

An effective game plan for personalized nutraceuticals should be straightforward and cover areas like hormone health, gastrointestinal imbalances, detox support, brain performance with nootropics, immune support, fitness formulas for recovery, stress, and sleep support.

Below are just a handful of well-studied nutraceutical compounds that I use with the participants in my program. I recommend using a clinical nutritionist or functional medicine practitioner who can carefully design each formula specifically for you based on the most recent nutrition science.

HEALTH CATEGORY	SUPPLEMENTS
ESSENTIALS	Multivitamin, Essential Fatty Acids, Probiotics, Vitamin D3/K2, Turmeric
FITNESS	Protein Powder, Hydration Support, Collagen Peptides, BCAA's, Beta-Alanine
METABOLISM	CoQ10, Alpha Lipoic Acid, Acetyl-L-Carnitine, Resveratrol, Irvingia Gabonensis, NMN/NR
DIGESTIVE	Enzymes, Berberine, L-Glutamine, Aloe Vera, DGL, Probiotics
COGNITIVE	Methylation Support, Alpha GPC, Uridine 5-Monophosphate, Phosphatidyl Serine
DETOX	N-Acetyl Cysteine, Liposomal Glutathione, Calcium D-Glucarate, Silymarin
IMMUNE	Greens Powder, Vitamin C, Zinc Chelate, Beta Glucans, Cordyceps, Shilajit, Peptides
STRESS	Ashwagandha, Rhodiola, Asian Ginseng, CBD, Cordyceps
SLEEP	L-Theanine, Myo-Inositol, Taurine, Magnesium

Summary – Final Food for Thought

You just received a master's degree in functional nutrition. I could have written an entire book on my approach to optimal nutrition. I also warned you at the beginning of the chapter that I was going to present a robust twelve-course meal of dense nutrition information in this chapter, so I "fully" expect your brain may be full and bloated. As you digest all this information, it's normal to feel overwhelmed. If these recommendations seem like a complex calculus equation, you're not alone.

The great news is the Nourish Target, EAT Plan, 80/20, and Intuitive Eating approach makes it simple to eat healthy. The strategy for hydration and supplements is designed for ease and practicality. With just a little practice, it will quickly become an effortless part of your routine which will result in incredible energy, mental clarity, and optimal digestion. And if you're still in doubt, eat clean food, not too much, only when you're hungry.

If you're interested in a personalized approach, I encourage you to work with a clinical nutritionist to assess your body chemistry and microbiome using functional lab panels to determine your precise macronutrient range and exact foods to emphasize. This will ensure a customized plan that aligns with your specific needs.

The "Essential Health Toolkit" includes a comprehensive list of the best foods to incorporate into your routine as well as detailed information on the top nutraceutical formulas for most symptoms, conditions, and health goals.

In the meantime, try the following game plan and start practicing now. You'll be surprised how easy it can be.

THE LAZARUS METHOD GAME PLAN

PLAY I: Your Simple EAT Plan

1. Begin by choosing and applying the aspect of the EAT Plan that you find the simplest to implement consistently.

2. Next, pick another element that you feel comfortable with and apply it for the following five days.

3. On the fifth day, integrate all aspects of the plan for a full day. At the end of this day, reflect and write down the state of your energy and how your gut feels.

Coach's Tip:

E - Use the *Nourish Target* green foods for the Essentials (What to eat)

A - Use the *Fullness Formula* steps for the Amount (How much to eat)

T - Use the *Intuitive Eating* strategy for the Timing (When to eat)

PLAY II: Hydrate Hustle

1. Integrate optimal water intake, salt, and electrolyte balance into your daily routine. Follow the principle of the "eight-by-eight strategy," which encourages the consumption of at least eight 8-ounce glasses of water a day (approximately 64 ounces or 2 liters).

2. Select three hydration strategies from the hydration chart and follow these three strategies every day for the initial three days.

3. Each week, add one additional hydration recommendation from the chart to your routine and build up to implementing all five recommended hydration strategies.

Coach's Tip:

Keep a log of the amount of water consumed each day for three days and write down the state of your energy and how your gut feels.

PLAY III: Nutraceutical Navigation

Review the nutraceutical/supplement charts and identify any health goals with the appropriate health categories. *For example, Gut Issues (Digestive), Weight Loss (Metabolic, Fitness) and Fatigue (Cognitive, Sleep).*

Create your own supplement game plan using the Nutraceutical Tier Chart. Write down your essentials, support formulas (based on your health goals or symptoms), and any potential prevention formulas.

Your Supplement Rx

Essential: _____

Support: _____

Prevent: _____

Coach's Tip:

Aim to limit the number of supplements to a range of two to six formulas.

Drawing from the Stoic wisdom of Epictetus, who advised, **"Focus on what you can control,"** your path now converges on a notable selection regarding your health.

Will you choose the direction that allows you to actively shape your health, making deliberate choices to take control of your health? Or will you opt for a path where outside circumstances play a larger role, testing your ability to respond and adapt?

This is a reminder that you have the power to focus on the aspects of your health and life that are within your sphere of control. Your health flows where your focus goes.

"Choose Your Own Health Adventure"

If you're drawn to **Identify Your Inner Voice and True Purpose**, *let your intuition guide you to page 149 in the Spark Chapter.* This section offers a glimpse of self-discovery, offering methods for identifying your life scorecard and an introduction to your avatar. It also introduces spark igniters, tools designed to stimulate personal growth and self-awareness.

If you're looking to **Elevate your Motivation and Inspiration**, *I dare you to turn to page 287 in the Challenge Chapter.* This section explores unique concepts like the universe test and your quantum coach, providing innovative perspectives on personal growth. You'll also learn about setting realistic challenges that involve establishing floors and ceilings to define and achieve your goals effectively.

If you can't wait to **Enhance Brain Function and Mental Clarity**, *navigate to page 255 in the Learn Chapter.* This section is dedicated to helping you diminish brain fog, enter your personal flow zone, and offer insight into achieving a mental makeover. It introduces the principles of neuroplasticity, providing you with tools to sharpen your cognitive abilities and enhance mental acuity.

If you want to learn how to **Increase Strength and Improve your Metabolism**, *run to page 219 in the Move Chapter.* Here, you'll explore the effective 2nd Gear Strategy, delve into the three foundational pillars of movement, review compound and functional movements, and discover the importance of incorporating play into your routine.

For those seeking to **Boost Energy Levels and Overcome Fatigue**, *chill out and to page 119 in the Rest Chapter.* This section will introduce you to the concept of your chronotype and circadian rhythm for optimal sleep. It provides detailed guidance on the RESTED Protocol, designed to optimize your rest and energy and two-minute timeouts, a strategy to rejuvenate and maintain sustained energy throughout your day.

If you want to prioritize **Being Present, Awareness, and Clarity**, *please focus on page 171 in the Connect Chapter.* This section is specifically tailored to enhance your mental fitness and sharpen your focus flashlight, a technique for cultivating mindfulness. You will also explore the happiness gap for true happiness and find your "thrive tribe" to achieve a heightened state of community and support.

CHAPTER 5

REST

In the fast-paced game of our modern life, sleep, often underestimated and overlooked, may stand as the foundation of health and performance. It's not merely a period of rest but an intricate biological process that repairs the mind and strengthens the body. In the pursuit of optimal health, sleep is not a luxury; it's a necessity that can dictate the course of your life.

Some fascinating new research has emerged, shedding light on the profound effects of the Rest element on various aspects of your health, including your metabolism, energy levels, brain function, gut health, hormones, and immunity. This neuroscience is important to know, but it can get complicated, so I've selected the most relevant concepts that you should know and practice applying.

During this chapter, you'll learn the concepts of circadian rhythms, sleep pressure, chronotypes, ultradian rhythms, and atelic activities. I will offer the most effective solutions using simple acronyms that will help you rest and recover immediately. These insights will provide a clearer perspective on how to prioritize rest, improve your sleep, and improve the other essential health elements in the Lazarus Method.

I'll Sleep on It

The most recent research and functional medicine guidelines have quantified the vital role of sleep in sustaining our overall health. For adults, the recommended range is seven to nine hours per night. Teenagers, who are navigating significant growth and developmental changes, should aim for eight to ten hours of rest, and school-aged children need nine to eleven hours to support their cognitive and physical development.

It's important to note that individual sleep needs might vary because of factors such as lifestyle, health conditions, activity levels, symptoms, and stress levels. It may be common knowledge, but aiming for eight quality hours of sleep is essential. By adhering to the sleep guidelines provided in this chapter, you can foster a foundation that promotes optimal performance, energy, and mental clarity.

Sleep Neurochemistry

Having lectured about sleep neurochemistry to patients and other physicians around the country over the years, I've come to realize it's a topic of interest for many people. Have you ever been curious about what signals to your brain and body that it's time to wind down and rest? Your nervous system's amazing autonomic mechanism is nothing short of spectacular. It dictates the natural rhythms within your body that you're not aware of every single day. Sleep is regulated by two mechanisms:

> **Circadian rhythm**, regulated by melatonin response to light and darkness, and is naturally twenty-four hours long on average.

> **Adenosine**, which rises consistently throughout the day and is depleted during sleep. This is a chemical that is responsible for sleep pressure.

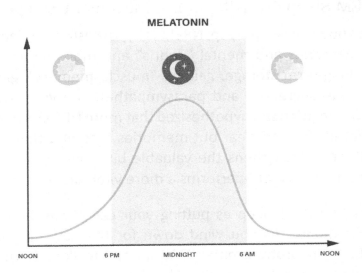

MELATONIN

NOON   6 PM   MIDNIGHT   6 AM   NOON

Circadian Rhythm

Your circadian rhythm is the natural internal process that regulates your sleep-wake cycle and other behavioral and physiological processes within a twenty-four-hour period. It's driven by an internal biological clock that aligns with the day-night cycle, affecting body temperature, hormone release, and other bodily functions. Essentially, the circadian rhythm is your body's way of synchronizing with the natural rhythm of the day, helping to determine when you feel awake or sleepy.

During the sleep phase of your circadian rhythm, a complex dance of neurochemistry unfolds, engaging various neurotransmitters, hormones, and brain structures to guide the body through different sleep stages. Sleep cycles last ninety minutes, starting with NREM, then transitioning to REM sleep. In total, there's an 80/20 NREM/REM sleep balance.

NREM Sleep (Non-Rapid Eye Movement Sleep)

Also known as deep sleep, NREM is hypothesized to clear out old memories and mental "debris" and move information into long-term storage, gaining "muscle memory," growth hormone secretion, and parasympathetic nervous system activation. It's been hypothesized that more NREM is needed earlier in sleep to clear out memories first, and then more REM later strengthens the valuable bits that are left. This suggests that NREM performs a more vital function.

Think of NREM sleep as putting your cell phone into "low power mode." As you wind down for the day, the brain's inhibitory neurotransmitter, GABA, and the sleep hormone, melatonin, act by reducing the brightness and silencing notifications. Your body goes into energy-saving mode, just as growth hormone promotes repair and restoration. The phone conserves its battery, focusing only on essential functions, and so does your body, allowing for physical rejuvenation.

REM Sleep (Rapid Eye Movement Sleep)

As sleep progresses through the night, a greater fraction of each cycle is spent in REM sleep. REM is responsible for forming new neural connections, problem-solving, dreaming, blunting emotional responses to painful memories, reading other people's facial emotions, strengthening the remaining valuable connections, and creatively forging novel connections. REM is when you dream, and your eyes move rapidly. This was initially thought to be a visual exploration of the dream field, but this turns out to be more related to the *creation* than passive observation of it.

It is similar to running essential updates on your cell phone. As GABA's effects diminish and acetylcholine becomes more prominent, the brain becomes more active, just like your phone downloading and installing new software while you sleep. Emotions and memories are processed, much as an update optimizes apps for better performance.

Meanwhile, cortisol prepares the body to awaken, just as your phone reconnects to all services and notifications, preparing to return to full functionality. At the end of the sleep cycle, you're ready to start the day refreshed, with everything updated and operating smoothly, just like your cell phone after a successful update.

Sleep Pressure

No, this isn't the pressure you put on yourself in the middle of the night when you can't sleep. Sleep pressure is a phenomenon that makes you sleepy and helps you to fall asleep. Sleep pressure builds up throughout the day and makes you sleepy in the evening. In a literal sense, sleep pressure basically "pressures" you to sleep.

At the heart of sleep pressure is the molecule adenosine, a byproduct produced in nearly all cellular activities within our bodies. From the flexing of your muscles to intricate nerve signaling, adenosine is consistently generated, silently accumulating in your brain as the day wears on.

As this accumulation of adenosine increases, it begins to exert its effects on your consciousness in two distinct ways. Firstly, it targets the centers of your brain responsible for alertness and wakefulness, attaching to nerve cells and reducing their activity. This has the effect of gradually diminishing your alertness, like a dimmer switch being slowly turned down.

Secondly, adenosine focuses its attention on the brain's sleep centers, stimulating nerve cells and amplifying the sensation of sleepiness. The more adenosine that is present, the stronger the pressure to sleep becomes, orchestrating a gentle but insistent call to rest.

As you sleep, adenosine is cleared from the brain, resetting this internal sleep-pressure gauge. When you awaken with reduced levels of adenosine, you find yourself refreshed, alert, and ready to begin a new cycle of activity and subsequent rest.

Adenosine Dam

Consider sleep pressure as the water inside a dam. As the day progresses, the dam's reservoir fills up with water, each drop representing the production of adenosine in your brain. With every task you perform and every thought you have, the water level rises, building up pressure against the dam's walls.

By the time evening arrives, the dam is brimming, the pressure is at its peak, and the urge to release this pressure corresponds with your need to sleep. When you finally succumb to sleep, it's like opening the dam's gates, allowing the water to flow out gradually, reducing the pressure, and making space for a new cycle of accumulation.

When you wake up, the reservoir is at its lowest, the pressure is released, and you feel revitalized and ready to begin a new day. Just as a dam regulates the flow of water, sleep pressure controls your rhythm of wakefulness and rest, ensuring that you respond to the natural buildup of your body's needs, and maintain the equilibrium that leads to optimal health.

Caffeine

Have you ever wondered why caffeine helps you wake up or delays sleepiness? It's really pretty simple. As adenosine is created in the brain and the pressure increases, it binds to adenosine receptors. This binding causes drowsiness by slowing down nerve cell activity.

To a nerve cell, caffeine looks like adenosine and binds to the adenosine receptor. However, caffeine doesn't slow down the cell's activity like adenosine would. As a result, the cell can no longer identify adenosine because caffeine is taking up all the receptors that adenosine would normally bind to. Instead of slowing down because of the adenosine's effect, the nerve cells speed up.

Caffeine basically acts like a false gate that looks the same but doesn't close. When caffeine binds to the adenosine receptors, it takes up the spots where adenosine would normally fit, leaving the flow of water uncontrolled. Instead of slowing down, the nerve cells speed up, creating increased alertness, much like how water would continue to flow if the actual gates in a dam were replaced by false ones that couldn't close.

Does this mean that caffeine is bad for you, and you should avoid it? Not at all. Caffeine can be used to your advantage when consumed appropriately. One of my favorite pleasures is an espresso or short Americano in the morning. It simply means that you should be aware of how it may affect your sleep patterns and be strategic when you consume it.

It is important to note that we each metabolize caffeine differently by a genetic variant called the CYP1A2. This variant affects the liver enzyme responsible for metabolizing caffeine and can influence an individual's ability to process caffeine, leading to differences in sensitivity and tolerance. This variant can be tested and provides insight into how you should consume caffeine.

You Snooze, You ~~Lose~~ Win

I'm sure you've experienced the invigorating sensation of waking up after a great night's sleep, feeling clear-headed, energetic, and prepared to conquer the day. On the other hand, a crappy night's sleep can leave you stuck in a fog, fatigued, and utterly exhausted.

These aren't just feelings; they are a reflection of profound disturbances within the body that affect everything from your metabolism to your mood. There are serious systemic imbalances that may occur when sleep is compromised. The difference between good and bad sleep is more than how you feel the next day; it's a matter of physiological harmony or hostility.

Sleep issues are directly tied to various physiological and psychological functions. From fatigue and weight gain to digestive function, brain activity, hormonal balance, and emotional well-being, the quality and duration of sleep play a decisive role.

I can attest to this personally as an insulin-dependent diabetic. I still occasionally struggle with low blood sugar levels in the middle of the night, which causes me to wake up and have a hard time returning to sleep. Not only am I exhausted the next day, but there's a drastic detriment to my brain, blood sugar, mood, digestion, and hormones.

Over the years, I've also witnessed countless patients whose terrible sleep habits resulted in all of these symptoms as well. Below are the five most common issues, shedding light on why prioritizing restorative sleep is essential.

- **Metabolism and Weight Loss:** Poor sleep can seriously impede metabolism and weight loss efforts. Insufficient rest leads to an imbalance in hormones like ghrelin and leptin, which regulate hunger and appetite. This imbalance often results in increased cravings for high-calorie, unhealthy foods, thereby affecting weight control. Additionally, a lack of sleep can reduce the body's ability to process sugars and fats effectively, slowing down metabolic functions. Together, these factors can significantly hinder weight loss and may even lead to weight gain.

- **Digestive Function:** Sleep plays a crucial role in supporting healthy digestive function. Inconsistent or inadequate sleep can disrupt the body's natural rhythms, impacting the secretion of digestive enzymes and the overall gut balance. This disruption may lead to issues such as bloating, indigestion, or constipation. Poor sleep has also been linked to inflammatory bowel conditions and can exacerbate existing digestive problems, emphasizing the importance of proper rest in maintaining digestive health.

- **Brain Function:** Cognitive performance, memory retention, and critical thinking are all heavily influenced by sleep quality. A lack of sleep can lead to impaired concentration, reduced problem-solving abilities, and a decrease in mental agility. The brain uses sleep to clear waste products and consolidate memories; without sufficient rest, these processes are hindered. Over time, chronic sleep deprivation may even increase the risk of neurological disorders, underlining the connection between sleep and optimal brain function.

- **Hormones:** Poor sleep affects the body's hormonal balance in several profound ways. Insufficient rest can disrupt the production of essential hormones such as cortisol, testosterone, insulin, and growth hormone. These imbalances can lead to a wide array of health issues ranging from increased stress levels and mood swings to compromised immune function and metabolic disorders. Hormones play an essential role in virtually every physiological process, and sleep is a key factor in maintaining this delicate equilibrium.

- **Mood:** Emotional well-being is closely tied to sleep quality. Lack of sleep often leads to irritability, anxiety, and a decreased ability to cope with stress. Chronic sleep deprivation has even been linked to the development or exacerbation of mood disorders such as depression. Adequate rest helps to regulate neurotransmitters and hormones that affect mood, promoting a more balanced emotional state. Prioritizing sleep is not only vital for physical health but is also instrumental in maintaining mental and emotional stability.

Chronotype

Are you an early bird or night owl? Most people know what they prefer but many people aren't aware of their chronotype. Chronotype refers to your unique natural sleep pattern, or circadian rhythm, which affects your preferred timing of sleep, wakefulness, and other daily activities. It is the manifestation of your internal biological clock, which regulates the timing of various physiological processes, such as body temperature, hormone release, and alertness levels, throughout the twenty-four-hour day.

There are three primary chronotypes:

1. **Morning type** (also known as "larks"): These individuals tend to wake up early, feel most alert and productive in the morning, and prefer to go to bed early. They often experience a decrease in energy levels and alertness in the late afternoon and evening.

2. **Evening type** (also known as "owls"): These individuals prefer to stay up late and wake up later in the day. They usually feel more alert and productive in the late afternoon and evening and may have difficulty falling asleep at an earlier bedtime.

3. **Intermediate type:** These individuals fall somewhere in between morning and evening types. They may have a more flexible sleep-wake pattern and can adjust to different schedules more easily than the other two types.

Your chronotype can be influenced by genetic factors, age, and environmental factors such as light exposure and social schedules. Understanding your chronotype can help you create your game plan, optimize your daily routine, improve sleep quality, and increase productivity by aligning your activities with your natural biological rhythms.

Many of my patients assume they know their chronotype, but you'd be surprised how many are wrong because of their bad sleep habits. Therefore, it's valuable to identify your true chronotype by assessing your natural sleep patterns and preferences. Consider not using an alarm clock, remove any caffeine for a week or so, and pay attention to when you feel most alert and when you feel tired during the day. If that sounds like torture or completely unrealistic for you, you can also use online questionnaires or assessments, such as the morningness-eveningness questionnaire (MEQ), to help determine your chronotype.

If you want to improve your sleep-wake schedule, do so gradually. Adjust your bedtime and wake-up time by fifteen to thirty minutes every few days until you reach your desired schedule. This will give your body time to adapt to your new routine and develop your new rhythm. I also suggest maintaining a consistent sleep-wake schedule, even on weekends or days off. This helps reinforce your body's new rhythm, making it easier to fall asleep and wake up at the desired times.

Try to limit exposure to bright light, especially blue light from screens, in the hours leading up to bedtime, and ensure that your bedroom is conducive to sleep by keeping it cool, dark, and quiet. You can use blackout curtains, white noise machines, or earplugs to help create the ideal sleeping conditions. Other effective considerations are moving throughout the entire day and preparing for sleep with the appropriate activities.

There you go. It's that easy. Sweet dreams!

You're likely rolling your eyes right now, thinking this is completely unrealistic and ridiculous. Who can make all these changes immediately? And you're right, not many can.

That's why I created a simple and effective method for optimal sleep.

Unlocking the Power of RESTED Sleep

At the core of the Lazarus Method lies an understanding that the journey to transformative health doesn't demand colossal changes. Instead, it invites you to embrace small, manageable shifts that, over time, culminate in profound health transformations. And what better place to begin than with our sleep?

RESTED is the acronym that encapsulates my approach to optimal sleep. Each letter is a beacon, guiding you toward nights of rejuvenation and repair. It doesn't ask you to overhaul your life overnight. Quite the opposite. It encourages you to start with bite-sized steps, ones that resonate with your unique life rhythm.

Many of my patients, when initially introduced to the six steps of RESTED, feel a bit overwhelmed because it's different from their typical routine. But here's the magic. I prompt them to embrace just three of these steps—whichever ones they find most approachable. One week at a time, they add another step, letting them create the momentum of this powerful process into their nightly routines.

The results, to put it mildly, are nothing short of astounding. Within a mere month, I've seen patients, once plagued by frustrating sleepless nights, completely transform their circadian rhythm. This resulted in waking up with energy and excitement, and it wasn't just confined to the bedroom. The benefits cascade into other aspects of their lives, and a palpable zest for life becomes evident. This may be one of the most radical improvements you may feel because of how important sleep is to all health elements.

But why does the RESTED practice hold such transformative power? Because at its core, it recognizes that sleep isn't just a passive act of closing your eyes. It respects the vital repairing, restoring, and revitalizing benefits of rest. It's an active commitment to your health. It's a nightly ritual where you honor yourself and reflect to recognize the wins and lessons of the day.

Each night of quality sleep is a step toward healing your body and reversing any underlying imbalances. As you embark on this journey, know that with each night using this protocol, you're not just sleeping; you're repairing your metabolism, hormones, brain, and gut.

The promise of RESTED sleep is not just about the hours spent in bed; it's about the life lived outside it. Embrace it, celebrate it, and watch as the world around you transforms.

RESTED PROTOCOL for OPTIMAL SLEEP

 ROUTINE: Establish a consistent sleep schedule. Avoid caffeine 10 hours prior to sleep, avoid large meals or alcohol 3 hours prior to bedtime.

 ENVIRONMENT: Create a sleep-friendly environment by keeping your bedroom cool, dark, and quiet. Keep your mobile device at least 10 feet away from your bed.

 SCREEN FREE: Limit exposure to blue light on screens and dim the lights at least 1 hour prior to sleep. Consider using blue light blocking glasses if you need to be on a device.

 TIME OUTDOORS: Spend time outdoors during daylight hours and aim for at least 10 to 60 minutes of direct sunlight exposure daily.

 EXERCISE: Engage in regular physical activity in the AM or early afternoon. Avoid intense exercise close to bedtime. Walking is best prior to sleep.

 DECOMPRESS: Stop any intense work 2 hours prior. Read a book, take a shower or bath, practice mental fitness, or write in a gratitude journal.

Kelly's Sleep Struggles

Kelly had a significant vulnerability when I initially evaluated her RESTED score. This was obvious from day one, and I knew I had to improve it ASAP. With a seemingly unending cycle of sleepless nights and stressful days, she relied on her nightly glasses of wine and late-night snacking after the kids went to bed. This would lull her to sleep, but she would often wake up in the middle of the night, her mind racing with thoughts and anxieties.

Mornings were a complete haze of pounding coffee and pastries just to shake off the brain fog that seemed to linger all day. Her fatigue became so overwhelming that she found herself dozing off during her kids' activities, a realization that both frightened and saddened her.

She was also resistant to changing her sleep routine at first. The simple solution of adjusting her nighttime routine seemed too straightforward for someone who felt so out of control, but she began to apply the small changes I asked her to make. She reduced her wine intake, replaced the snacking with a caffeine-free calming tea, minimized the endless scrolling on her phone before bed, and established a calming bedtime routine.

The immediate improvement in her sleep was surprising to her, and she was stoked. Gradually, she started to follow the RESTED protocol in its entirety, noticing how each aspect brought more clarity and vitality to her life. No longer waking in terror at night, no longer struggling with brain fog all day, and fully present for her children's activities, she was rejuvenated. With this success, she was eager to begin improving all the other health elements in the program.

***

Ultradian Rhythm

Now that you're familiar with your twenty-four-hour circadian rhythm and how important it is to your metabolic and cognitive health, it is a great opportunity to introduce another rhythm that you likely have never heard about. The term "ultradian" refers to occurrences "many times a day," and these ninety-minute rhythms are like mini versions of your circadian rhythm.

You can identify the right time to take an ultradian break by paying attention to natural dips in your concentration and energy levels, typically occurring every 90 to 120 minutes of sustained mental activity.

Imagine circadian rhythms as the full game, while ultradian rhythms are the short, intense plays happening many times throughout the game. Their main goal is to manage the cycles of energy production, output, and recovery in your metabolism.

Ultradian rhythms are to our biological clock what a time-out is to a game. In a game, a time-out allows the players to rest, strategize, and regain energy, which maximizes their performance. Similarly, ultradian rhythms, those fascinating biological patterns, are hardwired into your DNA by your "clock genes." They serve as the body's internal time-out system, governing how your body functions every single day.

When these rhythms are in sync, your body performs at its best, like a well-coached team. You have sustainable energy, are able to execute your game plan, be present, respond intentionally, and make quality health decisions aligned with your health goals. They're literally mini game changers!

However, if disrupted or ignored, similar to skipping time-outs or playing without a game plan, these rhythms can negatively affect your health. They have a powerful influence on your biological system, and understanding them can be as crucial as recognizing when to call a time-out in a game, ultimately leading to a winning performance in both health and life.

Good Coach, Bad Coach

Ignoring the body's need for an ultradian break is like refusing to call a time-out when your players are exhausted. When you step away from any of life's daily demands and take that necessary time-out, it's as though your body's internal training staff rushes onto the field, swiftly performing essential maintenance, refueling, and repairs. This ultradian healing response is like giving fresh energy to your players, rebalancing everything they need to win the game.

However, if you ignore the body's signals, like a coach who refuses to call a time-out when players are fatigued, the effects can be detrimental. White-knuckling through low-energy dips, and skipping those essential breaks, is like forcing the team to play without rest. The performance eventually recovers but never to its full capacity. The next peak is always lower, and the players won't perform as well. They won't feel as good, and they'll keep slogging along at a reduced capacity.

By the end of the day, those players—much like many individuals—become mere husks of their former selves. They return home, their energy so depleted that they collapse on the couch, resorting to unhealthy coping strategies like overeating or consuming alcohol. Relationships, too, suffer in this state of exhaustion; intimacy may become less frequent and satisfying, a game where both partners are too fatigued to play.

But this is not where it ends; the damage continues to accrue. Persistently ignoring the need for these vital time-outs can lead to burnout and physical ailments, which are the equivalent of long-term injuries on the field. These include fatigue, depression, cravings, digestive issues, inflammatory symptoms, persistent pain in the back and neck, hormonal imbalances, and even alterations to your DNA. It's like a team so worn that they become susceptible to constant injuries and long-term health issues.

The problem lies in the conventional norm that has long glorified the non-stop grind. The American work ethic has idolized the ceaseless hustler, always pushing through, enduring burnout as a badge of honor, and viewing rest as a weakness or a lack of commitment to the game.

However, embracing ultradian rhythm breaks is your brain coach strategically calling time-outs to replenish your team's energy and sharpen their focus. It's about recognizing that pauses are not admissions of failure but vital components to success. Implementing them can enhance productivity, decision-making, and inner strength, leading to a healthier, more fulfilling life.

Flow: The Assistant Coach

In the Learn chapter, we review the concept of a flow state, which is a mental state where a person is fully immersed in an activity, feeling energized and enjoying the process, with a sense of focus, confidence, and skillful performance.

During this state, a person might lose awareness of time and space, making a forced time-out seem counterproductive. It could be.

The key lies in tuning into your body, understanding intuitively when to take a time-out, and knowing when to continue, especially when engaged in productive deep work or flowing with creativity and enjoyment. Sometimes, we just need to defer to the assistant coach, who sees the game differently.

Two-Minute Time-Out

In Chapter 11, you will learn that your day can be broken down into four quarters. Well, when you take mini breaks in between quarters, you set yourself up for sustained energy. Ultradian rhythm break activities can be thought of as simple, quick two-minute time-outs used to rejuvenate your focus between responsibilities.

They can range from simple acts to more involved practices, all aimed at refreshing your body and mind. In the time it took me to write this section, I took a quick time-out to walk outside to adjust my eyes, take a few RISE breaths, and stare at a distant tree.

TIME-OUT Challenge

I want to share an effective strategy that I created for my patients to apply this concept. It's called the TIME-OUT Challenge, which serves as a helpful reminder for taking quick, periodic breaks to rejuvenate, aligning with the essential aspects of rest:

TIMEOUT CHALLENGE

This **TIMEOUT Challenge,** which serves as a helpful reminder for taking quick, periodic breaks to rejuvenate, aligns with the essential aspects of rest:

 Twenty4 The 20-20-20-20 is every 20 minutes, take a 20-second break, blink hard 20 times then focus your eyes on something at least 20 feet away. This helps mitigate symptoms associated with digital eye strain, such as dry eyes, blurred vision, and headaches.

 Integrate RISE breathing 5 times to recalibrate your autonomic nervous system.

 Move outdoors for a quick walk or grounding session and gaze as far as possible to reset your eyes and nervous system.

 Evaluate your daily game plan and what Quarter you're in.

 Opt for a quick stretche or a simple yoga pose. The hip flexor stretches, or downward facing dog are perfect.

 Use a hydration drink or healthy snack away from your work spot.

 Try a "Brain Break" which is form of NSDR *(Non Sleep Deep Rest)* or Yoga Nidra which promotes deep rest that isn't found in your typical mental fitness practice. The stages of body scan and breath awareness can be used to calm the nervous system in only 5 minutes.

These activities may seem simple and insignificant, but when integrated properly, they are great mental rest breaks that help bring a moment of presence and punctuate your day. They are not mere diversions; they are essential plays in the game of life, providing much-needed respite and recalibration.

Time-out activities transform you from a weary, worn-out player to a vital, engaged athlete, ready to tackle each new game with vigor and resilience. Ignoring these breaks is no longer an option; they are integral to maintaining a balance that allows you to perform at your best.

Chill the F*ck Out

The last concept of rest I want to introduce is the notion of your chill time and the idea of "telic activities." The word is derived from the Greek *telos*, meaning "end," and describes actions directed toward a specific endpoint. A telic activity refers to an action or behavior that is directed toward achieving a specific goal or end.

In this context, telic activities are undertaken with a particular outcome or purpose in mind rather than for the intrinsic enjoyment or experience of the activity itself. They are goal-oriented and often driven by a clear objective or target that the individual aims to achieve.

Think about it for a second. How much of your day is spent in the pursuit of accomplishing something? Whether it's taking care of duties at home, hours spent working, responsibilities with your kids or pets, chores or yard work, saving money for retirement, and even the work you put into your health, you spend much of your day trying to check a box so you can move on to the next obligation.

The concept of telic activities resonates with me and many of my patients, as it has enabled me to recognize that virtually every task I engage in throughout my day is aimed at achieving a particular goal. For instance, waking up early, meditating, teaching my kids, planning for our future, writing this book, creating the Lazarus Method online coaching program, meetings with my staff, doing kettlebell swings, prepping healthy food for the week, and even watching interesting documentaries. They're all directed at accomplishing something.

Can you relate to this scenario? It's undeniable that a large portion of our daily lives must be devoted to telic, or outcome-driven, activities. These activities are necessary to attain your personal definition of success and experience essential outcomes like optimal health.

However, the intent of introducing this concept to you is to make the argument that a fulfilling life isn't solely enriched by telic pursuits or checking boxes. I'm suggesting that the beauty and meaning in life may be the immense joy and depth of experience that can be discovered in atelic activities—those performed without any outcome in mind.

Telic Activities (Goal-Oriented): Purposeful Pursuits

Atelic Activities (Non-Goal-Oriented): Purposeless Pleasures

There are a million different ways to do nothing. Examples of such atelic activities might include:

> Relaxing on a beach and observing the waves.
>
> Playing catch or frisbee.
>
> Listening to the birds sing.
>
> Watching the clouds or stargazing.
>
> Hiking with no destination.
>
> People watching at the park.
>
> Practicing tai chi movements.
>
> Observing the fire at the fire pit.
>
> Dancing freely just because.
>
> Jamming on the guitar or piano.

Engaging in these atelic activities may initially feel strange or even unsettling if you're accustomed to a more goal-oriented approach. If you're like me, you'll likely think, *This is unproductive. I could be using this time more productively.* But, trust me, overcoming these internal demands for efficiency and embracing the initial unease of atelic activities can be profoundly rewarding.

When consumed by telic pursuits, by a relentless drive for results, you risk overlooking the simple joy of existing and the fleeting beauty of life's transient moments. It is through the apparent vulnerability of atelic activities that you may foster a delightful appreciation for the fragility of the present, passing moment—a moment that will never return—and of the people and surroundings that will never remain precisely as they are. It's a reminder to value our existence as it unfolds, in all its complex and ephemeral glory.

Sometimes we all need to move slowly so we can then move powerfully. Sometimes we need to take a moment to embrace life's purposeless pleasures, so forget Nike and just do nothing. So, sit on the sideline and simply observe the game of life. Be here now, and chill the f*ck out.

Summary - Sleep on This

The Rest element is positioned at the foundation of the Lazarus Method framework, symbolizing its crucial role as the bedrock for achieving optimal health. Some may even argue that it's the most vital prerequisite in the health equation. As an expert in nutrition and fitness, I guide my patients on their journey to become strong and lean, but I've observed that many reach a plateau or burnout. More often than not, this occurs because they either grapple with underlying rest-related issues or overlook the significance of this vital component.

My ultimate objective with the Rest element is not just to underscore its importance but also to pinpoint potential stumbling blocks in your rest routine and assist you in enhancing your rest playbook. Each individual's journey is unique, and the pace must be both realistic and practical. Kelly's experience is a perfect example of this approach because her poor sleep was a trigger for subsequent bad choices.

By prioritizing your rest routine and incorporating just a few of the RESTED and TIME-OUT concepts, immediate improvements can be made. You'll boost your energy, metabolism, and mental clarity. In the essential health playbook, chilling and snoozing doesn't mean losing. It is part of the winning game plan.

Here are a few simple "Rest Plays" you can try today and tonight that may help you immediately. Feel free to add them to your health game plan that you'll create in Chapter 11.

THE LAZARUS METHOD GAME PLAN

PLAY I: Optimize Sleep: The RESTED Sleep Challenge

1. Begin by selecting three principles from the RESTED approach that you find most manageable. Integrate these into your nightly routine for five days.

2. Gradually Add More Elements - Each week, introduce one additional RESTED principle to your routine. This step-by-step addition allows you to comfortably adjust to each new habit, enhancing your sleep quality without feeling overwhelmed.

3. By the final week, aim to incorporate all the RESTED principles into your nightly routine. Reflect on the changes in your sleep quality and overall well-being. This slow and steady approach ensures a sustainable improvement in your sleep habits.

Write Down your three initial RESTED principles:

1. _____

2. _____

3. _____

Coach's Tip:

Write Down your Target Date to integrate all six principles:

_____

PLAY II: Take a Timeout

This simple challenge, derived from the TIME-OUT method, is designed to integrate rest tactics into your daily routine. Select 2-3 tasks from the TIME-OUT list and integrate them over 10 days, experiencing firsthand how these simple actions can reduce fatigue and brain fog and significantly enhance your headspace.

Coach's Tip:

Summarize your headspace in one word before and after this challenge.

Initial Headspace: TIMEOUT Headspace:

_____   _____

Example:

Initial Headspace: TIMEOUT Headspace:
Overwhelmed   Persistant

PLAY III: Determine Your Chronotype

Use the Essential Health Toolkit to access the Morningness-Eveningness Questionnaire (MEQ) to help determine your chronotype. Answer the questions honestly and record your result. Modify your routine to stay in alignment with your chronotype.

Coach's Tip:

Write down one obstacle to modifying your routine based on your chronotype.

_____

Write down one solution to overcome this barrier.

_____

Inspired by the uplifting vibes of the talented musician Stick Figure, **"When you focus on the good things, all things under the sun, you free yourself from negativity, and then the good shall come. The choice is yours when you're ready."**

As your health journey's melody plays on, you may find yourself at an interesting juncture. Do you choose the path bathed in sunlight, embracing positivity and hope, or do you embark on a route that might challenge this brightness but offer profound growth?

The choice is yours when you're ready.

"Choose Your Own Health Adventure"

If you're drawn to **Identify Your Inner Voice and True Purpose,** *let your intuition guide you to page 149 in the Spark Chapter.* This section offers a glimpse of self-discovery, offering methods for identifying your life scorecard and an introduction to your avatar. It also introduces spark igniters, tools designed to stimulate personal growth and self-awareness.

If you're looking to **Elevate your Motivation and Inspiration,** *I dare you to turn to page 287 in the Challenge Chapter.* This section explores unique concepts like the universe test and your quantum coach, providing innovative perspectives on personal growth. You'll also learn about setting realistic challenges that involve establishing floors and ceilings to define and achieve your goals effectively.

If your primary goal is to **Lose Weight and Optimize your Digestion**, *turn to page 55 in the Nourish Chapter.* The recommendations provided in this chapter will help you improve your body composition and jumpstart your metabolism. The concepts that will help you are the Nourish Target, Metabolic Flexibility, Intuitive Eating, EAT Protocol, and the 80/20 Eating Principle.

If you can't wait to **Enhance Brain Function and Mental Clarity**, *navigate to page 255 in the Learn Chapter.* This section is dedicated to helping you diminish brain fog, enter your personal flow zone, and offers insight into achieving a mental makeover. It introduces the principles of neuroplasticity, providing you with tools to sharpen your cognitive abilities and enhance mental acuity.

If you want to learn how to **Increase Strength and Improve your Metabolism**, *run to page 219 in the Move Chapter.* Here, you'll explore the effective 2nd Gear Strategy, delve into the three foundational pillars of movement, review compound and functional movements, and discover the importance of incorporating play into your routine.

If you want to prioritize **Being Present, Awareness, and Clarity**, *please focus on page 171 in the Connect Chapter.* This section is specifically tailored to enhance your mental fitness and sharpen your focus flashlight, a technique for cultivating mindfulness. You will also explore the happiness gap for true happiness and find your "thrive tribe" to achieve a heightened state of community and support.

CHAPTER 6

SPARK

There is an elemental force waiting to be ignited or awakened. I call this force your "spark," and no, it is not located in a galaxy far, far away. It's a remarkable power deep within you. Your spark is an internal compass that guides your journey and enriches your existence. As unique as your fingerprint, your spark is the essential you, the authentic you, waiting to be discovered, nurtured, and unleashed.

Beneath the surface of your being, nestled within the core of your essence, your soul resides. This is an integral part of your spark. The soul is the wellspring from which your spark emanates, and its unique qualities, desires, and wisdom feed your spark, shaping it into a beacon of your true self.

The union between your soul and your spark creates an alignment that is undeniably powerful and fulfilling. When you live in alignment with your spark, you create a resonance between your external actions and your soul's deepest desires. This harmonious resonance engenders a sense of profound joy, peace, and fulfillment.

Let me be very clear, this is not a religious or deep spiritual strategy. Your belief and connection to a higher power represent a deeply personal and sacred bond, reflecting a unique spiritual journey that is entirely your own.

The spark is a universal energy that lives within you. You feel it at your core within yourself at various moments throughout your life, and it becomes particularly evident during health challenges, significant milestones, impactful encounters, and moments of great joy or sorrow.

No matter what your individual health goals are, be it losing weight, overcoming fatigue, boosting strength, clearing brain fog, or improving digestion, the vital spark element is something that cannot be disregarded or overlooked. This vital energy can be utilized for healing during periods of health challenges and harnessed to enhance your peak performance.

The Spark may be the X-Factor in your health playbook. There are seven elements in The Lazarus Method, and Spark is the epicenter. Nourish, Move, Rest, Learn, Connect, and Challenge all revolve around and support this core element. This is the essential play hidden deep in your playbook. It's what makes your playbook unique and different from everything else.

Spark Igniter

However, let's recognize the reality—not everyone knows what their spark is, or it's buried beneath the construct of conformity. It may remain dormant within you, or perhaps it's been silenced by life's many demands. Yet, there are also those among us who have found their spark but, for whatever reason, have chosen to neglect it. If that's you, please read on, as every spark, known or unknown, attended or ignored, has the potential to be lit and to transform your health and life.

This chapter is a process designed to help you uncover your spark if it's hidden and tend to it if it's been overlooked. It's not just to merely light your spark, but to fan it into a brilliant flame, a consuming fire that radiates from within, fueling a life filled with health, fulfillment, and meaning. Imagine living every day driven by this fierce internal flame, illuminating your path, warming your spirit, and inspiring those around you.

What does it feel like when your soul aligns with your realized spark?

When you live in alignment with your spark, everything seems to fall into place. Every step you take, every decision you make, resonates with the authentic rhythm of your soul. The discord between who you are and who you strive to be dissipate, replaced by a true alignment.

This doesn't mean that everything is perfect—in fact, it often reveals itself in the opposite way. Your spark is your compass, and no matter what health issues, obstacles, roadblocks, or dead ends you may encounter in your journey, you know there's a reason, and you carry an innate intelligence to overcome it.

You'll find a new sense of clarity and direction. Your path, possibly obscured by external expectations or self-doubt, becomes illuminated by the radiant light of your spark. You may notice a surge of energy, a newfound enthusiasm, and a sense of invincibility. You'll also find a comforting sense of peace and calm. When your spark is burning bright, you can and will overcome any health challenge in your life.

CHARACTERISTICS OF LIVING IN ALIGNMENT WITH YOUR SPARK	CHARACTERISTICS OF LIVING WITH THE ABSENCE OF YOUR SPARK
Embraces personal accountability to shape a distinct reality.	Adopting a victim mentality, forfeiting personal responsibility.
Fosters an abundance mindset, promoting optimism and possibilities.	Harboring a scarcity mindset, fixating on limitations and constraints.
Extracts lessons from every experience, fostering growth and wisdom.	Perceiving actions as mistakes, often blaming others rather than learning.
Exhibits gratitude, deriving joy from even the smallest moments.	Constant complaining, overshadowing potential positives in situations.
Ability to reframe and overcome any symptoms or health challenges.	Focusing on nagging symptoms and inability to take control of your health.

During my dark years when I was healing from my traumatic injury, I was using a victim mentality, avoiding personal accountability, entrenched in a scarcity mindset fixated on constraints. I placed blame on others, frequently complaining and overlooking any positives, and concentrating on persistent symptoms instead of proactively managing my health.

I also stumbled quite a bit personally in my younger years, making stupid decisions, having the wrong priorities, chasing the wrong desires, investing in the wrong relationships, stressing over stupid shit, drinking, late-night debauchery, neglecting school, and hanging with the wrong crowd. These bad decisions affected my health, led me to financial issues, destroyed quality relationships, and led me onto some unfortunate paths.

Do I regret having this victim mindset and these bad decisions? Certainly. Were they important lessons? Absolutely. But here's the silver lining within my unique spark. Each of these experiences were essential milestones, guiding me to where I stand today, wiser and clearer about my spark and with a clear perspective of my current health challenges.

Does this mean I have it all figured out? Not at all. It's actually the opposite – the more I learn, the less I understand. Throughout this confusion, my spark strengthens my ability to personal responsibility, maintain an optimistic mindset, learn from all experiences, appreciate life's moments, and reframe my health challenges.

**It can do the same for you,
whatever your health challenges may be.**

With many years spent in clinical practice, I've had the privilege of supporting numerous patients on their health journeys and quickly identified these traits in them, having experienced them myself. I provide this holistic playbook and help them identify and cultivate their distinctive spark, and when they embrace it, the health outcomes are incredible.

Be Yourself

We're all different, and we all have different stories to share. Here's a golden nugget of wisdom I'd like to share. It's perfectly okay if not everyone approves of you. When we're younger, we get applauded for fitting in—matching outfits, similar activities, the same music, and following identical trends. The aim for many young people can be conformity and popularity, and I was definitely one of them. But once you step into adulthood, you realize the attraction and power of being unique, even if it means some people might not approve.

It's not an easy pill to swallow, and quite a few never manage to digest it. They spend their lives on autopilot, adhering to society's expectations. And then, one day, they wake up with the realization that they've been spectators in their own lives. You're the play caller in the game of life. Don't be afraid to let your spark glow, even if it means being different from your current peers!

Unleashing your potential to be different is like unlocking the secret play—it gives you the strength to tackle difficult tasks that others shy away from. This courage not only adds a layer of significance and purpose to your life but also paves the way to success that may seem daunting to many. I call this our internal scorecard. It's an internal record that lies deep within us that tallies up every action we take.

But let's dial it up a notch. Embracing others' disapproval can lead you to true freedom. It's only when you're okay with not pleasing everyone that you truly liberate yourself from the confines of others' viewpoints. Strive to do what feels right for you, even when it might shake up the game board.

**REJECTION IS EXPECTED AND
ALWAYS SUPERIOR TO REGRET**

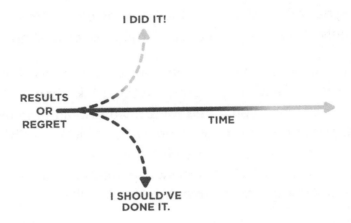

Welcome the Resistance

Why should you value the embrace of potential disapproval from others? Well, it holds significant importance. In today's society, the prevailing default lifestyle is not healthy. Opting for a healthy lifestyle and making healthy choices is the exception these days. The default lifestyle tends to revolve around consuming unhealthy foods, leading a sedentary existence, excessive alcohol consumption, endless hours of screen time, materialistic pursuits, talking about others, and simply rushing to keep up with social expectations.

This is a systemic issue with our current culture. Fifty years ago, you would have had to go out of your way to make unhealthy choices. The food was real, we moved constantly, we weren't tied to technology, and the pace was slower. Fast forward to our current situation and you now have to go out of your way to be healthy these days.

Certain people may not support your new health game plan. Accepting the potential disapproval of others regarding your newfound healthy choices is part of the essential health playbook. It's when you become comfortable with the idea of making better decisions and not satisfying every one that you genuinely break free from the constraints of others' opinions.

Have you ever found yourself in a situation like this? Perhaps there was a time when you chose not to drink when everyone else was, or when you opted for a salad instead of joining in on the pizza feast at the table, only to be labeled as "boring" or even receive a derogatory comment such as "look who's eating healthy now." Occasionally, it manifests in subtler ways, such as a slight eye roll from another or a deliberate chuckle.

This is a common story my patients share when they start making different choices. It occurs not only among colleagues but also among friends, family members, and even partners. Often, individuals' own insecurities about their health choices become evident when you're actively striving to improve your health. I've even seen loved ones unintentionally and subconsciously sabotage their partners' health progress based on their own health issues.

Accept this critique and negative feedback; they're growth phases to improvement. Don't shy away from being teased or criticized for making healthy choices. Once you're confident with your new choices, there's absolutely nothing that can stand in your way. You'll be in alignment with your spark, and that is the ultimate superpower!

Your Avatar

We've all heard about the ego, but few actually truly understand how we interact with it on a daily basis. The ego represents your sense of self. It is shaped by personal experiences, societal influences, and psychological development and is concerned with maintaining identity, fulfilling desires, and seeking social recognition within the physical realm.

I call this our avatar. No, it's not our blue alter-egos soaring through Pandora on Mountain Banshees. It's that version of ourselves that we show to the world; every interaction, whether it's with a stranger or a close friend. It represents that version of us that is driven by external validation and seeks to gain approval or recognition from others. This could be in a casual conversation with a coworker, a shallow conversation with an acquaintance while grabbing coffee, or a close friend to whom we silently compare ourselves.

Similar to how an avatar in a virtual world may focus on accumulating points or achievements to impress others, the ego seeks to accumulate accomplishments, possessions, and status symbols in the physical world. I call this our external scorecard, and it drives many people to spend much of their daily energy to rack up points on their scorecard.

Our avatar is not a true reflection of who we are at our core, but it is an important protective mechanism that allows us to engage with the world with confidence. If it's not properly realized or trained, it can lead us astray from our genuine desires and aspirations, causing us to prioritize external validation over our internal scorecard.

By constantly seeking validation from others, we may lose touch with our inner voice, passions, and true values. Like an avatar chasing after virtual rewards, the ego may lead us to make choices that do not align with our authentic self, hindering our health and personal growth.

Corey's Inner Voice

A quintessential people person, Corey had the gift of making anyone feel like they'd been friends for years. His large stature and outward confidence suggested a man who was "large and in charge," fully in command of his life.

However, beneath this strong posture was a web of complexities. A devoted father of three and entrenched in a high-pressure career in finance, Corey was no stranger to stress. But as our conversations deepened, we uncovered an even more intricate layer affecting his behavior and daily choices.

During one of our meetings, Corey opened up. "You know, it's crazy. I've always felt this pressure since childhood. Being the oldest of three, there were a lot of expectations," he shared.

"Expectations like...?" I prompted.

"Being the perfect role model for my siblings, excelling in sports, getting good grades. That kind of programming gets hardwired early on," he admitted. "And lately, it's been resurfacing—in the middle of the night, during my commute, even on conference calls. I've been brushing it aside because I've got tons of responsibilities, but I'm starting to see how it's affecting my health."

This led us to discuss the concept of his external scorecard and avatar, the version of Corey that he presented to the world in every interaction, whether with strangers or close friends. This avatar was fueled by the need for external validation and approval, a tendency he'd carried since childhood.

"Brother, trust me, I get it. We all have an avatar. I've grappled with mine, too," I said, aiming to normalize what he was going through. "This is one of your superpowers, and you've used it to accomplish great things. The key is awareness without judgment."

I offered him various spark resources (provided at the end of this chapter) designed to heighten his self-awareness, and it was at that moment that I knew Corey was poised for a breakthrough. He was ready to confront the limitations he had unwittingly set for himself, and I was confident that with this newfound awareness, everything else would start to fall into place.

Your Inner Voice

It is essential to recognize this tendency of the ego and strive to align ourselves with our internal scorecard, which reflects our true desires, aspirations, and values that resonate with our soul. If you're not properly trained to be aware of its effect, your avatar may influence many aspects of your life, such as:

Health:

Your avatar can interfere with your soul's true desires when it comes to prioritizing external appearances, societal standards, or comparison with others over the soul's genuine need for holistic well-being and self-love.

For example, someone may engage in extreme dieting or intense exercise regimens driven by the ego's desire for a certain body image or societal acceptance, disregarding the soul's true desires for balance, self-compassion, and nourishment. This can lead to a disconnection from the body's natural signals and a neglect of the emotional and spiritual aspects of health.

Career choices:

Your avatar may interfere with your soul's true desires when it prioritizes external validation, societal expectations, or financial success over following one's true passions and purpose.

Think about your job. Do you see it as just a way to earn money? Do you like it, but only if you're doing well and getting promoted? Or is it the main thing in your life, something you would do even if you didn't get paid? If your job feels like something you would do for free, you're more likely to be happy in your career and your life.

Relationships:

Your avatar may interfere with your soul's true desires in relationships when it prioritizes control, validation, or power dynamics.

For instance, someone's ego may prevent them from truly connecting and nurturing a healthy relationship because they are driven by their own insecurities, need for dominance, or fear of vulnerability. This can hinder the soul's genuine desire for love, intimacy, and emotional connection.

Material possessions and status:

Your avatar may interfere with the soul's true desires by placing excessive importance on material possessions and external markers of success.

When the ego is focused on acquiring wealth, possessions, or social status for the sake of ego gratification, it can distract from the soul's deeper longing for contentment, inner fulfillment, and authentic connections with others.

Spark vs. Noise

In the game of life, your avatar assumes the role of a committed defense, focused on protecting its own image and seeking outside validation. It acts as a shield against potential criticism or rejection, guarding the status quo. However, it can sometimes become overly cautious and hesitant to take risks and explore the depths of your true potential.

On the other hand, the soul takes charge as a dynamic offense, fearlessly venturing forward to embrace new experiences, growth, and self-discovery. It uses an internal scorecard, propelling us toward our deepest desires, passions, and purpose. The soul's offense pushes boundaries, ignites creativity, and guides us toward fulfillment, unveiling the true essence of our being.

The soul and ego speak to you all day, especially when you make new health choices. These voices can be loud at times and quiet whispers at other times. Balancing the ego's defense with the soul's offense, you can navigate a lot of the noise and life's health challenges with authenticity and joy, embracing both the protective strength of the ego and the expansive power of your spark's true desires.

Values and Beliefs

Everyone has different values, beliefs, and priorities. Some people have no idea what theirs are, and others have complete clarity. Regardless of where you stand, it's a vital initial step to achieving optimal health and performance. It's the first step in the Lazarus Method Program because if you don't know what's important to you and why, it's very difficult to begin to make decisions that align with it.

Completing the questions at the end of this Chapter may uncover cognitive conflict because it might reveal your current decisions are not in alignment with what you truly want. It happens all the time. It's an exercise to identify your current values and what's truly important to you. There are no wrong answers. In fact, the answer you're searching for is usually found in the area you're avoiding. Read that again.

Personal Success

Have you ever thought about your own version of success? How do you personally define success? It's also essential to understand the aspects of your success, as this awareness directly impacts your ability to make health decisions that foster and sustain success. Without this knowledge, it becomes challenging to light your inner spark effectively.

The meaning of success varies from person to person. An answer from a typical individual about their concept of success might yield an image of wealth, an impressive vehicle, millions of followers, and admired by many. Yet, for others, success could mean maintaining good health, a nurturing family, supportive friends, and a fulfilling career, or it could simply be about living minimally, finding true happiness without any possessions, and achieving satisfaction in life.

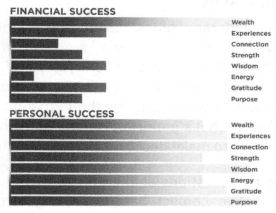

The Spark Scoreboard

Setting Health and Personal Goals:

Just like a team in a game sets goals for themselves, you can establish health and personal goals aligned with your spark. Regularly assess how you're progressing toward these goals and evaluate the steps you've taken. Are you moving closer to your desired outcome? Are you making consistent efforts and adjustments? By assessing your progress, you can gauge how effectively you're playing the health game and whether you're staying true to your internal scorecard.

Reflecting on Alignment with Values:

Similar to how players in a game adhere to their team's strategies and tactics, you can reflect on how well your actions and choices align with your core values. Take time to evaluate whether your daily decisions and behaviors resonate with your spark's internal scorecard. Are you living in alignment with your values of kindness, compassion, integrity, or growth? By regularly assessing your alignment with your values, you can ensure that you're playing the game of life with integrity and authenticity.

Cultivating Self-Awareness:

Just as athletes practice self-awareness during a game to gauge their performance, you can cultivate mindfulness and self-awareness in your daily life. Take moments to pause, observe your thoughts, emotions, and actions without judgment. Assess how present and mindful you've been throughout the day. Are you fully engaged in the present moment or caught up in worries or distractions? By being aware of your state of mind and headspace.

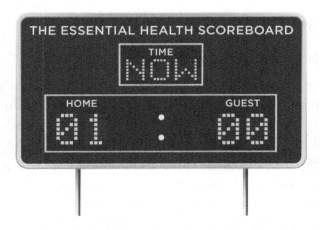

Summary - The Epicenter

The Spark element is obviously the most personal element in the essential health playbook. It's your values, purpose, your life's mission, and an internal compass that guides your journey and enriches your existence. It's why you're playing the game in the first place.

Discussing one's purpose, life mission, or internal compass carries an inherent responsibility—a responsibility I don't take lightly. Who am I to talk about something so deeply personal and sacred?

The reason why I placed the Spark in the center of all the essential health elements is because your spark is the secret play. Remember, the winning gameplan is...*you.*

In any holistic health framework, the center is always based around the individual and the energies that supply it. The Lazarus Method emphasizes this central tenant as well. It is influenced by the six other health elements. What food and information you consume, where you place your attention, your movement habits, your sleep, and ability to rest, your flow states, your connections with yourself and your tribe: they all shape your spark. They either nourish it or diminish it. Let's review a few simple ways to nourish it.

THE LAZARUS METHOD GAME PLAN

PLAY I: Health Goals

Write down your top three current health goals.

1. _____

2. _____

3. _____

Coach's Tip:

Label each health goal with the appropriate Essential Health Elements

Example: <u>Improve Energy (Rest, Nourish)</u>

PLAY II: Your Values & Beliefs

Your values, beliefs, and priorities are what dictate your daily decisions. Use the hierarchy of values below and answer the following questions.

Family (FAM), Health (H), Social/Entertainment (SE), Career (C), Finances (F), Spirituality (S), Personal Development (PD)

What do you think about most?

1st: _____   2nd: _____

What are you inspired about?

1st: _____   2nd: _____

How do you spend your time?

1st: _____   2nd: _____

Example: What do you think about most?

1st: CAREER   *2nd: FAMILY*

Coach's Tip:

We use a comprehensive worksheet with participants in our programs, and it often exposes common misalignments of what is truly important to each person and their daily decisions. Be honest with yourself. It's normal to feel cognitive dissonance.

PLAY III: Personal Success

Let's determine how success looks for you. What is your first intuitive definition of success? Write down five descriptions to define personal success.

1. _____

2. _____

3. _____

4. _____

5. _____

Coach's Tip:

Read about Internal Scorecards (IR) and External Scorecards (ER) in Chapter 11 and place an IR or ER next to each description.

Drawing from John Wooden's wise words, **"There is a choice you have to make in everything you do. So, keep in mind that in the end, the choice you make, makes you."**

Our choices define us. This means that the consistent choices you make that are in alignment with your values, beliefs and personal success will lead to a life of purpose, and fulfillment. On the other hand, repeatedly making bad health choices may create cognitive dissonance, anxiety, or depression. Keep that in mind as you choose and read the next chapter.

"Choose Your Own Health Adventure"

If you're looking to **Elevate your Motivation and Inspiration,** *I dare you to turn to page 287 in the Challenge Chapter.* This section explores unique concepts like the universe test and your quantum coach, providing innovative perspectives on personal growth. You'll also learn about setting realistic challenges that involve establishing floors and ceilings to define and achieve your goals effectively.

If your primary goal is to **Lose Weight and Optimize your Digestion,** *turn to page 55 in the Nourish Chapter.* The recommendations provided in this chapter will help you improve your body composition and jumpstart your metabolism. The concepts that will help you are the Nourish Target, Metabolic Flexibility, Intuitive Eating, EAT Protocol, and the 80/20 Eating Principle.

If you can't wait to **Enhance Brain Function and Mental Clarity**, *navigate to page 255 in the Learn Chapter.* This section is dedicated to helping you diminish brain fog, enter your personal flow zone, and offers insight into achieving a mental makeover. It introduces the principles of neuroplasticity, providing you with tools to sharpen your cognitive abilities and enhance mental acuity.

If you want to learn how to **Increase Strength and Improve your Metabolism**, *run to page 219 in the Move Chapter.* Here, you'll explore the effective 2nd Gear Strategy, delve into the three foundational pillars of movement, review compound and functional movements, and discover the importance of incorporating play into your routine.

For those seeking to **Boost Energy Levels and Overcome Fatigue**, *chill out and to page 119 in the Rest Chapter.* This section will introduce you to the concept of your chronotype and circadian rhythm for optimal sleep. It provides detailed guidance on the RESTED Protocol, designed to optimize your rest and energy and two-minute timeouts, a strategy to rejuvenate and maintain sustained energy throughout your day.

If you want to prioritize **Being Present, Awareness, and Clarity**, *please focus on page 171 in the Connect Chapter.* This section is specifically tailored to enhance your mental fitness and sharpen your focus flashlight, a technique for cultivating mindfulness. You will also explore the happiness gap for true happiness and find your "thrive tribe" to achieve a heightened state of community and support.

CHAPTER 7

CONNECT

"Everything changes once we identify with being the witness to the story, instead of the actor in it."
- Ram Dass

In the relentless pulse of today's high-speed world, prioritizing true connection is not just a matter of importance, but a necessary cornerstone for holistic health. We all naturally crave meaningful connections, and this chapter explores four key areas where connections should be nurtured and fostered:

Connection to nature for restoration.

Connection to ourselves for understanding our minds.

Connection to our tribe for our relationships with family and friends.

Connection to our community for our function within society.

This chapter serves as a compass, helping you explore these concepts and guiding you toward valuable interactions that improve your health and enrich your life. It values these connections not as optional but as fundamental—core pillars that support your optimal health. By prioritizing these four connections, you'll have a sustainable approach to mindfulness and personal growth.

Connection to Nature for Restoration

Have you ever experienced the clarity that comes from spending time immersed in nature? It's actually a timeless phenomenon that exists cross-culturally for us as humans. Spending time connecting with the Earth brings us clarity in our relationships, professions, health, finances, and more. Done right, it helps us come back to who we truly are and reconnect with our spirit—that thread of meaning, purpose, and vision that is like rocket fuel for life itself.

There's an undeniable potency that grips you when you wander along the shoreline and observe each unique wave. Equally powerful is the raw serenity of the untamed wilderness, its pulsating life force echoing in your soul. Or maybe it's when you're perched on your surfboard, suspended in a timeless dance with the waves, anticipating the ocean's rhythmic bounty. From epic sunrises to mystical sunsets, there's an energy available that can revitalize you if you're willing to absorb it.

It's in these moments of quiet contemplation that the symphony of nature plays its most mesmerizing soundtrack. These experiences serve as a vital reboot, realigning our perspective on existence, underscoring what truly matters, and revealing the universal beauty that permeates our world every single day of our lives.

In addition to these reflective spiritual moments, connecting with nature also has a profound impact on your health, a relationship that goes beyond the immediate sensory experience and extends to the realm of your genetic makeup. Even short times in nature can lead to stress management, boosting mood, immune system strengthening, and an overall increase in vitality, all underpinned by complex biochemical processes that can modify gene expression. If you could wrap all the benefits in a single capsule, it may be the most potent form of medicine we have available.

For instance, sunlight exposure triggers the body's synthesis of Vitamin D, which is not just essential for bone health and immune function, but also plays a role in gene expression. Moreover, the unique scents of nature and calming natural sounds, such as the waves crashing, rustling of leaves, birdsong, and flowing water, along with physical activities like hiking or boarding, not only reduce anxiety and enhance sleep quality but also stimulate epigenetic changes that may boost cognitive function, fostering creativity and problem-solving abilities.

WAYS TO CONNECT WITH NATURE	
Beach Strolls	Walking along the beach not only connects you to nature but also provides awesome exercise. The soothing sound of waves, the feel of sand beneath your feet, and the smell of the sea are nature's medicine.
Water Sports	If you live near a lake or pond, engage in watersports such as kayaking, surfing, cliff diving, paddleboarding, or swimming. These activities provide both an adrenaline rush and peaceful interaction with the water and surrounding environment.
Fishing Trips	A fishing trip can provide a quiet, contemplative time spent in nature. Whether you're by a pond, lake, or ocean, fishing offers a unique form of relaxation and connection to the peaceful water environment.
Camping in the Wilderness	Plan a camping trip in the deep wilderness where you can unplug completely from modern technology. Spending a few days and nights surrounded by nature can have a profound reset on your perspective.
Guided Nature Tours	Participate in guided nature tours that can take you on hikes through deep forests, to majestic waterfalls, or around tranquil lakes. This provides an opportunity to learn more about the ecosystem, observe wildlife, and immerse yourself in the wilderness.

WAYS TO CONNECT WITH NATURE	
Beach/Park Yoga	Practice yoga or meditation on the beach or park during sunrise or sunset. The peaceful environment aids in focusing your mind, and the stunning view of the sun over the water is an added bonus.
Take Walks in Green Spaces	Schedule daily walks in parks, woods, or other green spaces. This will give you the dual benefits of exercise and the calming effect of being surrounded by nature. If possible, take different routes each time to add a sense of adventure.
Playing or Training Outdoor	Swap the gym for an outdoor workout once or twice a week. Playground workouts, yoga, games, or recreation at a park. Play like when you were a kid.
Picnics	Instead of eating inside, pack a picnic and head to a local park or natural area. This will not only give you the opportunity to spend time in nature but will also create a more mindful eating experience.
Start a Garden	Whether it's a small herb garden on your balcony or a full-fledged vegetable plot in your backyard, gardening can be a therapeutic activity that connects you with nature. It also provides physical exercise and, if you grow edible plants, fresh and healthy food.

NATURE PYRAMID

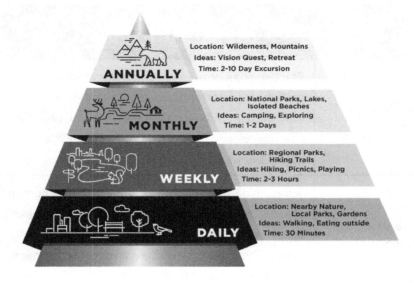

Location: Wilderness, Mountains
Ideas: Vision Quest, Retreat
Time: 2-10 Day Excursion
ANNUALLY

Location: National Parks, Lakes, Isolated Beaches
Ideas: Camping, Exploring
Time: 1-2 Days
MONTHLY

Location: Regional Parks, Hiking Trails
Ideas: Hiking, Picnics, Playing
Time: 2-3 Hours
WEEKLY

Location: Nearby Nature, Local Parks, Gardens
Ideas: Walking, Eating outside
Time: 30 Minutes
DAILY

Nature Pyramid

The Nature Pyramid serves as a straightforward guide for individuals to integrate these strategies. I frequently ask my patients to explore this tool, and together we brainstorm engaging ways to ascend the pyramid's various levels. Some of my patients have even planned specialized excursions and retreats that have been transformational, both for their health and their overall outlook on life. Regardless of your prior experience or comfort level with the outdoors, the Nature Pyramid can chart a simple yet effective course for your connection with nature.

I remember a compelling story about an individual who had a life-changing experience in nature. In the summer of 1993, when I was sixteen years old, I ventured to the Grand Teton wilderness in Wyoming for a month-long trip. I was incredibly excited about the opportunity to venture into the expansive landscapes, breathe in the clean air, and spend hours immersed in bird-watching.

Yep, you guessed it—that's all total bullsh*t.

I was sent to a survival camp for "bad behavior." My parents saw this as an opportunity for me to reconnect with myself and gain some much-needed perspective. Needless to say, I wasn't thrilled. Actually, I was really pissed off. I was preoccupied with the idea of missing typical teenage summer activities—partying, pulling pranks, and loitering in the local grocery store's parking lot while blasting Pearl Jam and Cypress Hill.

They sent me to the reputable National Outdoor Leadership School (NOLS) for thirty-two days. NOLS is an immersive program that teaches wilderness survival skills such as wilderness first aid, navigation, and creating shelter, as well as other skills like teamwork, problem-solving, and leadership.

The month I spent removed from any distractions or petty problems served as a transformational rite of passage. With all the usual distractions of modern life removed, I was immersed in an unfamiliar state: boredom. This vast expanse of emptiness became a canvas for introspection.

This boredom provided profound clarity. An overwhelming sense of gratitude surrounded me, making me deeply aware of the value of relationships, comforts, possessions, and life experiences. There, isolated and devoid of distractions, the blessings of my life were illuminated in stark contrast to my immediate environment. The rawness of nature and the essentials—water, shelter, safety, and food—realigned my perspective on what truly mattered.

Connecting to nature is a portal to holistic health. The act of detaching from our bustling lives and reconnecting with nature reduces stress, enhances cognitive clarity, improves immunity, and can support hormone balance.

In an era dominated by constant stimulation and relentless pursuits, it's essential to occasionally step back. By immersing ourselves in nature and embracing moments of simplicity, we not only revitalize our mental and physical energy but also rediscover the richness of life that's often overshadowed by the noise of our routines.

Here's the great news: you don't have to embark on a month-long wilderness survival journey to reap all the health advantages of nature. By adhering to the simple principles in the Nature Pyramid, you can experience the restorative effects of spending time outdoors.

Grounding

Grounding, also called "earthing," is a holistic practice based on the idea that physically connecting to the Earth's natural energy can be beneficial to your health. This is often done by walking or standing barefoot outside, preferably on grass, soil, sand, or any natural substance, so you have direct contact with the Earth.

The theory is that the Earth's surface carries a natural electric charge and that being in direct contact with it can help neutralize free radicals and reduce inflammation throughout the body. Grounding may provide a range of health benefits that might include:

Improved Sleep: Some people who practice grounding report that they experience better quality and duration of sleep. The idea is that the natural electromagnetic fields from the Earth can help regulate the body's internal clock and melatonin secretion, promoting healthier sleep patterns.

Reduced Inflammation: Grounding is said to neutralize free radicals in the body, which in turn may reduce inflammation. Chronic inflammation is linked with many health conditions like heart disease and arthritis, so practices that could reduce inflammation are often seen as beneficial.

Stress Relief: Engaging in grounding practices, particularly outside in a natural setting, can be calming and help reduce stress. This might be due to a combination of the physical practice, the mental focus it requires, and the general benefits of spending time in nature.

Connecting with nature also instills a sense of belonging, an understanding that we are part of a complex ecosystem. This spiritual connection helps us recognize the beauty and diversity of life, in turn cultivating respect and responsibility for the environment. Stepping outside and embracing the natural world is not just a refreshing break from our routine—it's an essential part of our biological heritage and a potential key to better health at the molecular level. Simply put, it has the ability to put all things in perspective and serves as a neurological reboot.

Spending mere minutes in nature is essential for human health from an evolutionary lens because our physiological and psychological systems have evolved to thrive in these environments. As our modern lives become increasingly disconnected from nature, it is vital to prioritize this time.

***

Connect to Yourself

Before I explain how and why you should make an effort to connect with yourself, nature, tribe, and community, it's key to point out that to truly connect also means to consciously disconnect. It signifies intentionally unplugging from the noise, from life's distractions—the ceaseless digital chatter, the relentless pursuit of material success, and the numbing pace that often substitutes for substantive engagement. As we detach from these attention-diverting elements, we create space to immerse ourselves in the depth of our own minds, the rhythm of nature, the support of our tribe, and the spirit of our community.

Disconnection is not about isolating oneself but about selective engagement, allowing us to refocus on the crucial aspects of our lives that truly cultivate health. The paradox of connection in our modern era is that, in order to emphasize what truly matters, we must first master the art of strategic disconnection.

Micro Distractions, Macro Impact

Have you ever experienced a moment when you're intent on looking up crucial information on your phone, only to find yourself suddenly sidetracked by an inconsequential notification or an irrelevant text?

This scenario exemplifies a modern phenomenon I call a "micro distraction," a common occurrence in our daily lives. These distractions, seemingly small and harmless, have the insidious ability to hijack our attention, diverting us from our initial intentions and objectives. They interrupt our thought process, impeding the important task at hand.

In today's fast-paced, digitally driven world, our smartphones and devices are constant sources of these micro distractions. Each ping, buzz, or flash of the screen has the potential to pull us away from meaningful activities, disrupting our immediate concentration and productivity.

A "macro distraction" operates on a larger scale compared to its micro counterpart, yet its effect remains strikingly similar. These are major distractions that divert us not just from immediate tasks but from our overarching goals, such as making good health choices or adhering to our long-term goals. Macro distractions encompass a wide range of activities and phenomena, including relentless toxic news cycles, mindless television watching, involvement in friend drama, and the infinite scroll of social media.

Unlike micro distractions, which are brief and often momentary, macro distractions have a more profound and prolonged impact. They not only consume our time but also influence our thoughts, emotions, and behaviors, often in ways that are misaligned with our deeper values and long-term health goals.

The insidious nature of macro distractions lies in their ability to reshape our priorities without our conscious awareness. Over time, they can subtly shift our daily routines and habits, steering us away from our intended path. Recognizing these distractions is the first step toward regaining control. By being mindful of the time and energy we devote to these activities and understanding their impact on our health goals, we can proactively disconnect from them, which aligns with our health intentions and overall life objectives.

An effective antidote for macro distractions is a "Technology Cleanse" that helps break the dopamine addiction to these distractions and facilitates a connection to what's beneficial to your health goals. If you think that disconnecting from these distractions could benefit you, don't forget to check out the practical steps outlined at the end of this chapter.

Monk Mode

Speaking of disconnecting, have you ever heard of the trendy term "monk mode?" It's a short period of focused self-improvement, often characterized by discipline and minimal distractions. The concept draws inspiration from the lifestyle of monks, who dedicate themselves to spiritual growth and discipline.

During monk mode, individuals may concentrate on various aspects of health and personal development, such as learning new skills, improving physical fitness, or advancing in their careers. Distractions like television or social media are often minimized or eliminated to enhance focus and productivity.

Strategic disconnection from the noise and true connection to what really matters allows you to interact with the world in a more mindful and purposeful manner. By teaching you to intermittently disconnect, it equips you with the ability to discern between mere distractions and what truly contributes to your personal growth and happiness.

It's not just about accomplishing more tasks or endless biohacking but about being present and connecting with what truly matters. Consider this periodic disconnection as your "micro monk mode."

Mental Fitness

Connecting to self is simply tuning in to you. How do you feel, and how's your headspace? Simple, right? Not at all. It's very challenging, and it requires practice. I call this mental fitness, and it involves cultivating the skill of becoming a witness and observer of your own thoughts and emotions.

It's not about quieting your mind completely but about understanding the intricacies of your consciousness. This practice guides you to a state of balance and peace. It encourages the recognition of the illusory nature of self and promotes living more fully in the present moment.

Mental fitness will help you to develop a sense of calm amidst this constant flow of thoughts and emotions. By observing the entire freeway rather than fixating on individual cars, we learn to detach from specific thoughts and maintain a more balanced perspective. This approach encourages a calmer, more focused state of mind, allowing us to navigate the high-speed traffic of our thoughts and emotions more effectively.

Let's quickly revisit the quote at the beginning of the chapter and provide context. "Everything changes once we identify with being the witness to the story, instead of the actor in it." As the main actor in your life's story, you may become directly involved in every emotion, thought, and experience. This attachment may often lead to stress, anxiety, and a lack of objectivity, as you're so immersed in the role that you're playing that you can't see beyond it.

Becoming the witness, on the other hand, means observing your thoughts, emotions, and experiences without getting entangled in them. This perspective allows you to watch your daily life unfold as if you were an audience member, creating a sense of detachment that fosters clarity and calmness.

Movie Premiere! Featuring... You

Let's say you're frustrated because you're constantly exhausted, unfulfilled with your work situation, or disappointed in yourself for repeatedly making poor choices despite previous resolutions to change.

Here's a different way of viewing this situation. You feel the frustration of fatigue; you recognize exactly how it feels, the heaviness in your body and lacking the energy to do things you need to. You observe the feeling of disappointment, like a weight in the heart, a mix of sadness and frustration when your reality falls short of expectations. You feel the features of frustration and disappointment, but you are not frustrated or disappointed. There's a difference.

It's like watching a movie where you are the main character in a familiar scene; you recognize and understand the emotions and events unfolding. However, there's a cushion that provides a transparent perspective on the circumstances. This allows you the distance you need to change your typical emotional response.

This concept encapsulates a profound shift in perspective, moving from an emotionally invested actor to a calm and objective witness. By embracing this shift through the practice of mental fitness, you gain the ability to navigate your life with greater clarity, resilience, and wisdom.

Everything does change when you can identify with being the witness, as it opens a new path toward self-realization. The practice of training your mind to become the witness is a game changing play in essential health playbook, allowing you to live your life in a more conscious and intentional way. This is the ultimate power of your mind and practicing mental fitness will help this become your reality. Chapter 11 will offer a game plan so it's easy to add this to your new playbook.

I'm no Yoda

Lau Tzu shared great wisdom, "Knowing others is intelligence. Knowing yourself is wisdom. Mastering others is strength. Mastering yourself is absolute power."

There were many reasons why I began to train and master my mind. It was all of the anecdotes from Zen masters revealing how enlightened they had become, it was attempting to understand my previous traumas, and it was just the plain curiosity of consciousness. It was also to simply quiet the noise.

I felt like an imposter trying to meditate because, for some reason, it didn't feel natural. I felt like there were a lot of rules; I had to sit this way, in this specific posture, and do nothing. It was intimidating because it was unfamiliar, and I didn't want to feel frustrated. Plus, simply sitting in a specific position sounded like torture to me. I was dead wrong.

I redefined this process as mental fitness, which was the way I was going to train my mind, like a muscle, to be ready for life's inevitable cognitive tests. I reframed it as a short trial to investigate my headspace. Mental fitness is the regular exercise of the mind to enhance awareness and mental clarity in the face of life's heavy lifting.

Just as physical fitness sculpts your muscles for resilience and strength in the arena of sports or the trials of life, so too does mental fitness shape the contours of your mind. With regular practice, it instills calmness, sharpens awareness, and roots you firmly in the present moment. It's a kind of mental athleticism that allows you to confidently navigate life's unpredictable courses. Without this mental conditioning, you run the risk of being governed by your thoughts and emotions, reacting impulsively rather than responding mindfully.

Therefore, mental fitness is as vital as sharpening your athletic competence, turning you from a mere bench player in your own mental game into a seasoned, experienced quarterback calling the plays in your cognitive huddle.

My experience showed me that it was possible to view myself and the world differently. I realized I could have a clearer mind than I had at that time, which was influenced by my injury, upbringing, and habits. This led me to learn about techniques to understand my mind better through self-reflection.

Why Train Your Mind

There are so many reasons to practice mental fitness, but here are two simple ones. First, it helps deal with a cluttered mind. Everyone experiences unhappiness at different points in life. Although happiness comes, it also goes. Given enough time, feelings of frustration, annoyance, anger, sadness, and fear surface. Most of us regularly experience a negative headspace.

Our mental distress is a lot like constantly replaying past games or worrying about future matches, forgetting to play the game that's happening right now. We're so caught up in strategizing and replaying that we don't notice we're missing the current play on the field of our thoughts. Mental fitness provides a way to stay in the game and gain a profound understanding of these emotions. It involves understanding the nature of our thoughts and disconnecting our self-identity from them.

> *Recognize your emotions because they become your thoughts.*
>
> *Examine your thoughts because they become your spoken words.*
>
> *Assess your spoken words because they become your focus.*
>
> *Watch your focus because it will become your actions.*
>
> *Evaluate your actions because they become your daily habits.*
>
> *Review your daily habits because they will become your lifestyle.*
>
> *Your lifestyle is what you repeatedly do—it determines your health.*

Another reason to meditate is to enhance our pure awareness. We don't often remind ourselves about the beauty of life, our blessings, the wonderful people around us, and our fortune to have them. Instead, we're engrossed in a narrative of inadequacy, always seeking something more.

We constantly tell ourselves that if only we could alter some aspects of our lives—look better, be healthier, have more money, change jobs, find a partner, or have a better social life—then life would be perfect. We imagine that once our lives are perfect, we can finally focus on the present moment and feel content. However, our happiness appears to be contingent upon satisfying those desires.

Happiness Gap

Be mindful of the happiness gap, as we all have a tendency to fall into it. This theory, which has been supported by empirical research, suggests that happiness is determined by the gap between one's expectations or aspirations and their actual experiences or outcomes. Individuals with high expectations but low levels of achievement or satisfaction tend to feel less happy than those with lower expectations who achieve similar outcomes. This theory highlights the importance of managing our expectations and being mindful of the impact that our aspirations can have on our health.

You achieve a goal, and almost immediately, you might start asking, "What's next?" I fall into this trap all the time. The pursuit of mental fitness involves understanding the workings of this dissatisfaction and our ongoing quest for happiness. In Chapter 11, you'll learn the power of setting floors and ceilings for individual goals, which removes frustration within the happiness gap and replaces it with fulfillment and accomplishment.

Mental fitness involves being present to fully immerse yourself in the world experience, finding pleasure in your interactions with others and in the blessings all around you. It's about enjoying the act of behaving more intentionally and appreciating the mental state that such good intentions create. Mental fitness is about having the ability to be a witness and observe your thoughts and emotions. This state allows you to proactively choose how you want to respond rather than react as a reflex to each stimulus.

How to Practice Mental Fitness

Mental fitness begins with a decision to practice it. You follow the process that speaks to you, which can be mindfulness, transcendental meditation, mantra meditation, sit spots, visualization, or any other way to focus your attention. Many start by closing their eyes and focusing on their breath. In doing so, most people feel their awareness is located in their head, and they direct their focus toward their meditation object. If they're focusing on their breath, they'll feel it at their nose's tip, their chest, or their abdomen's rise and fall.

The main challenge is staying focused and not getting distracted by thoughts. Which you will, and that's the point. When you're distracted by thoughts, become aware of it, and go back to your anchor. The more you practice, the stronger your mind will become. That's why it may be called the ultimate cheat code, "mind porn," or even the Jedi mind trick. *Everything changes the moment you realize you have the power to control your mind and not let it control you.*

For me, the experience itself wasn't so directly relevant to what I later came to consider the true purpose of mental fitness, but it revealed for me the fact that it was possible to have a very different experience of myself and the world and my sense of being in the world.

Your Focus Flashlight

Let's practice for one minute. Your attention can be compared to using a flashlight. Imagine your attention as the beam of a flashlight, and you have the ability to point at it wherever you choose. Right now, your attention is on these words. But with a little guidance, you can direct that beam elsewhere. Let's explore how.

Your seat: Think about the feeling of your seat against your body. This is like shining the flashlight on something close by, focusing on the present physical sensation.

Temperature: Now move the beam to the temperature on your skin. This shift in focus helps you become aware of your immediate environment.

Dinner last night: Directing your attention to what you had for dinner last night is like aiming the flashlight into a dark room filled with memories. It's a journey back in time, albeit a short one.

Current sounds: Lastly, let's shine the flashlight on the sounds around you. Listen closely and focus on them. This is like focusing on the present once again but in a different way, listening to subtle noises that you might not usually notice.

Controlling your flashlight is mental fitness. You learn to control where you shine the flashlight of your attention. It's not just about picking something to focus on; it's about deciding how to hold that focus as long as possible. Like holding a physical flashlight steady, it might be challenging at first. But with practice, you'll become more skilled at keeping the beam where you want it.

In daily life, your flashlight might be darting all over the place, from one thought to another, one conversation to the other, or from one task to the next. Mental fitness practice teaches you how to hold it steady, focusing on what's essential at the moment, whether it's a sensation in the body, the breath, or a specific thought or emotion. This control leads to greater awareness, calm, and ultimately, mastery over your own mind.

He Knows Kung Fu

I can't emphasize enough how transformative the Connect element has been for so many individuals who have gone through my program. It seems that we're all craving authentic, genuine relationships and a deeper understanding of ourselves. Over the years, I've witnessed countless epiphanies from patients who began to practice mental fitness. While both Kelly and Corey made significant strides by prioritizing mind training, there's one individual whose transformation was nothing short of extraordinary: Trevor.

Trevor was a thirty-eight-year-old single man who held a demanding role as a regional sales manager for a well-known software company in the Bay Area. With around 180 people reporting to him and a relentless travel schedule, Trevor seemed perpetually distracted. Conversations with him were challenging, to say the least; he'd check his phone and watch continuously, interrupting me to fast-track to "the diet stuff" and even taking calls mid-meeting despite my respectful requests for him to focus on the conversation.

Rather than allowing my resentment with his scattered attention to frustrate me, I reframed it as my challenge. I took a different approach, dedicating significant time to discussing the mechanics of his mind and its repercussions on both his professional and personal relationships. I initially recommended guided meditation apps for short five-to-ten-minute sessions. Unfortunately, it was a major fail.

Going back to the drawing board, I spent a lot of time comparing his scattered attention to a flashlight, aimlessly pointed here and there. I explained that his mind was training him and listed all the reasons why he needed to train it. It would improve his sales numbers, his dating, and the whirlwind in his head, causing constant anxiety. I even made him a promise: if he set achievable floor goals for mental training, he would experience a moment of pure clarity.

What happened next still moves me to tears as I write. Trevor not only met the mental fitness tasks I set for him but experienced a spontaneous epiphany. For a brief moment, he became a dispassionate observer of his own thoughts and experienced pure awareness. He texted me that very day, exclaiming, "Bro, whatever Jedi mind sh*t you're giving me, I'm in!"

Encouraged, we doubled down on his mental training. I increased the length and frequency of his meditation sessions and guided him to identify "sit spots" for deeper mindfulness. The change was like a scene from *The Matrix* when Neo downloads martial arts training and realizes that not only does he know kung fu, but believes he cannot be beaten.

At our next meeting, Trevor was all ears.

I explained, "Imagine your life as a movie. If you're the main actor, every emotion, thought, or experience directly affects you. You're caught up in the drama, and it's easy to get lost. Now, think about becoming the witness to your own story. You still experience everything, but you're not swept away by every emotion or thought. You observe, you understand, but you don't lose yourself."

Trevor nodded slowly. "Like watching a movie of my own life?"

"Exactly. The quote I always find pertinent is: 'Everything changes once we identify with being the witness to the story, instead of the actor in it.'"

"So instead of getting worked up about every little thing, I'm just observing and learning?" he asked.

"Yes! You are not your thoughts or emotions; you're simply observing them. This change will allow you to respond and not react. There's a huge difference."

Trevor was quiet for a moment, then his eyes brightened. "I finally get it. Last week, when I had that huge presentation, I was a total wreck. But halfway through, I remembered that *I just feel nervous, but I'm not nervous.* I now realize the difference."

I replied, "That's a huge breakthrough, brother! You started to become the witness. How did that change the experience for you?"

"It was liberating, to be honest. I could see my nervousness as just a feeling that was there, not as a definition of who I am."

"This is just the beginning, Trevor," I emphasized. "The more you practice being the witness, the more empowered you become in every aspect of your life. You won't just live your story; you'll start to understand it."

"So what's next?" he asked.

"The sky's the limit. Keep practicing, keep observing. And in our next session, we'll explore some specific techniques to deepen this awareness."

We added more and more techniques, and he soaked it all up. The transformation I witnessed over the subsequent twelve weeks was astounding. Trevor was reborn mentally. Our conversations were no longer one-sided affairs; he was fully present, attentive, and remarkably focused. Even better, his newfound mental equilibrium had a transformative impact on his professional relationships.

It was, without a doubt, one of the most significant mental turnarounds I've ever facilitated in my program, and it underscores the immense power and potential of focused mental fitness training.

Consciousness

"Control of consciousness determines the quality of life." - Mihaly Csikszentmihalyi, *Flow: The Psychology of Optimal Experience*

Consciousness has been a central topic of interest for centuries. It raises several fundamental questions: What does it mean to be conscious? What is the nature of the self? What's the relationship between consciousness and the physical body?

I seriously contemplated adding the concept of consciousness into my health manifesto. I truly believe you can't define mental fitness without at least introducing the concept of consciousness. It's a key part of the Lazarus Method and needs to be introduced. So, what is the definition of consciousness? I'm still trying to define it for myself and always attempting to describe it to my patients.

Consciousness is a complex and multifaceted concept that is often defined differently depending on who you ask and the context. However, in a broad sense, consciousness refers to the state of being aware of, and able to think and perceive one's surroundings and experiences. It is often associated with the ability to experience feelings, thoughts, and perceptions.

In the field of psychology, consciousness is a continuum that ranges from full awareness to deep sleep. In neuroscience, it is linked to the functioning of the brain and nervous system, particularly in areas like the cortex and thalamus. Philosophically, it involves discussions about the nature of the self, personal identity, and the mind-body problem, with consciousness often seen as a subjective and first-person experience that's difficult to reduce to purely physical or functional explanations.

Consciousness remains something of a mystery, with many questions about its nature and origins still unanswered, but I'll provide a simple definition for you. It is pure awareness without any intermediary thoughts, feelings, or perceptions. This form of consciousness is typically associated with states of deep meditation or enlightenment and involves a dissolution of the sense of a separate self, leading to a more unified or non-dualistic experience of reality.

What does all this perception mumbo jumbo mean? Well, our exploration here serves a practical purpose: to guide you towards greater energy and clarity in your daily life. By understanding and tapping into this pure, unfiltered awareness, you can improve your energy and sharper mental clarity.

Awareness

Awareness may be the most powerful technique for your playbook. It's your ability to notice and understand what's happening around you, including thoughts and feelings. My friend and meditation expert, Cory Muscara, has a great way of describing awareness using what he calls the three layers of experience. He has revealed that there are three main things happening at any given moment.

1. Your experience.

2. Your awareness of your experience.

3. The story you tell yourself about your experience.

Recognizing these three layers is crucial for living a more intentional life. Awareness is the part of you that knows what is happening as it's happening and your ability to directly know and to be cognizant of events, thoughts, emotions, or sensory patterns. In this sense, awareness is a specific and pointed consciousness and a skill you can leverage when making different choices for your health.

Intuition

Intuition is often described as that "gut feeling" that guides you in certain situations. It's like an internal compass, gently nudging you in the right direction. Sometimes it's a strong sensation, like an inner voice loudly telling you "Yes" or "No." At other times, it's subtle, like a quiet whisper or a slight uneasiness.

Consider a common situation: meeting someone for the first time. Even without their saying much, you might get an instant feeling of comfort and ease or perhaps a sense of unease and discomfort. This immediate response isn't based on logical thinking or analysis; it's your intuition at work.

Another example is when you're faced with a tough decision, and you've weighed all the pros and cons, but something still doesn't feel right about the choice that seems logically correct. That's your intuition suggesting you might want to think again. Do not ignore your intuition; it's simply data processed too quickly for your conscious mind to comprehend.

Even when everything looks perfect on paper, if something feels off, that's your intuition signaling you. It's not always easy to explain why or how you know something. But this intuitive understanding often leads to more fulfilling paths and decisions. Trusting this innate guidance will empower you in your day-to-day life.

Building your intuition starts with one thing: trust. Try to be aware of your gut feelings or the feelings that come to you out of the blue, wherever you are. You might feel like you don't want to go somewhere or you don't want to engage with a certain person. Always believe in these feelings, even if you can't make sense of them logically. Intuition comes from a higher understanding that's there to help guide you and keep you safe. Let yourself trust what you feel deep down. Grow the skill of trusting your intuition.

The future you will thank you for listening to your intuition, for upholding boundaries that supported your inner growth, for saying no to things that did not align with your values, for taking the time to build your self-awareness, and for staying true to your vision of optimal health.

Mind Medicine

Another way to explore your consciousness is by using "mind medicines" or psychedelics. Think of it like going on a journey guided by these substances, where you can discover new landscapes of your consciousness, awareness, and intuition. These mind medicines can help you see parts of yourself you didn't know existed. Each gives you a unique chance to discover more about yourself and the amazing potential you have inside.

In simpler terms, what it means is that there are a handful of "consciousness compounds" that can change the way your mind, thoughts, and behaviors are structured. There are hundreds of these medicines that have been used for thousands of years in almost every culture.

The use of various mind medicines for therapeutic and spiritual purposes can be traced back thousands of years. Various indigenous cultures, particularly in Central and South America, have a long history of using them in spiritual and shamanic rituals. Archaeological evidence, including cave paintings and artifacts, suggests that such use may date back to at least 5,000 to 7,000 years ago.

Recent research on psychedelics has shown promising results for their therapeutic potential in treating a range of mental health conditions. Psilocybin, a natural compound with a history rooted in ancient spiritual and healing practices, has emerged as a groundbreaking therapeutic agent, showing remarkable potential in treating mental health disorders such as depression, anxiety, and addiction and offering profound insights into the human psyche.

MDMA, DMT, and LSD can also positively impact the mind by interacting with various neurotransmitters and their associated systems. MDMA is known for its ability to elevate mood and enhance emotional bonding by increasing the release of serotonin and oxytocin, leading to feelings of empathy, closeness, and happiness. DMT, often associated with intense visual experiences, may modulate neural circuits involving serotonin, influencing perception and consciousness. LSD's interaction with serotonin receptors results in altered sensory perceptions and potentially profound introspective experiences.

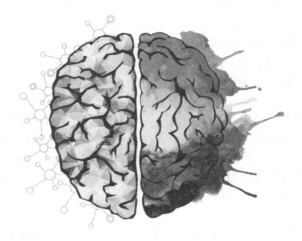

These mind medicines allow you to reshape the stories and behaviors that have influenced your life. These stories and behaviors, like unproductive or toxic programming, traumatic experiences, depression, anxiety, and addiction, are often symptoms of underlying issues. Psychedelics warm up your mind, making it possible to change your perspective of those stories. Most of these stories, such as a near-death experience, childhood trauma, or the absence of a parent, were not consciously chosen by you; they were situations absorbed from, or influenced by, your environment.

Psychedelics act like a softening agent for the clay of your mind, allowing you the flexibility to reshape long-standing narratives. These narratives, such as past traumas or family dynamics, were often imprinted upon you by external circumstances rather than chosen by you. Once the mental clay is softened, the critical aspect is how you choose to remold it.

The importance of having an expert guide you through the process of using psychedelics is key. Proper "set and setting"—your mindset and the physical and social environment in which you have the experience—are crucial factors that an experienced guide can help optimize. This ensures not only a safer experience but also one that is more likely to yield therapeutic benefits.

Furthermore, proper integration of your experience is vital for long-term positive outcomes. The Multidisciplinary Association for Psychedelic Studies (MAPS) is a great resource that can provide the essential framework for reflection and interpretation.

Microdosing is the act of consuming sub-perceptual (unnoticeable) amounts of a psychedelic substance. Many individuals who have integrated microdosing mushrooms into their weekly routine report higher levels of creativity, more energy, increased focus, and improved relational skills, as well as reduced anxiety, stress, and even depression. When paired with a clear intention and a proper health game plan, these consciousness compounds can amplify your frequency of awareness, gratitude, and love.

Tear off That Label

A single "mind medicine" experience has the potential to reveal deeper insights into the essence of reality than thousands of hours of scientific research. The following story exemplifies the magnitude of these mind medicines. It pertains to the concept of the "label theory" I introduced in Chapter 2, where individuals start to exhibit behaviors and attitudes that align with the condition they believe they have.

I attended a health "retreat" a few years back with the intention to reconnect with myself and nature using a specific mind medicine. This retreat offered one of the best gifts I've ever received, a brand-new view about... myself.

The experience and its unfolding are beyond my explanation, but there's a well-known adage in these circles: "the medicine doesn't give you what you want, it gives you what you need." Evidently, this revelation was something I needed far more profoundly than I could have ever anticipated.

Throughout the experience, a relentless and echoing voice persisted in my mind, which I initially tried to dismiss as it diverted me from my planned journey. Every time I ventured deeper into this experience, this voice got louder and grew increasingly insistent, reaching a state that left me with no other option but to stop and listen.

What was the voice saying? The voice delivered a transformative, five-word message that forever altered the trajectory of both my health and my life.

"I am Not a Diabetic."

Now, you might be thinking, "Is that all? Was that the life-altering message?" You might have anticipated something more profound or esoteric, like "I embody pure love" or "I am a reflection of the cosmos." But it was a straightforward, succinct phrase, precisely what I needed. All it required from me was to take a moment and be present to hear it.

You see, in the months following my injury, I was told I was an insulin-dependent diabetic with digestive failure, and I was going to struggle with my health for the rest of my life. It was not only a label, but it was also a curse. Ever since that moment, even though I didn't realize it, I lived my life as a diabetic with digestive failure. I was obsessed with blood glucose numbers, insulin shots, CGM readings and this data became almost an extension of myself, dictating my daily routines and decisions.

Insulin shots became a stressful, unavoidable ritual. Each injection was a stark reminder of my dependency on external means to regulate my body's functions. This obsession with numbers and medication not only consumed my time but also profoundly influenced my mental and emotional state, reinforcing my diabetic identity.

This fear dictated my life. Each unexplained blood sugar surge and digestive twinge sent waves of paranoia coursing through me. This persistent fear not only overshadowed my daily life but also steered my decisions, relationships, and overall well-being, trapping me in a cycle where my identity was inextricably linked to my medical label.

This mind medicine experience didn't miraculously heal my crushed organs or remove the diabetes diagnosis. It didn't give me the answers to the universe or give me what I wanted from the retreat. It "gave me what I needed" and allowed me to tear off that label and destroy that curse. It offered a new awareness and outlook for my health challenge.

Since shedding this medical label, I've integrated my experience with the combination of mental fitness techniques, fortifying this fresh outlook. This journey that I've shared with you exemplifies the transformative strength of self-connection. It's a testament to the immense power of your consciousness, awareness, intuition, and mental resilience, highlighting how these facets can profoundly reshape your life's narrative.

You don't need to seek out a health retreat or use mind medicines for self-connection. Simply dedicating time to self-reflection and engaging in mental fitness exercises can unlock the profound potential of your consciousness, awareness, and intuition. This focused introspection can bring clarity, helping you to transcend any medical labels you might have been given or internalized.

***

Connection to Tribe: Family, Friends, Community

If there's one crucial insight that mind medicine offers, it's the importance of our tribe, family, friends, and community. In the era of accelerating digital interconnection, the innate human need for real, tangible, face-to-face connections, community, and a sense of belonging continues to hold its significant place. Tons of anecdotal and scientific studies have underscored the immense physical, psychological, and emotional health benefits that stem from a sense of community, support, love, and belonging.

The "Law of Five" is a concept that holds considerable relevance in the realm of leadership and personal or professional growth. This principle suggests that your personality and behavior are influenced significantly by the five individuals with whom you spend the most time.

This principle asserts that our closest acquaintances exert a considerable influence over us, shaping our habits and lifestyles. It's quite likely that you and your closest companions share many common habits, both beneficial and detrimental. Yet, many of us tend to disregard this reality. "If you look at the people in your circle and don't get inspired, then you don't have a circle; you have a cage." — Nipsey Hussle

We may trick ourselves into believing that we can hang out with individuals possessing poor health habits, focusing solely on the positive traits we aspire to adopt and disregarding the rest. It's possible but can be difficult. Inevitably, you may integrate some of those undesirable habits.

Consider this: if you are a fitness enthusiast, there's a high probability that a majority of your close friends also prioritize fitness. If your tribe loves to explore and challenge their minds and set high goals, you'll be inspired to do the same. If your closest acquaintances are characterized by ambition and motivation, you are likely to exhibit these traits as well.

If your closest friends complain about everything and are constantly making excuses for their poor choices, it's quite likely you may eventually do the same. In essence, our closest companions have the potential to shape us significantly, just as we can shape them, across all aspects of life—be it physical, financial, spiritual, or professional. If you're the wisest person in the room, you're in the wrong room.

Small minds discuss people. Average minds discuss events.

Great minds discuss ideas. Brilliant minds discuss opportunity.

Therefore, it is crucial to be discerning about the individuals you keep within your sphere of influence. I recommend that you critically evaluate your companions and be deliberate about who you allow to remain in your immediate vicinity. This advice may seem harsh, but it's important to recognize that these personal health influencers can either distract or support your health playbook. It's productive to have teammates who support and inspire you to be healthier. Identify them and add them to your playbook.

Your Real Social Network

Influences are not restricted to the individuals around us; they extend to the books we read, the podcasts we listen to, and the social media profiles we follow. Instagram, Facebook, TikTok, X, and YouTube may unconsciously mold your perception and reality as profoundly as real-world interactions. These digital narratives are a hotbed of emotions.

So, whether you realize it or not, every time you log on to these social media platforms, you're absorbing the emotional content in your feed. Therefore, I encourage you to reflect on the reality you desire. Audit your social media profiles and be mindful of whom you follow—not just in your physical world but digitally as well.

Have you ever heard of a social media digital detox? I've personally observed the transformative impact of a social media digital detox, a valuable challenge within the Lazarus Method that consistently garners enlightening feedback from participants. Almost all of my patients have come to understand the importance of being discerning when it comes to health advice, as not all opinions warrant your attention, and much of the information out there is designed to convince you of something or sell you something.

Make wise choices. If you're not present and aware, these accounts may shape your reality. Notable philosopher and psychonaut, Terence McKenna, offered us great advice to "Stop consuming images and start producing them." This means shifting from being a passive observer to an active creator.

Collective Consciousness

The choice to be an active creator allows you to contribute to our collective consciousness. In some spiritual, philosophical, and metaphysical traditions, collective consciousness is understood as a shared, unified consciousness that connects all beings. This concept transcends the sociological framework and proposes a much more interconnected, universally shared mindset.

Under this interpretation, collective consciousness isn't just about shared cultural norms or social beliefs. Rather, it suggests that all beings—humans, animals, perhaps even the entire universe—are part of a single, interconnected whole.

In this view, our individual consciousness (our thoughts, emotions, experiences) are not entirely separate but rather contribute to this larger collective consciousness. The implication here is that what each of us thinks, feels, and does can influence the collective consciousness.

For instance, if many individuals cultivate positive thoughts, emotions, or actions, that could contribute to a shift in the collective consciousness toward more positivity. Similarly, widespread negative or harmful attitudes could have a negative impact on the collective consciousness. The concept of collective consciousness in this spiritual or metaphysical sense is often associated with practices associated with the quantum field and the energy of the universe.

Think of individual consciousness as drops of water. Each drop of water is unique and has its own identity. It has its own characteristics, just as each person has their own thoughts, emotions, and experiences.

Now, imagine each of these individual drops of water falling into the ocean. Once they merge with the ocean, they're no longer separate drops but part of a larger, unified body of water. They still exist, but they're now part of something bigger—the collective body of the ocean.

In this analogy, the ocean represents collective consciousness. Each individual drop—each person's individual consciousness—contributes to the overall composition and state of the ocean. The ocean is impacted by the accumulation of all the individual drops, just as the collective consciousness is shaped by the thoughts, feelings, and experiences of each individual.

Have you ever considered what frequency of energy you're donating to this collective body of water? It might seem odd, and you might even be skeptical, but I've seen incredible health outcomes when my patients connect with this collective energy.

Connect to Your Community

This collective energy reminds us that we're all in this together! Connecting to your community encompasses more than just residing in a particular geographic location. It involves engaging and actively participating in the local fabric of life through interaction with your neighbors, affiliations with local organizations, and contributing to the cultural and social life of your local community. This engagement fosters a dynamic, interactive relationship between you and your community.

CONNECT TO YOUR COMMUNITY

Fostering relationships with neighbors	One of the fundamental aspects of community connection involves cultivating relationships with neighbors. This could mean helping a neighbor with yard work, having casual conversations, or organizing block parties or community events. These interactions, no matter how small, create a bond of mutual respect, support, and understanding among community members, which in turn fosters a sense of safety and security.
Local organizations and institutions	Involvement in local organizations, like community centers, religious groups, recreational clubs, or volunteer groups, provides a platform to meet like-minded individuals, share experiences, and work toward common goals. These organizations are often the backbone of a community, providing support services, recreational activities, and platforms for community discussions.
Social, cultural, and civic participation	Engaging in the cultural and social life of one's community can be achieved by attending local festivals, performances, public meetings, or participating in local clubs or groups. On a civic level, involvement may include participating in local governance, attending town hall meetings, or voting in local elections. These interactions not only provide a sense of camaraderie but also facilitate understanding and respect for diverse viewpoints, traditions, and experiences within the community.

Health Community

A health community represents a collaborative circle of individuals that might include family, friends, acquaintances, or even complete strangers from anywhere around the world. Bound together by shared health goals and a commitment to prioritize health, this community serves as a support system, discussing common symptoms, answering questions, offering encouragement, and inspiring each other to achieve more.

There's a network of like-minded people who actively engage on our innovative coaching platform. Our community is not just a place to share ideas but an environment that fosters collaboration, growth, and the pursuit of optimal health. From integrating the concepts laid out in the book to opening discussions on various health-related topics, we've cultivated a thriving community eager to learn and share. Consider this your **"Thrive Tribe!"**

Beyond the platform, there are various channels of communication where we connect on a more casual level. For instance, the Oura Circle, where twenty members transparently share their sleep and activity scores, promotes a culture of accountability. We also share healthy restaurants, hidden biking trails and interesting health podcasts to inspire curiosity and comradery.

The goal is to be a part of any community where you can exchange health insights. This could be on holistic health, nutrition, natural medicine, meditation, competitions, restaurants, biohacking, or exciting fitness ideas. The power of any community is that it's not merely a static group but a dynamic network always open to new people and perspectives. It's about sharing each other's health playbooks and adding new plays.

I encourage you to become a part of any enriching community. Whether you choose to join the Thrive Tribe in the Lazarus Method Network, find an established group that resonates with your health interests or challenges, or embark on the journey to create your own circle of health enthusiasts, there's immense value in connecting with others who share your playbook and passion.

Summary – Connecting the Dots

The Connect chapter presented four essential areas: nature, self, tribe, and community, emphasizing their role in your holistic health. It explored how to connect with nature using the nature pyramid. It emphasized the importance of understanding consciousness, awareness and intuition with your focus flashlight and provided guidance on how to train your mind with mental fitness.

The chapter also made you star of your own box office blockbuster and warns you about the happiness gap that often lies in front of us and the plays to avoid it. It covers why and how to connect to your tribe and community and evaluates if your teammates use another or a similar health playbook. Finally, it extended an open invitation to become part of our "Thrive Tribe," and share your thoughts with a welcoming community who apply this playbook in their own way.

Putting these connections into practice will enhance your headspace and health. Now, it's time for you to connect the dots and engage with what matters most to you.

THE LAZARUS METHOD GAME PLAN

PLAY 1: Disconnect with a Tech Cleanse

The goal of this cleanse is to help you intentionally unplug from the noise and distractions that pull you away from your core values and health goals. These steps help reconnect with what's truly important to you and your health.

Coach's Tip:

A Tech Cleanse may reveal a dopamine addiction to these platforms. Be aware of it and consider if these platforms are distracting you from your health goals. Write down two solutions to avoid the distractions.

T H E   L A Z A R U S   M E T H O D

TECHNOLOGY CLEANSE

Introduction: Welcome to The Lazarus Method Technology Cleanse. The goal of this cleanse is to help you intentionally unplug from the noise and distractions that pull you away from your core values and health goals. By performing these 5 steps during this 48-hour experience, you'll have taken meaningful steps to reconnect with what's truly important to you and your health.

CLEANSE COMPONENTS

Objective: List your primary health goals. These could be related to any of The Lazarus Method essential health elements including nutrition, supplements, movement, sleep, rest, mental fitness, performance, or overall happiness.

1 News Detox:
Detox from the continuous news & propaganda cycle.

2 Social Media Fast
Take a break from the posts, likes & alerts.

3 Contact Purge
Remove 10 contacts from your phone.

4 App Rearrangement & Deletion
Delete & rearrange all unused Apps.

5 BONUS: 24-Hour Phone Removal
Experience your life without your phone for a day.

PRE-CLEANSE ASSESSMENT

Before you begin the cleanse, take a moment to rank your current technology distractions (1st being the most distractive and 5 being the least).

	1	2	3	4	5
Social Media	☐	☐	☐	☐	☐
News	☐	☐	☐	☐	☐
Email	☐	☐	☐	☐	☐
Games	☐	☐	☐	☐	☐
Shopping	☐	☐	☐	☐	☐

Others:

_____ ☐ 1 ☐ 2 ☐ 3 ☐ 4 ☐ 5

_____ ☐ 1 ☐ 2 ☐ 3 ☐ 4 ☐ 5

_____ ☐ 1 ☐ 2 ☐ 3 ☐ 4 ☐ 5

1.   NEWS DETOX

Detox from the continuous news and propaganda cycle that fuels fear and anxiety. In today's fast-paced society, news is almost inescapable. While staying informed is important, the constant influx of news *(especially negative news)* can lead to increased levels of stress, fear, and anxiety. Check the following boxes to detox from the news:

☐ **Identify Sources:** List the news sources you regularly check.

☐ **Log Out/Unsubscribe:** Log out of news apps or temporarily unsubscribe from news notifications.

☐ **Set Boundaries:** Choose a designated time to catch up on necessary news after the detox, preferably from unbiased sources.

2.   SOCIAL MEDIA FAST

Take a break from the posts, likes, & alerts that may distract you from your priorities. Social media platforms are designed to capture your attention. The endless scrolling, likes, and notifications can distract you from real-life priorities and can even lead to feelings of inadequacy or unhappiness. Check the following boxes for your social media fast:

☐ **List Platforms:** Enumerate the social media platforms you use most often.

☐ **Notification Off:** Turn off all social media notifications.

☐ **Log Out:** Log out of all social media apps or temporarily uninstall them.

3.   CONTACT PURGE

Remove 10 contacts from your phone that no longer serve your health or goals. Over time, we accumulate contacts that may no longer align with our current life situation or aspirations, leading to unnecessary digital clutter. Check the following boxes to purge your old contacts:

☐ **Review Contacts:** Scroll through your contacts list.   ☐ **Identify and Remove:** Select 10 contacts that you no longer interact with or who don't serve your current health or life goals.

4.   APP REARRANGEMENT & DELETION

Delete all unused apps and rearrange the remaining ones to focus on what truly matters. Unused or distracting apps not only consume storage space but can also serve as a constant source of distraction. Check the following boxes to improve your Apps:

☐ **Inventory:** Take stock of all the apps on your phone.   ☐ **Delete:** Remove any apps you haven't used in the past month.   ☐ **Rearrange:** Move essential and goal-supportive apps to your home screen.

5.   BONUS: 24-HOUR PHONE REMOVAL

Experience your life untethered and unfiltered without your phone for an entire day. Our smartphones have become almost like an extra limb. A full day without it can offer a powerful perspective on how reliant we are on technology. Check the following boxes for a phone cleanse:

☐ **Plan Ahead:** Inform necessary contacts that you'll be unavailable.

☐ **Set Up Auto-Responses:** Activate auto-responses for calls and texts, if possible.

☐ **Safeguard:** Put your phone in a safe but inaccessible location.

POST-CLEANSE REFLECTION

1.   What positive changes did you notice during and after the cleanse?

2.   What challenges did you face and how did you overcome them?

3.   What are the next steps you'll take to maintain a balanced relationship with technology?

PLAY II: Mental Fitness: Train your Mind for the Breath Battle

Dive into a Breath Battle, where you challenge yourself to train your mind with a daily contest of focus. For the next 10 days, dedicate a few minutes each day to sit quietly and concentrate solely on your breathing. Each time your thoughts drift, gently bring your attention back to your breath.

Document your progress and turn it into a competition with yourself by aiming to increase your focused time day by day. Track your daily scores based on the length of uninterrupted focus and watch as your mental stamina improves over the three weeks.

Before beginning the challenge, set a personal goal for the longest duration of focused time you aim to achieve on the final day, day 10, and write it down as your target.

Mental Fitness Goal: _____ Minutes on Day 10

Coach's Tip:

Visualize training your mind like training a muscle. Watch your mind get stronger and sharper in only 10 days.

PLAY III: Connect to Nature

Craft your personalized nature plan using the Nature Pyramid, selecting and noting a unique natural spot for daily, weekly, monthly, and annual visits corresponding to each layer of the pyramid. This approach ensures a consistent and escalating connection with nature, from everyday spots to special yearly destinations.

DAILY: _____

WEEKLY: _____

MONTHLY: _____

ANNUALLY: _____

Coach's Tip:

Use the All-Trails App to find a trail near you and plan a 2nd Gear Strategy.

Ralph Waldo Emerson offered timeless wisdom when he said, **"Life is a journey, not a destination."**

As you arrive at this point in your health adventure, reflect on the road ahead. Will you wander along the path of contemplation, receiving each concept and lesson along the way, or will you stride boldly towards a specific health goal, focusing on the solution?

In this adventure, each step is a part of the journey, reminding you that the path you take is as significant as the destination you seek.

"Choose Your Own Health Adventure"

If you're drawn to **Identify Your Inner Voice and True Purpose**, *let your intuition guide you to page 149 in the Spark Chapter.* This section offers a glimpse of self-discovery, offering methods for identifying your life scorecard and an introduction to your avatar. It also introduces spark igniters, tools designed to stimulate personal growth and self-awareness.

If you're looking to **Elevate your Motivation and Inspiration**, *I dare you to turn to page 287 in the Challenge Chapter.* This section explores unique concepts like the universe test and your quantum coach, providing innovative perspectives on personal growth. You'll also learn about setting realistic challenges that involve establishing floors and ceilings to define and achieve your goals effectively.

If your primary goal is to **Lose Weight and Optimize your Digestion**, *turn to page 55 in the Nourish Chapter.* The recommendations provided in this chapter will help you improve your body composition and jumpstart your metabolism. The concepts that will help you are the Nourish Target, Metabolic Flexibility, Intuitive Eating, EAT Protocol, and the 80/20 Eating Principle.

If you can't wait to **Enhance Brain Function and Mental Clarity**, *navigate to page 255 in the Learn Chapter.* This section is dedicated to helping you diminish brain fog, enter your personal flow zone, and offers insight into achieving a mental makeover. It introduces the principles of neuroplasticity, providing you with tools to sharpen your cognitive abilities and enhance mental acuity.

If you want to learn how to **Increase Strength and Improve your Metabolism**, *run to page 219 in the Move Chapter.* Here, you'll explore the effective 2nd Gear Strategy, delve into the three foundational pillars of movement, review compound and functional movements, and discover the importance of incorporating play into your routine.

For those seeking to **Boost Energy Levels and Overcome Fatigue**, *chill out and to page 119 in the Rest Chapter.* This section will introduce you to the concept of your chronotype and circadian rhythm for optimal sleep. It provides detailed guidance on the RESTED Protocol, designed to optimize your rest and energy and two-minute timeouts, a strategy to rejuvenate and maintain sustained energy throughout your day.

CHAPTER 8

MOVE

Imagine there is a magic pill that eases anxiety and depression, improves focus, boosts your mood, provides joy and pleasure, helps you sleep, causes you to lose weight, have better sex, and guarantees you live longer. Oh, and it's available whenever you want; it's completely free and has no known side effects. Well, I'm here to inform you that this magic pill exists...

It's called "movement."

Yep, it's the ultimate wonderdrug. Food may be the most abused anxiety drug, and movement may be the most underutilized antidepressant. And the more you use it, the more stamina, strength, and flow will follow. So, let's discuss how you can leverage this wonder drug and take advantage of this phenomenon called movement.

I've intentionally used the word "movement," and I named it the Move element for a handful of reasons. It's important to note that movement, exercise, and fitness are used interchangeably in this chapter.

Fitness continues to be one of the most captivating and sought-after subjects across various age groups and demographics.

The relentless desire to achieve a lean, strong physique and an overall appealing appearance fuels universal interest. With society's increasing focus on health and well-being, the fitness industry has exploded into an incredible $96 billion market and is expected to grow to $434 billion in the next five years! This massive growth has led to the emergence of innovative trends, equipment, classes, and business models that cater to diverse fitness goals and preferences.

However, it's essential to recognize that not all offerings within the growing fitness industry are equally beneficial or genuine. While some products, methods, and services demonstrate ingenious solutions to fitness challenges, a significant portion may be categorized as mere gimmicks. These may promise quick fixes and dramatic results but often lack scientific backing or practical efficacy. As the industry continues to expand, discerning between valuable fitness strategies and fleeting trends becomes a critical skill for anyone embarking on a journey toward physical wellness and personal transformation.

Movement Specialist

I have been infatuated with the science and benefits of movement my entire life. This started as a child with a love of games and sports and eventually transitioned to organized sports at competitive levels. I even traveled all over the United States and internationally, competing with some elite athletes.

This passion inspired me to pursue an undergraduate degree in exercise science and transitioned into teaching undergrad students exercise physiology at the Cal Poly exercise physiology lab. This high level of education and experience provided essential data to understand an individual's fitness level, functionality, and performance capacity.

The assessments in the lab included the VO2 max test (maximal oxygen uptake test), which measured the maximum amount of oxygen a person can utilize during intense exercise and is considered the gold standard for assessing cardiovascular fitness. We also used body composition analysis, biomechanical assessments, muscular strength and endurance tests, and functional movement screens, which are essential for designing personalized training programs.

Learning and teaching these concepts was crucial for my ability to provide personal training programs for clients while I was in graduate school. Before my time as a healthcare provider, I worked with clients and continued to learn and apply my knowledge and exercise training methodology.

I currently review and apply the most current movement protocols. I'm excited to share my expertise, perspective, and unique approach to movement with you so you can apply it to build strength, lose body fat, and supercharge your metabolism.

Movement Philosophy

The truth about achieving strength, fitness, and a powerful physique is that it does not necessitate a complex, expensive, or flashy approach. My personal philosophy on optimal movement is founded on engaging in a routine that is consistent yet flexible, enjoyable, and infused with elements of play and recreation. This routine is not a rigid structure but one that can adapt to whatever life throws at you. It's a proven approach that aligns with ancestral norms, the most current research, and the essential pillars of movement.

In my experience as a personal trainer and healthcare practitioner, I have observed a recurring theme: many individuals, maybe even you, exhibit a reluctance or even an aversion to exercise. This phenomenon can be attributed to a handful of reasons. One prevailing factor seems to be a misconception that exercise is inherently painful, tedious, or inconvenient.

There's often a lot of confusion and a diminished sense of confidence in knowing what to do and how to do it when it comes to exercise. These factors, along with other considerations, lead many of my patients to associate the word "exercise" with discomfort or agony. For this reason, I've shifted the terminology from "exercise" to "movement," reframing it in a more positive and approachable light.

Recognizing this common challenge, I have leveraged my personal experience and training to formulate a game plan for you that aims to redefine and invigorate the experience of movement. I integrate these components with each of my patients in a personalized manner, and you can apply them as well.

Ancestral Movement

Our ancestors didn't exercise; they moved all day. Ancestral movement refers to the study and practice of human physical activities that align with our evolutionary heritage. It represents an approach to movement and fitness that recognizes the adaptations and needs developed throughout human history. Here is a basic summary of the background and history of ancestral movement:

From an evolutionary standpoint, the human body has evolved to perform specific tasks essential for survival, such as hunting, gathering, climbing, and long-distance walking or running. These fundamental movements shaped our ancestors' daily lives and had direct implications for their health and well-being.

Mismatch Theory

The modern sedentary lifestyle is often in stark contrast to our ancestors' active way of living. This has led to the "mismatch theory," where our current lifestyle does not align with our evolutionary adaptations, potentially leading to various health issues. With the advent of agriculture, human movement patterns started to change, focusing more on repetitive tasks. This shift began to reduce the diversity of movements, leading to a gradual decline in overall physical fitness and health.

The Industrial Revolution further removed humans from their ancestral movement patterns, as mechanization replaced many physical labor tasks. The rise of sedentary jobs marked a significant departure from the varied physical activities our bodies evolved to perform.

In recent years, there has been a resurgence of interest in returning to more natural, play-oriented, functional movement patterns. This has been driven by an understanding of the importance of diverse and natural movements for overall health. Programs emphasizing ancestral or primal movement patterns focus on replicating the functional movements that were integral to our ancestors' lives.

The science of ancestral movement has grown, examining the biomechanics, physiological responses, and health outcomes associated with these natural movement patterns. Research validated the benefits of ancestral movement practices, providing a scientific basis for this approach. By examining the evolutionary pressures that shaped human physiology and movement patterns, let's focus on fun, playful, and effective movements that align with our evolutionary design and create strength and resilience.

Play and Recreation

"We do not stop playing because we grow old; we grow old because we stop playing." - George Bernard Shaw

Another component of the ancestral movement is play. If you ask a child about the important things in life, play is at the top of their list. So how does this concept of play relate to us as adults? There is an increasing body of evidence to suggest that the type of playful physical activity we usually associate with young children will also offer substantial health, mental, and physical benefits for you.

Play doesn't need justification. Engaging in playful movement nurtures practical skills like strength, balance, agility, coordination, speed, and mental focus. It's more than just a nostalgic pastime; it's an integral part of human development and well-being, regardless of age.

Play serves as a key to unlocking the mind, sampling boundless possibilities, and discovering fresh levels of creative opportunities. It's vital to our well-being, yet it's often underrated. In reality, play is essential to human development—a biological imperative tied to our survival.

One of the most critical aspects of play and recreation is the fun factor. By participating in activities that bring joy, excitement, and challenge, you're more likely to view exercise as an enjoyable aspect of your life rather than a chore or obligation. Play acts as a natural antidote to the pressures of modern life.

But who has time to play? How do I play as an adult? With the relentless demands of work and family commitments, it often appears that there's no room for play in our daily routine. Believe me, there's always time, even if it's just a few minutes, and it's a game-changer when you manage to do it. I recommend a game of tag, playing your favorite sport, dancing, a playground workout, capture the flag, dodgeball, an impromptu game of frisbee, or even crawling on the floor. It may sound silly, but once you make it a part of your movement routine, the benefits are incredible.

***

Pillars of Movement

The Three Pillars of Movement in the Lazarus Method provides a well-rounded and innovative approach to fitness. They integrate key aspects of physical well-being, infusing individuality and enjoyment into the process. These pillars represent a holistic and forward-thinking approach to fitness, with potential benefits for every person.

Utilizing the Lazarus Method's Three Pillars of Movement empowers you to train your heart for enduring stamina, amplify your power for incredible strength, and find your flow with natural fluidity. Let's review the importance of each pillar, then read on to see how you can apply them.

1. Cardiovascular, Pulmonary, and Endurance:

This pillar focuses on enhancing cardiovascular and pulmonary endurance through a distinctive strategy that involves targeted heart rate zones and specific intensity levels. It emphasizes the essential role of stamina in your overall health and performance.

2. Strength, Resistance, and Power:

This pillar combines traditional aspects of strength training with functional movement patterns, with an emphasis on enjoyment and creativity. It involves a diverse range of exercises to build muscle, enhance power, and foster functional fitness.

3. Flexibility, Mobility, and Stability:

This pillar emphasizes the importance of flexibility, mobility, and stability through fundamental stretches, foam rolling protocol, and core strength exercises. By combining these key aspects in your routine, you can enhance fluidity, reduce the risk of injuries, and attain overall body functionality.

Movement Gears

Movement is medicine. But you have to choose the right dose and the right medicine. Every pillar of movement can be categorized into one of several different zones based on your heart rate. There are five distinct heart rate zones numbered from 0 to 5. Each represents a different intensity of effort, uses a different energy system in the body, and corresponds to one type of movement you make.

These zones are more than mere numbers; they are tailored pathways to your fitness. These heart rate zones are similar to the gears of your vehicle, with each specific zone symbolizing a varying degree of exertion. There are also five gears in your vehicle, and all are used as you drive around town and when you're on the highway.

When your car is in park or in neutral, you're in Zone 0. This represents a state of complete rest, where there's little to no physical activity, and the heart rate is at its lowest. This could be when you're sitting or lying down, not engaged in any significant movement.

As you accelerate, you move to first gear or Zone 1. These would be activities of daily living such as getting dressed, brushing your teeth, getting in and out of the car, cooking, and walking around your house, and the heart rate remains relatively low. It also includes a concept that is relatively unknown in metabolic activity called non-exercise activity thermogenesis, or NEAT for short.

Zone 2 represents a moderate level of activity, comparable to a car moving in second gear. Activities falling under this category could include brisk walking or light jogging, with the heart rate slightly elevated but conversation still possible.

Recent research has revealed that Zone 2 is an important gear that is often missed or overlooked.

Zone 3, or third gear, is a moderate to high level of activity. This could involve activities such as running or cycling at a steady pace. Your heart rate has noticeably increased, and maintaining a conversation becomes more challenging.

Zone 4, or fourth gear, is a high-intensity activity. At this level, the activities could be high-intensity interval training (HIIT). Your heart rate is high, and conversation is difficult to maintain.

Zone 5 represents maximum or near-maximum exertion and is comparable to a car flooring it on the highway in fifth gear. This is where you're pushing your body to its limit with activities such as sprinting at full speed, high-intensity interval training, or lifting heavy weights to exhaustion. The heart rate is at or near its maximum, and maintaining a conversation is nearly impossible.

The goal of comparing the different exercise zones to movement gears is to make it easy for you to integrate all your favorite movements. This comparison is not only intuitive and relatable but also makes your movement plan more accessible and straightforward. Once my patients align their gears with the three core pillars, they have a seamless strategy that simplifies the path to strength and flexibility.

Stuck in the Same Gear

I've worked with many patients who began my program with a dysfunctional movement routine. Some of these individuals were essentially robots in the gym, running at the same pace on the treadmill for twenty minutes, meandering to a shoulder machine to lift the wrong weight, and eventually making it to a squat machine where they checked their email for five minutes. Some go to a gym to check the box and literally spend more time in the shower than on the floor.

I've worked with others who only take the same spin classes at the same time every day, people who only do yoga on Monday and Friday, some who bench press and do curls every day, and others who take a stroll for thirty minutes and call a day. I respect anyone who prioritizes moving, as we all have different capabilities, schedules, and opportunities. I want to share a new perspective on optimal movement and motivate them to try other activities.

Take a moment and envision yourself navigating the same road in your car, day after day, at the exact same time. The route and scenery are unchanged. You find yourself trapped in one gear without the need or opportunity to shift either up or down. Each route has the same tedious stretch and landscapes, mirroring yesterday, the day before, and countless days before that. This drive turns into a lackluster loop in the same gear, traversing the same path, draining what could have been a daily adventure of joy and excitement.

This stagnant repetition is a striking metaphor for the experiences of many individuals who lack the variety in movement necessary to achieve their fitness goals. Without diversity in your exercise routine, you can lose the opportunity to feel the effects of that "wonder drug" that will help you lose weight, build strength, have fun, and maintain consistency, turning what could be a monotonous chore into an invigorating pursuit.

Taking the first step is usually the hardest, but I guarantee it will change your health immediately. If you're stuck in the same gear, I want you to consider adding a new gear to your routine to experience the benefits of the other forms of movement. No matter where you are on your journey, let's explore these dynamic gears together. I'll present a wide array of options, all designed to resonate with you and ignite your path forward. Your perfect fit is just around the corner, and I'm here to help you discover it!

Pillar 1: Cardiovascular, Pulmonary, and Endurance

This type of movement is segmented into distinct heart rate zones to offer a more personalized and effective approach. By understanding and utilizing these zones, you can tailor your activity to align with your specific goals, whether it's weight loss, building stamina, cardiovascular health improvement, or peak performance.

The Blue Zone: Your Second Gear

The energy source your body taps into changes as the intensity of your movement increases. For lighter exercises in first and second gear, your body mainly burns fat. As you shift up to third gear, your body starts to utilize carbohydrates more. At the highest intensity, fifth gear, your body uses creatine phosphate to create ATP, an immediate energy source.

ZONE	INTENSITY	HEART RATE	PRIMARY ENERGY SOURCE
Zone 1	Very Light	50 - 60% HR max	Fat
Zone 2	Light	60 - 70% HR max	Fat/Glucose
Zone 3	Moderate	70 - 80% HR max	Fat/Glucose
Zone 4	Hard	80 - 90% HR max	Glucose
Zone 5	Maximum	90 - 100% HR max	Glucose/Creatine Phosphate

This chart outlines different exercise zones, each defined by how hard your heart is working and where your body gets its energy from during that activity. Zone 1 is the lightest level of exercise, like a leisurely walk, where your heart is working at 50 to 60 percent of its maximum rate and mainly uses fat as its energy source. Zone 2 is slightly more intense, perhaps a brisk walk or light jog, where your heart is at 60 to 70 percent of its maximum, and it starts using some glucose (sugar) along with fat for energy.

As you move up to Zones 3 and 4, the activity gets more challenging, like a steady jog or running. Your heart is working harder, between 70 to 90 percent of its maximum. In these zones, your body continues to use both fat and glucose, but as the intensity increases, especially in Zone 4, it relies more heavily on glucose. Finally, Zone 5 is your maximum effort, like sprinting, where your heart is at 90 to 100 percent of its max. In this zone, your body primarily uses glucose, and something called creatine phosphate for quick bursts of energy.

Second gear is especially notable because the moderate intensity of movement in this zone stimulates mitochondrial function in your cells. That is ideal for your cellular engines that facilitate energy and longevity. Pushing harder shifts the energy source toward carbohydrates.

Unfortunately, many people often overlook second gear, jumping straight to third, fourth, or even fifth gear. There's a common notion that exercise has to feel hard and uncomfortable to be effective, leading many to focus on high-intensity workouts.

It's easy to overshoot second gear. A casual jog might feel like a "normal" pace, leaving you slightly out of breath, but it's likely placing you in third gear or higher. Second gear doesn't feel strenuous, and you could potentially maintain that level for hours, which might lead people to believe it's not very effective.

However, this underestimation of your second gear may be causing many to miss out on its significant health and performance benefits, as suggested by numerous studies. Zone 2 exercises, while deceptively easy, hold key value in an effective fitness program.

Here are a few of the benefits you can expect by incorporating Zone 2 into your routine.

Boost Metabolic Health

Zone 2 significantly enhances metabolic health, largely because of its ability to strengthen mitochondrial function, size, number, and performance, thus leading to more effective workouts and burning fat more efficiently.

Endurance and Performance

Zone 2 training effectively enhances endurance and performance. Increasing the mitochondrial density in the skeletal muscles prevents the need to rely on glucose for energy and mitigates lactate buildup, contributing to better performance and lactate clearance.

Prevent Injury and Aid Recovery

Zone 2 training reduces the risk of injury and promotes recovery because of the minimal stress it places on the body compared to high-intensity workouts, making it a valuable addition to any fitness regimen.

Simple Second Gear Strategy

How do you drive in second gear?

The concept of incorporating Zone 2 physical activities into daily routines for optimal health outcomes is practical and effective. By viewing common tasks as opportunities for exercise, individuals can engage in second-gear activities without having to set aside significant additional time for exercise.

Consider the act of carrying groceries home from the store. By choosing to walk instead of driving or using public transport, you're elevating your heart rate into Zone 2. Instead of viewing this as a chore, consider it a part of your weekly exercise regimen. If the store is too far to walk, parking farther away and walking the extra distance could serve the same purpose.

Household responsibilities are another great example. Tasks like sweeping, vacuuming, mopping, and gardening can elevate your heart rate into Zone 2. By intentionally investing a little extra effort into these tasks—moving faster, scrubbing harder, or incorporating squats and lunges while cleaning—you can turn them into effective workouts.

Another daily opportunity could be taking stairs instead of elevators. Climbing stairs is an excellent form of exercise that falls within Zone 2, and consciously choosing stairs over elevators whenever possible can greatly contribute to your weekly Zone 2 movement goals. Walking or cycling to and from work, or even simply during lunch breaks, is another practical way to incorporate Zone 2 activities into your routine.

The beauty of these strategies lies in their practicality. They require little additional time commitment, making them suitable for even the busiest individuals. With a little creativity and a shift in perspective, daily tasks, responsibilities, and chores can become opportunities for effective Zone 2 workouts.

Striving for consistency is the key to your movement, rather than pushing yourself to extremes and risking burnout; and as with any new habit, it takes practice and consistency. Once these habits become a regular part of your daily routine, they will help you lean up and boost your energy.

**NO NEED TO GRIND,
CONSISTENCY IS THE KEY.**

YOU DON'T HAVE TO BE EXTREME

BURNOUT

TIME

YOU HAVE TO BE CONSISTENT

TIME

* * *

Pillar 2: Strength, Resistance, and Power

Strength, resistance, and power play a critical role in the development of muscle mass, impacting the overall body composition in various positive ways. Stimulating muscle growth through progressive resistance not only enhances appearance by toning and sculpting the body but also boosts your metabolism.

This increase in metabolic rate aids in reducing body fat and increasing lean muscle mass, contributing to a healthier body structure. Strength also has a beneficial effect on bone density, functional fitness, athletic performance, and daily life tasks, making it essential for physical well-being.

This pillar is a multifaceted approach to fitness that integrates traditional strength training with compound movements and functional movement patterns, highlighting enjoyment and creativity. By employing a diverse range of strength exercises, it aims to build muscle, enhance power, and foster functional fitness.

In other words, this pillar will get you strong, sturdy, and shredded!

Lift Heavy Things

Strength training is the process of using resistance to build the strength, endurance, and size of skeletal muscles. The key is progressive overload, where the muscles are gradually challenged by increasing the resistance over time.

Strategies to Implement:

- **Individualized programming**: Tailoring workouts to your goals, fitness level, and specific needs.

- **Progressive overload**: Gradually increasing the resistance, repetitions, or intensity to challenge the muscles.

- **Compound movements**: Including exercises that engage multiple muscle groups, like squats and deadlifts, to enhance overall strength.

Resistance Training

Resistance training involves exercises that cause muscles to contract against external resistance, such as dumbbells, resistance bands, or body weight. This can lead to improved muscle tone, strength, and endurance.

Strategies to Implement:

- **Use various tools**: Dumbbells, kettlebells, resistance bands, or even body weight can be used for diverse and engaging workouts.

- **Focus on form**: Proper alignment and execution minimize the risk of injury and optimize results.

- **Incorporate functional movements**: Exercises that mimic daily activities can make resistance training more practical and effective.

Power Training

Power training focuses on executing movements quickly and explosively. It's vital for athletes but can be beneficial for anyone looking to enhance their physical capabilities.

Strategies to Implement:

- **Plyometric exercises**: Movements like jump squats and box jumps can increase explosiveness.

- **Olympic lifting**: Exercises such as the clean and jerk can be used to develop power but should be taught by a qualified instructor.

- **Combine strength and speed**: Using resistance with explosive movements can enhance both strength and power.

Functional Movement Patterns

Functional movement patterns are exercises designed to train muscles to work together, preparing them for daily tasks by simulating common movements used at home, work, or in sports. These patterns involve multiple joints and muscle groups, ensuring coordinated and efficient movements. They aim to improve strength, stability, mobility, and coordination, mirroring natural body movements like bending or reaching.

Functional exercises, which are customizable, enhance core strength, mobility, flexibility, and engage multiple muscle groups, making everyday tasks easier and reducing injury risk.

Here are some examples:

Deadlift: Bending over to pick up a paperclip or a box off the ground utilizes the same hip hinge and back strengthening motion as performing a deadlift. This movement engages the glutes, hamstrings, lower back, and core.

Front Squats: Crouching down to get in or out of your vehicle or to tie your shoelaces mirror the movement of a front squat. This involves the quadriceps, glutes, hamstrings, and core muscles, with an emphasis on maintaining an upright chest.

Lunges: Stepping up onto a high curb or climbing stairs activates the same muscles used in lunges, working the quadriceps, glutes, hamstrings, and calves.

Push-pulls: Opening a heavy door or pushing a shopping cart involves a push-pull motion similar to exercises like push-ups, rows, or chest presses. These movements engage the chest, back, shoulders, and arms, replicating everyday tasks.

Overhead press: Reaching up to place an item on a high shelf or changing a light bulb involves the same motion as an overhead press. This exercise works the shoulders, triceps, and upper chest, promoting strength in movements that require reaching overhead.

Plank: Holding a suitcase or carrying groceries requires core stability, similar to holding a plank position. This exercise helps build endurance in the core muscles, aiding in tasks that require prolonged engagement of the midsection.

Functional Movement Screen

I've been testing my patients' ability to perform these movements in my practice using a functional movement screen (FMS). The FMS test is a standardized assessment tool used to evaluate the quality of your fundamental movement patterns. The goal of this screening is to identify your asymmetries, limitations, or weaknesses in mobility and stability that might predispose you to injury or hinder performance.

I use the functional movement screen to develop personalized training programs to improve performance by focusing on your individual needs and capabilities. I recommend finding a trainer or practitioner who uses this assessment to help you personalize a functional routine.

Compound Movements

Compound movements are movements that engage multiple joints and muscle groups at the same time. They are important to strength development, as they allow for greater weight loads and challenge multiple muscles at once. This efficiency helps in building functional strength, enhancing metabolism, and improving the body's overall ability to perform both daily tasks and sports.

Here's a great way to think about compound movements. Imagine all the keys on a piano represent the muscles in your body. Playing a single note with your index finger is like isolating one muscle, such as a single bicep curl; it's simple and clear but lacks the depth and richness of a full piano chord with all your fingers.

When you play a chord on the piano, you use multiple fingers to press several keys together to create a unique, harmonious sound. In a similar manner, a compound movement involves engaging multiple joints and muscle groups simultaneously to produce a powerful and efficient motion.

The ultimate goal of a compound movement is to use multiple muscles to compose a beautiful piece of music using as many keys as possible. By using various combinations of keys, or in this case, muscles, you can produce unique and powerful movements that not only contribute to overall strength, but also to the functional harmony of the body.

Just as a pianist learns to skillfully play chords to bring a piece to life, incorporating compound movements into your fitness routine helps you to coordinate and utilize as many "musical keys" or muscles as possible. This approach leads to a symphony of movements that builds strength, enhances performance, and creates a well-balanced physique, mirroring the complexity and beauty of a well-played piece of music.

These movements can be broadly categorized into four main types, each targeting distinct muscle groups. By incorporating these four main compound movements, you can create an efficient strength routine workout that simulates real-life actions. Here's a simplified and elaborated breakdown:

1. **The push**: Think of exercises like bench press or a push-up. These are like pushing a heavy door open. The push trains the pressing muscles, primarily engaging the chest, triceps, and shoulders. It's all about using force to move something away from your body.

2. **The pull**: Imagine pulling a rope or doing a pull-up. This trains the back muscles, focusing on the rhomboids, lower traps, latissimus dorsi (lats), and even the biceps. The pull is the opposite of the push; it's about bringing something closer to your body.

3. **Knee flexion**: This involves bending the knee and engaging the muscles of the legs. Exercises like squats and lunges are perfect examples. Knee flexion trains the quadriceps, hip flexors, and adductors in the leg. Think of sitting down or crouching to pick something up.

4. **Hip hinges**: Deadlifts and hip thrusts are examples of this movement. Hip extension is about straightening the hips and involves the muscles of the glutes, hamstrings, and lower back, like the erector spinae. It's similar to standing up after bending over or picking something heavy off the ground.

The pillar of strength, resistance, and power offers a balanced approach that goes beyond muscle building. It emphasizes functional fitness, enjoyment, creativity, and real-world application. By incorporating these strategies, you can create a fulfilling and effective training regimen that meets your unique needs, whether you're looking to gain muscle, increase power, or simply look great naked.

***

Pillar 3: Flexibility, Mobility, and Stability

Flexibility, mobility, and stability improve the body's range of motion, allowing muscles and joints to move unrestricted and pain-free using the strength of the core muscles to support and stabilize you. Including these crucial movements promotes proper coordination, balance, and posture, reducing the risk of injuries, improving the alignment of the body, and increasing overall functionality.

There are hundreds of techniques and ancient practices to include this pillar into your movement routine. Below is a list of some of my favorites that are effective, fun, and challenging. I personally use them and provide coaching guidance for my patients. Your objective is to identify the techniques that speak to you and incorporate them into your movement routine.

Stretching strategies: Stretching can be categorized into various forms, including static, dynamic, ballistic, PNF, passive, active, isometric, and mobilization, each with distinct techniques and purposes. These different methods are used to enhance flexibility, warm up muscles, cool down after exercise, and improve overall physical performance and mobility.

Foam rolling: Also known as self-myofascial release, this involves using a cylindrical foam roller to apply pressure and massage various muscle groups, aiding in the release of muscle tightness and trigger points. The practice enhances flexibility, reduces muscle soreness, improves circulation, and supports overall recovery.

Functional movement patterns: Exercises such as deadlifts, squats, lunges, bear crawls, crab walking, and crawling engage multiple muscle groups and mimic our ancestral everyday activities, promoting overall strength, stability, mobility, and coordination. These movements can enhance athletic performance, reduce the risk of injury, and improve quality of life across various age groups and fitness levels.

Plank progressions: Series of increasingly challenging exercises that build upon the basic plank position, enhancing core strength, stability, and endurance by introducing variations and modifications to engage different muscle groups.

Yoga: Combines physical postures, breathing techniques, meditation, and philosophical principles to unify the mind, body, and spirit. It is often used for improving flexibility, strength, balance, and mental clarity and can be practiced in various styles and levels to suit individual needs and preferences.

Pilates: Focuses on controlled movements that target core strength, flexibility, and overall body awareness. Performed on a mat or specialized equipment, Pilates emphasizes proper alignment, breathing, and balanced muscle development to support efficient and graceful movements.

Tai Chi: Traditional Chinese martial art that emphasizes slow, controlled movements, deep breathing, and mental focus, often described as "meditation in motion." Practicing tai chi can improve balance, flexibility, and strength, reduce stress and anxiety, enhance mental clarity, and provide therapeutic benefits for various health conditions.

***

Ava's Movement Makeover

In Ava's initial assessment upon joining my program, her strengths were immediately apparent, particularly in the elements of Nourish, Rest, Connect, and Spark. A soft-spoken yet highly intelligent young professional, Ava was not lacking in motivation; what she needed was personalized guidance. However, her most notable area for improvement was evident in the Move component of the program. After an insightful discussion, the reasons for this vulnerability became clear.

Her perspective of exercise was a combination of confusion, fear and hesitance. She never spent much time playing sports growing up, so she was uncertain what to do. She knew she should be doing more than just walking and occasional yoga videos at home, but the gym environment was intimidating to her, and the idea of hiring a personal trainer felt overwhelming.

It was clear that she understood the importance of incorporating some type of weight training into her routine. However, her self-guided research on YouTube did not work, and the fitness gurus she followed on her social media platforms were too much for her to follow. As a result, she was unable to establish a structured or effective movement routine.

She was already feeling helpless and frustrated because her weight was steadily increasing despite her efforts to eat less, increasing her frustration. During the initial consultation, I listened intently to her concerns and apprehensions. I explained how the program utilizes the Three Pillars of Movement.

Her words echoed the sentiments of countless others. "I'm lost, and don't know where to start," she confessed. "I have the time. I just need a routine I enjoy that includes weights and all the other things."

I assured her, "It's not about right or wrong; it's about finding what works for you. Are you ready to try a new approach centered around fun and hitting different gears?"

Ava also mentioned a sense of urgency; her vacation in Mexico with college friends was just a few weeks away, and she wanted to feel her best. Eager to make a change, she fully committed to the gym schedule and strength training regimen I had carefully tailored for her. Initially, she felt out of place, unfamiliar with the gym's layout and equipment. However, within just a few days, that discomfort faded. Armed with a plan, her confidence started to soar.

As those weeks flew by, Ava had already made noticeable changes. The day before her vacation, she faced her wardrobe with newfound confidence. Gone was the need to hide behind long dresses; she boldly chose a tank top and shorts, feeling the results of her hard work. She radiated self-assurance, anticipating the adventure ahead with excitement.

But the true litmus test came the first morning of her vacation when her college friends woke up, grabbed coffee, and planned to meet at the hotel gym. In years past, they would have assumed Ava would opt for an early breakfast or a quiet morning with a book. But not this time. Ava had been waiting for this moment, eager to reveal her new self in a familiar setting.

As she walked into the gym, her confidence was palpable. Not only did she know her way around, but she also had a workout plan that was distinctly her own. Rather than sitting it out or awkwardly attempting to keep up, Ava took the lead. She even shared her personalized circuit training plan with her friends, transforming the workout into a fun experience.

The difference in Ava was massive, not just in her appearance but in her aura of confidence and accomplishment. Her friends noticed, and she felt it too—empowered, ready for whatever else the trip had in store for her. She was no longer the same person who had walked into my office weeks before, full of fear, apprehension and self-doubt. Ava had not just prepared for a vacation; she had transformed the part of her identity that she had been most self-conscious about.

Ava's fitness journey is a powerful illustration of a widely observed phenomenon, where the initial stages of pursuing a new health goal are often marked by a mix of high fear and low confidence. This emotional landscape is not uncommon; many of us experience similar feelings when standing at the threshold of a new challenge.

In Ava's case, her intention to get fit was initially overshadowed by apprehension and self-doubt, a barrier familiar to myself and maybe even you. However, as she embarked on her fitness routine, a significant shift occurred. With each step forward, Ava's fear began to diminish, and her confidence started to build.

This gradual transformation is evidence to the power of taking action, highlighting how the act of just simply starting can progressively convert fear into a growing sense of confidence. Intention is nothing without action, but action is nothing without intention. Read that again.

Eventually, Ava reached a point where fear became a faint echo, and confidence took the forefront, a journey that serves as an inspiring example for anyone feeling similarly hesitant about embarking on a new fitness endeavor.

INTENTION IS NOTHING
WITHOUT ACTION,
BUT ACTION IS NOTHING
WITHOUT INTENTION.

Upgrade your Fitness Game Plan

As you finish this chapter, thoughts may be swirling in your mind. You probably began this chapter believing it would be a straightforward path to fitness. You were looking for something simple and easy to implement into your daily routine. Now, presented with numerous movement concepts, you might find yourself overwhelmed and questioning how you can possibly apply all of these techniques.

Despite the abundance of concepts and techniques provided, the key to mastering them is actually quite simple. It's all about being efficient with these movements and integrating them seamlessly into your routine. Yes, it may seem complicated at first glance, but it will soon become second nature.

Recognizing that individual needs and preferences are unique, my method ensures that your journey to fitness is tailored to align with your specific goals and circumstances. By combining time-honored principles with modern scientific insights, the Lazarus Method offers a balanced and effective roadmap to fitness.

This approach breaks away from the trends and gimmicks that often dominate the fitness landscape. It offers a sustainable and genuine path toward strength, health, and performance. By prioritizing essential, enjoyable, and accessible aspects of movement, the Lazarus Method demystifies the tedious process of becoming fit and strong, making it an achievable goal for anyone willing to commit to the process.

> **Flexible**: Life is dynamic, and so should your fitness routine. The Lazarus Method embraces flexibility, allowing you to navigate through your day with a sense of balance and poise, adapting to your needs and evolving with you.
>
> **Enjoyable**: Forget the mundane and the repetitive. With our unique movement patterns and zone strategies, every session is infused with creativity, novelty, and fun. We believe that enjoyment isn't just an added bonus; it's a vital component of sustainable success.
>
> **Infused with play and recreation**: Remember the joy of movement as a child? The freedom, the laughter, the pure delight in being alive? Try to rekindle that spirit through your focus on play and recreation. My approach isn't about rules and regimens. It's about reconnecting with your body, engaging with the world, and rediscovering the pleasure in movement.

Summary - Your Personal Fitness Playbook

Like Ava, if you want more guidance or are looking for a fun and engaging way to incorporate these movements, or you're in search of a more customized plan tailored to your specific goals and fitness level, consider working with a personal trainer in your local area.

Your path to movement and fitness may be filled with various concepts and techniques, but the application is easy once you understand how to be efficient with these movements. With a bit of consistency and the aid of the tools I've provided, you can make all of this part of your regular routine.

I also highly recommend trying the Lazarus Method fitness app. This app has been designed to provide all of these movements in an interactive and enjoyable manner. It's like having a personal trainer right in your pocket, guiding you through each step, ensuring that you not only perform the exercises correctly but also enjoy the journey toward achieving your fitness goals.

You'll be hooked on your ultimate wonderdrug, guaranteed to provide enduring stamina, amplify your power for incredible strength, and find your flow with natural fluidity. Use the fun and diverse fitness plays on the next page to get started.

THE LAZARUS METHOD GAME PLAN

PLAY I: Climb the Pyramid

Select Your Movement: Select any 2nd gear activity from the Movement Pyramid, like brisk walking, hiking, or light jogging in the Blue Zone 2.

Set Your Schedule: Decide on the number of days per week you will do this movement for 30 minutes.

Three-Week Commitment: Plan to stick with this routine for three weeks.

First Week Frequency: In the first week, perform your chosen movement twice.

Progressive Challenge: Each week, aim to surpass your previous week's performance. This could mean increasing the number of repetitions, the duration of the exercise, or the intensity.

Tracking Progress: Keep a record of your daily performance to monitor your improvement over the three weeks.

Coach's Tip:

Determine your maximum heart rate, by subtracting your age from 220 and calculate your 2nd Gear Range by times it by 65%. Monitor your heart rate when you're in 2nd gear and aim to stay between 65% of your max heart rate.

Example: 45-year-old, Max HR of 175, 65% is 114 beats per minute. Write down your 2nd Gear Target HR:

_____

PLAY II: Play Cards

Get out a deck of cards. This is a bodyweight workout, and the reps correspond to the cards you pull.

1. Start a 20-minute timer.

2. Draw a card and perform the movement corresponding to the suit, with the card number indicating the number of reps. Face cards are 10 reps, Aces are 11, and number cards are as per their face value.

   - Hearts: Push-ups

   - Spades: Air squats

   - Diamonds: Burpees

   - Clubs: Lunges (total, not per leg)

3. After completing the reps, quickly draw the next card and continue the workout.

4. Keep going until the 20-minute timer goes off.

Coach's Tip:

Have fun, and consider grabbing a partner and splitting the deck!

PLAY III: Fun & Functional

Five-Minute AMRAP for 4 rounds (As Many Rounds As Possible): Create a list of 3-4 compound exercises, such as push-ups, deadlifts (with a kettlebell or dumbbell), and plank-to-push-up.

Set a timer for 5 minutes and perform as many rounds as possible of the exercises in sequence. Rest for 2 minutes, and then start where you left off. Write down how many rounds you hit and beat your score each week for three weeks.

Coach's Tip:

Use the Lazarus Method Fitness App for a handful of fun and functional workouts.

A foundational philosophy within the essential health playbook is that **"The best defense is a good offense."**

This strategic approach to your health, focusing on proactive decisions, serves as an effective offense. Simultaneously, a quality offense also acts as a formidable defense, equipping you to face life's inevitable setbacks, barriers, and challenges with resilience.

Will you prioritize the essential elements of health with an offensive or defensive strategy in mind? Both approaches are valuable, and as the head coach of your health journey, it's up to you to choose the strategies that best suit your needs.

"Choose Your Own Health Adventure"

If you're drawn to **Identify Your Inner Voice and True Purpose**, *let your intuition guide you to page 149 in the Spark Chapter.* This section offers a glimpse of self-discovery, offering methods for identifying your life scorecard and an introduction to your avatar. It also introduces spark igniters, tools designed to stimulate personal growth and self-awareness.

If you're looking to **Elevate your Motivation and Inspiration**, *I dare you to turn to page 287 in the Challenge Chapter.* This section explores unique concepts like the universe test and your quantum coach, providing innovative perspectives on personal growth. You'll also learn about setting realistic challenges that involve establishing floors and ceilings to define and achieve your goals effectively.

If your primary goal is to **Lose Weight and Optimize your Digestion**, *turn to page 55 in the Nourish Chapter.* The recommendations provided in this chapter will help you improve your body composition and jumpstart your metabolism. The concepts that will help you are the Nourish Target, Metabolic Flexibility, Intuitive Eating, EAT Protocol, and the 80/20 Eating Principle.

If you can't wait to **Enhance Brain Function and Mental Clarity**, *navigate to page 255 in the Learn Chapter.* This section is dedicated to helping you diminish brain fog, enter your personal flow zone, and offers insight into achieving a mental makeover. It introduces the principles of neuroplasticity, providing you with tools to sharpen your cognitive abilities and enhance mental acuity.

For those seeking to **Boost Energy Levels and Overcome Fatigue**, *chill out and to page 119 in the Rest Chapter.* This section will introduce you to the concept of your chronotype and circadian rhythm for optimal sleep. It provides detailed guidance on the RESTED Protocol, designed to optimize your rest and energy and two-minute timeouts, a strategy to rejuvenate and maintain sustained energy throughout your day.

If you want to prioritize **Being Present, Awareness, and Clarity**, *please focus on page 171 in the Connect Chapter.* This section is specifically tailored to enhance your mental fitness and sharpen your focus flashlight, a technique for cultivating mindfulness. You will also explore the happiness gap for true happiness and find your "thrive tribe" to achieve a heightened state of community and support.

CHAPTER 9

LEARN

The Learn element within the Lazarus Method is not just an instructional game plan; it's a core philosophy that encapsulates the beauty and complexity of human growth. While often overlooked or misunderstood, it is by far the most didactic element in this playbook (and by picking up this book, you're already doing it!)

At its essence, the Learn element promotes openness to new information, perspectives, and insights concerning health, performance, and life itself. It extends beyond merely acquiring new information and dives into the cultivation of a mindset that prioritizes fresh experiences and profound perspectives.

Learning is often experienced as a state of flow, a phenomenon where you feel a sense of pure joy and clear mindedness. As you flow, you become fully engaged with your intentions, and your execution may become effortless. Whether your goal is weight loss, overcoming brain fog, or getting fit, being in a state of flow can make reaching your health goals a journey of joy and excitement.

I advise my patients to never stop learning because life never stops teaching. Being a constant learner, regardless of age or life phase, is integral to this process. The Learn element encourages you to delve into the rich history of humanity, explore the insights of brilliant heroes and leaders who shaped the world, and embrace the wisdom they imparted. By connecting the past with the present, you can apply timeless lessons to your daily life.

Furthermore, the Learn element emphasizes engagement with cutting-edge health strategies discovered over the last decade. It invites you to critically analyze these advancements, adapt them to your unique circumstances, and implement them in a way that aligns with your individual needs.

The playbook includes several vital aspects essential for optimal health and personal growth. These aspects are neuroplasticity, achieving flow states, maintaining healthy skepticism, and embracing the philosophy of "fail often, learn lessons." When these aspects are properly integrated into your routine, they lead to a higher level of perspective and understanding and will allow you to execute your health playbook with confidence.

The More I Learn, the Less I Understand

"The more I find flow, the more I want more." This was a mantra I created many years ago, and after you read this chapter, my hope is that it resonates with you as well. It's characterized by a continuous openness to acquiring new information and embracing novel experiences. This approach to flow and learning emphasizes the importance of nurturing your curiosity and adaptability, allowing you to find your flow and evolve. In other words, take a proactive role in understanding new ideas that relate to your health.

There are many fascinating topics to learn about right now; biotracking wearable devices, longevity strategies, the metaverse, AI technology, cosmopoiesis, biology of belief, human consciousness, crypto, quantum field, UAPs, innovation, sustainable living, and of course, personalized medicine—to name a few.

Learning about health can also be a powerful catalyst for positive change in your life. When you equip yourself with knowledge and apply your health game plan from this playbook, you're more likely to make informed decisions that lead to lasting improvements in your health. Understanding the science behind healthy habits and the impact of lifestyle choices on your body empowers you to take charge of your well-being.

As you gain insight into the connection between your choices and your health, you become more motivated to apply your game plan. Moreover, learning about health helps you develop a sense of responsibility and self-awareness, encouraging you to be proactive in maintaining and improving your health. Learning plus application equals lasting changes. That's a winning formula.

Level Up Your Playbook

Knowledge is power, and learning about health will allow you to update your playbook and strengthen your game plan. By educating yourself about nutrition, movement, sleep, mindfulness, and natural medicines, you will be better equipped to make informed decisions that lead to lasting improvements in your health.

Seek out reliable sources of information in books, podcasts, masterclasses, articles, and expert advice. Consider attending retreats, engaging in workshops, or participating in health-focused programs that emphasize education and support as key components of success. Surround yourself with people that you can learn from, including friends, family members, and professionals who share your goals and can offer guidance. By fostering a supportive network, you will create an environment that nurtures your growth and helps you overcome challenges along the way.

Observation

American psychiatrist William Glasser suggested that we learn:

10 percent of what we read,

20 percent of what we hear,

30 percent of what we see,

50 percent of what we see and hear,

70 percent of what we discuss,

80 percent of what we experience,

95 percent of what we teach others.

Half of what we learn is what we see and hear. We don't see things as they are. We see them as we are. Observation is a powerful tool in the playbook, allowing us to recognize our unique perspectives. We can absorb and integrate information without direct involvement. It is a fundamental part of experiential learning, often fostering insights that cannot be gathered from text-based materials alone. Observational learning raises critical thinking, increases awareness of the world around us, and enhances our ability to understand and empathize with others' experiences.

A simple way to leverage this approach is through active observation in daily life. Actively observing your environment can be a rich source of learning. Whether it's noticing how your coworker manages a stressful situation, an acquaintance at the gym having a bad day, or an ecstatic friend after receiving exciting news. It could even be how a chef handles their knife, observing how a successful meeting is conducted, or studying the patterns in nature. There's always something to learn from what's happening around us.

A familiar example might also be "people watching," in which we actively observe strangers' behaviors, mannerisms, and actions. There's great insight from these interesting experiences. If we can set aside our own judgments of the person, we can gain valuable insight into effective and ineffective ways to communicate with others. All of this observation insight is a form of learning that may help you engage with the world around you.

The simple act of observation will also allow you to notice the signs and signals in your life. The cosmos are giving you signs every day in your sleep, while watching others, in your conversations, in books or podcasts, in the clouds, in epiphanies, everywhere. Pay attention to them and piece them together. You will likely notice a pattern. The universe is communicating with you. Or perhaps it's not the universe; maybe it's just simply observing what you're thinking about. Either way, it's an insightful learning experiment.

No Flow: The Missing Link?

I argue that some of the greatest moments in our lives are not the passive, easy times. I believe the best moments may occur when a person's body or mind is stretched to its limit in a voluntary effort to accomplish something new and worthwhile. But as we age with structured education, work demands, and societal expectations, learning can feel like a chore, diminishing the intrinsic joy it once provided.

This leads to a reluctance to venture beyond our comfort zones, causing us to miss out on achieving flow states—those moments of deep engagement and happiness that come from learning new tasks. As a result, we may settle for transient pleasures instead of the deeper satisfaction that comes from continuous growth and learning.

Lucas is a great example of the transformative power of embracing the power of learning and rediscovering the joy of flow states. I met him in my Napa clinic in 2018. Back then, he was a middle-aged single gentleman suffering from a host of health issues—both physical and emotional. On the surface, he seemed content, a man settled into the routines of adult life. But as we dug a little deeper, a different picture emerged.

Lucas reminisced about his childhood with great fondness. He was a curious kid who had been an inventive child, building intricate models out of LEGO blocks or taking apart toys to see how they worked. Those little pieces of plastic weren't just toys; they were gateways to uncharted worlds. As he pieced them together, he felt a surge of accomplishment, his young mind completely absorbed in the task. Even though he didn't realize it at the time, he was in a flow state, completely engrossed, happy, and content.

Lucas told me that this curiosity changed when he entered his school years, and the focus shifted from learning to grading. His passion for discovery was replaced by the need to score well in exams. Though he excelled academically, he felt a void growing within him. The focus had moved from the joy of learning to the obligation of proving himself.

The flow states of his childhood were all but gone, and when we started working together, he had been caught up in a nine-to-five job for years. The grind had stripped away the enthusiasm he once had. He told me, "It pays the bills, but it's boring as hell and doesn't excite my soul." I realized right there that Lucas's job was draining his energy from all the essential health elements, and his lack of excitement in learning new things overlapped with his personal life and health.

Post-work hours found Lucas in the comfort of his living room, binge-watching shows with microwave popcorn and a Diet Coke as a quick escape. Though it provided a fleeting sense of relief, it wasn't fulfilling. Like a sugary snack that offers instant gratification but no nourishment, this form of entertainment couldn't quench his underlying thirst for new interests and fulfillment.

The Rope That Tied it All Together

Lucas was so surprised and a bit embarrassed that his Learn score was a 3/10 from our initial exam. I explained how important learning, neuroplasticity, and flow states were for him, and he decided it was time for a change. I encouraged him to rediscover that missing piece and to embrace learning new interests that would bring him closer to a flow state.

To say Lucas's choice to rediscover his flow state was unexpected would be an understatement. I had imagined he might gravitate toward activities like model airplane building, complex puzzles, or even coin collecting. But Lucas had a different plan in mind.

He chose—wait for it—jump roping as his path back to flow!

At first glance, this may seem like a simple, even childish activity, but Lucas saw it as a learning challenge waiting to be conquered. You see, he had never been good at it as a kid, tripping over the rope more times than he could count and even being made fun of in elementary school. This old "failure" beckoned him; it was a chance to reclaim a lost skill and prove to himself that growth was still possible.

I loved this idea! I modified my movement plan for him on the Lazarus Method fitness app and substituted it with jump rope progression. I needed to have the challenge slightly above his skill level for him to find flow. He started off slowly, his first few attempts loaded with stumbles and missteps, even triggering old memories of shame from school. The rope whipped against his legs, leaving temporary red marks that seemed like badges of courage. But each falter only fueled his obsession to improve.

Lucas began practicing religiously, dedicating time each morning and evening to practice his technique. As the weeks rolled by, I updated his challenge so he was constantly in flow. If the challenge was too high, it would likely lead to frustration, and if it was too low, he'd be bored. That's the key to finding flow; having the learning challenge slightly exceed your skill level to facilitate the pure joy of accomplishment.

After only three weeks, he reached a momentous milestone I set for him: fifty consecutive double-unders. The sensation was electric, and Lucas felt it—that magical state of flow. He was completely absorbed, stretched to his limits, and it felt liberating. He was not only mastering the mechanics of the jump rope; he was also reclaiming his innate love for learning again and rewriting his personal narrative with the jump rope.

This accomplishment in jump roping did more than just improve his "Learn Score" in my program; it was also transformational for his body composition and metabolism. He lost 12 pounds, boosted his endurance, and had more energy than he'd had in a decade. He reignited his passion for learning and shattered the self-imposed barriers that had held him back for years. Lucas had rediscovered the profound joy that comes from embracing learning challenges, from pushing oneself to the edge of possibility and then leaping over it.

Lucas's transformation didn't just stop at fifty double-unders; it permeated every facet of his life, reigniting his enthusiasm for challenges both big and small. His entire family was so blown away with his new skill, they even questioned how he learned it so fast. He shared a quote with his family that he and I discussed, "Never stop learning because life never stops teaching." He introduced the concept of flow states to them and inspired them to find flow in their own way.

Lucas is a vivid reminder that no matter where we are in life, the flow state is accessible to us all—as long as we're willing to step out of our comfort zones and seize the opportunities to learn.

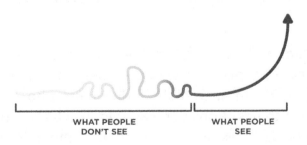

NEVER STOP LEARNING BECAUSE
LIFE NEVER STOPS TEACHING.

WHAT PEOPLE
DON'T SEE

WHAT PEOPLE
SEE

**

Learning Begins with Questioning, Not with Certainty

Learning is more than mere assimilation of knowledge; it's also about questioning conventional wisdom and challenging the popular narrative. By viewing information with a skeptical eye, we empower ourselves to make informed, deliberate decisions that align with our values and personal definition of success. Aristotle offered us a piece of wisdom when he reminded us, "It is the mark of an educated mind to be able to entertain a thought without accepting it."

There are millions of daily mental stimuli that compete for your attention at every single moment of your day. These external distractions are abundant in our daily experiences, including the "news," radio, your mobile device, social media algorithms, billboards, every conversation you have, and the multitude of events and objects you observe. Some are valuable; many are distractions.

Pause for a moment and assess where your attention gravitates on a typical day. If you're like most of my patients, you might find that your focus is primarily on work, family, social engagements, gossip, current events, or dramatic news. These aspects often dominate our minds, leaving little room for contemplation of more profound and enriching subjects.

How often do you dedicate your attention to exploring interesting concepts, marveling at unbelievable phenomena, or learning from incredible individuals who are doing remarkable things? Consider how seldom we allow ourselves to engage with experts who discuss thought-provoking topics without an underlying bias or hidden agenda and who present facts and insights purely to inform and enlighten.

Challenge Conventional Wisdom

"It ain't what you don't know that gets you into trouble. It's what you know for sure that just ain't so." – Mark Twain

Learning also involves adopting a critical and discerning mindset that questions the veracity of information, particularly in the realm of health. This perspective emphasizes the importance of challenging conventional wisdom and scrutinizing the underlying motivations behind the dissemination of information, as it is often driven by commercial interests or persuasive intentions.

I encourage you to develop analytical and critical thinking skills to effectively evaluate the credibility of various sources and the validity of their claims. By maintaining a healthy skepticism and questioning the current health trends, you are better equipped to make informed decisions that align with your personal health and well-being.

The foundation of this learning approach lies in the recognition that not all information is equally reliable or trustworthy. The responsibility is on the individual to actively seek out diverse perspectives and consider the context and potential biases in the information being presented. This may involve examining scientific research, consulting experts, and engaging in open-minded discussions to foster a more comprehensive understanding of health-related issues.

This definition of learning underscores the importance of cultivating a discerning and critical mindset to navigate the complex landscape of health information. By questioning "medical facts," conventional wisdom, and the motivations behind information dissemination, you can challenge the popular narrative, develop a better understanding of health issues such as fatigue, weight loss and digestive issues. This will allow you to make properly informed decisions when it comes to solutions.

Rage Against the Machine

In a world where information is more readily available than ever before, it has become increasingly difficult to discern what is accurate, unbiased, and reliable—especially with health and medical advice. The concept of skepticism in the face of overwhelming information is crucial in maintaining a healthy and informed understanding of the world around us.

Biased information: Information can be biased because of various factors, such as the source's motivations, the intended audience, or the selective use of data. Bias can manifest in subtle ways, making it difficult to recognize without critical thinking. For example, a news source may have a political leaning that influences its coverage, or a company may present data to promote its products.

Misinformation and disinformation: Misinformation refers to false or inaccurate information that is unintentionally spread, whereas disinformation is false information deliberately disseminated to deceive or mislead. These can be a result of mistakes, hoaxes, or malicious intentions and can have significant consequences if left unchecked.

Echo chambers and filter bubbles: Social media and other digital platforms can create environments where individuals are exposed only to information that aligns with their existing beliefs. This leads to a reinforcement of those beliefs and an unwillingness to consider alternative perspectives, exacerbating polarization and misinformation.

Cognitive biases: Human beings are susceptible to cognitive biases, which are mental shortcuts that can lead to irrational or illogical conclusions. Confirmation bias, for example, drives people to seek and accept information that confirms their preexisting beliefs while disregarding contradictory evidence.

An important part of the Learn element is to challenge the popular narrative, even the fact checkers. It has become increasingly clear that the popular narrative is a perspective from someone or some entity, and there's likely an agenda behind it.

It's crucial not to accept everything shared by various sources without critical evaluation. Cultivate a healthy skepticism, fact-check claims yourself, and seek information from people you trust and multiple credible sources to form a well-informed understanding of the world around you.

Most people rely on the news, social media, and their inner circle for news and information. I believe it's wise to be skeptical of the sources below and challenge everything.

News: Nearly every news source varies in terms of reliability and has a bias. Most are funded by special interest groups designed to convince you of something. It's crucial to consume news from reputable outlets that adhere to journalistic standards and have a track record of accurate reporting.

Social media: Social media platforms are notorious for spreading misinformation and amplifying echo chambers. While they can be useful for staying connected and informed, it's essential to exercise caution and verify information before accepting it. Be mindful of the credibility of the person or organization sharing the content.

Commercials: Advertisements are designed to sell products or services and may present biased or exaggerated claims. Period. It's important to maintain a healthy skepticism toward commercials and conduct independent research before making decisions based on their content.

Documentaries: Documentaries can provide valuable insights, but they are not immune to bias or selective presentation of facts. Assess the credibility of the filmmakers and their sources and consider watching multiple documentaries on a topic to gain a more comprehensive understanding.

Friends and family: People close to you may unintentionally share misinformation or biased perspectives. While it's essential to maintain trust and open communication, it's also important to critically evaluate the information they share, especially if it seems questionable or contradicts other reliable sources.

Hero's Journey

Reflect on the stories of people who have faced incredible challenges and failed in many of the endeavors that might intrigue you. Think about those who have found success or enlightenment in universal human experiences like fear, apprehension, wisdom, triumphs, and the profound search for meaning. These narratives are not mere entertainment; they hold the power to motivate and inspire us. They encourage us to take the first step or to push through our internal barriers. We should learn from them.

Understanding how others have faced similar dilemmas and overcome them connects us to a shared human experience. This connection is more than a fleeting emotion; it's a pathway to growth and self-realization. It's why the process of learning from others and absorbing their wisdom and insights, is not just beneficial but crucial.

You are the hero of your own health journey, bravely navigating your own path to wellness. This playbook serves as a guide for you and the heroes before us have shared how they have succeeded. In these tales of perseverance, resilience, and enlightenment, you may find a path to your own potential and a spark that ignites your own unique journey.

***

Reach Your Health Goals with a Mental Makeover

Flow states, also known as "being in the zone," refer to a mental state of complete absorption and focus on a particular task or activity. In a flow state, individuals experience heightened concentration, creativity, and performance.

At various points in our lives, we find ourselves deeply engrossed in an activity, experience, or project. These are the moments where our surroundings and the passage of time seem to fade away. Whether it's practicing martial arts, engaging in a challenging board game, surfing or snowboarding, creating music, drawing or other creative design work, gardening, playing golf, or even just playing freely, we experience a profound immersion that transcends the ordinary.

These experiences light up the pleasure chemicals in our brain and offer immediate value to our health. Understanding the health benefits associated with flow states and learning how to enter them can lead to pure joy, improved concentration, productivity, and overall health. Health benefits include:

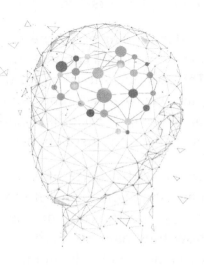

Improved concentration: Flow states can promote a sense of fulfillment and satisfaction, as individuals feel deeply engaged and purposeful in their activities. This heightened sense of well-being can contribute to reduced stress and improved overall mental health.

Enhanced performance: Flow states enable individuals to perform at their peak, leading to increased efficiency and effectiveness in completing tasks or solving problems.

Increased creativity: Flow states facilitate the generation of innovative ideas and solutions, fostering a higher level of problem-solving abilities.

Reduced stress and anxiety: Being in a flow state allows individuals to become fully immersed in an activity, temporarily setting aside other concerns, worries, and anxieties. This state can serve as a form of mental respite, leading to reduced stress levels.

Greater resilience: Regularly experiencing flow states can help individuals build mental resilience and adaptability, allowing them to better cope with challenges and setbacks.

FUN FLOW FACTS	
Flow is fun	Research has revealed that time spent in flow is consistently rated as the best experience available to humans. In fact, so joyous and ecstatic is the experience, that it produces an incredibly powerful drug-like drive to get *more* flow. Flow is addictive, and once you feel it, you want more.
Flow is accessible to you	Flow is a universal experience in humans. It arises in anyone, anywhere, regardless of health, weight, intelligence, class, or culture, provided certain initial conditions are met. That's where flow fact number three comes into play.
The conditions are the challenge and skill balance	This is the idea that flow shows up most reliably when all of our attention is focused on the task at hand and the challenge of that task *slightly* exceeds our skill set. In other words, we need to be slightly challenged when we're performing our favorite activity or project.

One of the underlying mechanisms of flow is the concept of neuroplasticity. This is the brain's remarkable ability to adapt and reorganize itself in response to new experiences, learning, and challenges. This process allows the brain to form new neural connections and pathways, which offers significant health benefits, primarily in the areas of learning, memory, cognitive flexibility, and reducing cognitive decline.

Additionally, neuroplasticity enhances cognitive flexibility, allowing the brain to adapt and reorganize itself, which aids in effectively switching between tasks and adapting to new situations. Engaging in activities that promote neuroplasticity also helps slow down age-related cognitive decline, thereby preserving mental acuity and overall brain health.

Think of it this way:

Neuroplasticity can be compared to skiing on a mountain with fresh powder versus skiing on previously established tracks. When skiing on fresh powder, you have the freedom to carve new paths, explore new routes, and adapt to the unique terrain. This experience represents the brain's ability to form new neural connections and pathways in response to new challenges, experiences, and learning.

On the other hand, skiing in previous ski lanes is like relying on existing neural pathways that have already been established in the brain through prior experiences and habits. While skiing in these lanes may be more comfortable and familiar, it does not offer the same opportunity for growth and adaptability as venturing into the fresh powder.

Engaging in new activities and experiences, like skiing on fresh powder, fosters neuroplasticity, allowing the brain to continuously adapt, learn, and improve its cognitive performance.

Finding Your Flow

Achieving neuroplasticity and flow requires the right balance of challenge and skill, along with a conducive environment and mindset. You don't need to be a pro at it either. Lucas's jump roping experience is a perfect example. Picking up a hobby or interest where you're a total newbie can be a blessing in disguise. It teaches you humility, which is arguably one of the best gifts you can give yourself.

Here are some strategies to help you enter a flow state:

Choose a meaningful and engaging activity: Select an activity that you are passionate about and find intrinsically rewarding. This will help you become fully immersed and focused on the task at hand.

Balance challenge and skill: The activity should be challenging enough to require your full attention and skill but not so difficult that it leads to frustration or anxiety. This balance helps create the optimal conditions for entering a flow state.

Eliminate distractions: Create an environment that minimizes external distractions, such as noise, interruptions, or clutter. This will allow you to focus fully on the activity and maintain a state of deep concentration.

Set clear goals: Establish specific, achievable goals for the task or activity. Having a clear sense of direction and purpose can help you maintain focus and motivation.

Practice mental fitness: Develop the ability to be present and fully engaged in the moment. Mindfulness techniques, such as deep breathing or meditation, can help cultivate the necessary focus and awareness required to enter a flow state.

LAZARUS METHOD LAW

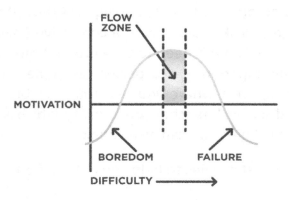

Damian's Climb to the Top

I've heard some amazing stories over the years from my patients who found flow. My patient, Damian, was caught in a whirlpool of stress, and his work responsibilities were a relentless burden. With deadlines looming and tasks piling up, he felt a constant gnawing anxiety. He was in defense mode and struggling to find the energy to complete his work.

That's when he shared a surprising invitation that came from one of his close friends: an afternoon away from work to go rock climbing. For someone who had never scaled a cliff and had work bearing down on him, the idea was not just ludicrous; it seemed downright irresponsible considering all he was dealing with. But something nudged him to accept, so he did.

The climb began with a mix of apprehension and excitement. Damian was far from a seasoned climber; every move required careful deliberation and acute focus. The ascent was not even that challenging, only about thirty feet, but for him, it felt like a mile. But each grip, each foothold, drew him further from his troubles and closer to something inexplicably freeing.

Forty minutes and thirty feet felt like a fleeting moment. As Damian reached the top, he was struck by an overwhelming sensation. His mind, previously cluttered with concerns, was crystal clear. A surge of confidence coursed through him, and dopamine surged through his body. He had stumbled upon an accidental flow state where the perfect challenge matched what little skills he had. He had temporarily forgotten about all his work problems and all his mundane responsibilities.

Standing atop the small cliff, Damian thanked his friend over and over, not just for an adventure but for a revelation, one that revealed the power of establishing new neuronal connections, finding his zone and new mental landscape. The drive home was a journey through a transformed landscape, not of the world around him but of his new headspace. Motivated, excited, and recharged, he was ready to face his work drama with a newfound energy he hadn't felt in years.

What Damian found that day was more than a simple escape; it was a unique form of focus and a lesson in the profound impact of flow on the human spirit. The way he told his story was incredible and stands as real-life proof of the untapped reservoirs of strength that lie within us, waiting to be discovered through the right challenge at the right moment. That's what the Learn element is all about. It's about having new experiences that accelerate a new perspective on life.

Flow Facilitator

The essential health playbook emphasizes straightforward actions that can be taken, including choosing purposeful and captivating activities, finding the right balance between difficulty and ability, minimizing distractions, establishing well-defined objectives, and cultivating mindfulness. By implementing these strategies, you can establish the ideal circumstances for entering a flow state, ultimately reducing brain fog and unleashing your cognitive potential.

Challenge, Fail, Learn

Take a moment to reflect on a situation when you ventured into something new and didn't succeed. This could be a new year's resolution or a health goal like losing weight, joining a new gym, or starting a new diet.

Remember the emotions that surfaced from that experience and the lessons it taught you? What did you learn?

Is there a new challenge or opportunity you're eager to pursue right now, but the fear of not completing it lingers, bringing back those past feelings?

There are no failures in life, only lessons. This concept is an empowering and optimistic perspective that encourages personal growth and resilience. This outlook reframes setbacks and perceived failures as valuable opportunities for self-improvement, self-awareness, and the acquisition of new skills and knowledge.

By adopting this mindset, you will cultivate a growth-oriented attitude, which emphasizes the importance of learning from experiences rather than dwelling on negative outcomes. This approach enables you to view challenges and obstacles as essential components of your personal development journey, helping you to build resilience, adaptability, and a deeper understanding of your own capabilities.

When perceived failures are treated as lessons, you will become more inclined to take calculated risks and step outside of your comfort zone. You are more likely to approach new situations with curiosity and an open mind, viewing each experience as a chance to learn and grow, regardless of the outcome.

This perspective cultivates self-compassion and a healthier view of failure, encouraging the understanding that setbacks are a natural part of learning. This approach, embracing the idea that there are no failures, only lessons, fosters a growth mindset, resilience, and adaptability.

As you implement the health recommendations in this playbook, you may face challenges, such as choosing unhealthy food, excessive snacking or drinking, overuse of your phone, or missing morning workouts due to late nights.

By viewing these not as failures but as lessons, you transform these setbacks into opportunities for making improved healthy choices in the future.

Final Lesson

Embarking on a journey of health and wellness begins with learning from our mistakes and accessing the right sources of knowledge. By tapping into a variety of educational resources, you equip yourself with the tools to make informed decisions about your health. From the immersive learning experiences of health podcasts and the depth of insight found in books, to the practical wisdom of masterclasses and the diverse perspectives gained from conversations and travel, each medium offers unique benefits.

RECOMMENDED RESOURCES	
Podcasts	Podcasts provide an engaging and convenient way to access a wealth of information on diverse topics, from science and technology to history and personal development. They often feature expert interviews and in-depth discussions, allowing listeners to delve deep into subjects of interest. With the ability to listen on the go, podcasts are a time-effective learning tool that can be easily incorporated into daily routines during commutes, exercise, or household chores.
Books	Reading is a fundamental tool for acquiring knowledge and stimulating intellectual curiosity. Books, articles, and other written materials provide access to the expertise and insights of countless authors and thinkers, enabling readers to explore new ideas, deepen understanding, and challenge their preconceived notions. Reading also helps to develop critical thinking, communication, and analytical skills, which are essential for lifelong learning and personal development.

RECOMMENDED RESOURCES

Masterclass	Masterclasses, workshops, and retreats may all provide structured, in-depth platforms for teaching ideas, concepts, and tools crucial for adopting a healthy lifestyle. They bring together expert knowledge and practical advice in a conducive learning environment. Events often encompass topics such as nutrition, exercise, spirituality, stress management, and sleep hygiene, among others. You can learn from the experiences of other participants and also share insights with fellow attendees.
Conversations	Conversations with different people offer a wealth of perspectives that can contribute to improved health. By challenging our preconceptions, understanding our biases, and broadening our understanding, we can gather a new perspective that may help us make better decisions. It's also super powerful to listen to how other people live their lives, and it may inspire you to try similar ideas.
Traveling	Traveling offers an invaluable opportunity to immerse oneself in different cultures, environments, and experiences. It allows individuals to break free from the confines of familiar surroundings and gain new insights, ideas, and perspectives. The perspective-expanding benefits of traveling do not require lengthy vacations or visits to exotic destinations. Exploring nearby regions or taking short trips can also provide valuable opportunities for new experiences and broadened perspectives, allowing you to learn from different cultures and environments, even within a local context.

Summary – Fail Often, Find Flow

The "Learn" element, an analytic part of the playbook, is designed to encourage a continuous journey of discovery and growth in health and personal performance. It stresses the importance of embracing new knowledge and perspectives and cultivating a mindset that is always open and receptive to learning. This includes finding your flow, neuroplasticity, healthy skepticism, and the guiding principle of "fail often, learn lessons."

This upgraded game plan allows you to use your new playbook to eliminate brain fog, increase mental clarity and creativity, and make better health choices by learning from your mistakes.

Let's apply some simple ways to integrate flow and knowledge into your routine.

THE LAZARUS METHOD GAME PLAN

PLAY I: Find Flow

1. Write down one activity you love, find rewarding, or are interested in trying.

_____

2. Assess your Challenge and Skill: Quickly rate the activity:

Challenge Level (1-5): _____

Skill Level (1-5): _____

Is there a balance? (Yes/No): _____

If not, how can you improve the balance?

_____

Coach's Tip:

Write down one way you can practice this activity:

_____

PLAY II: Connect to Nature

Select and listen to any health Podcast: Write down one thing you learned and one way you can integrate it into your routine.

Lesson:

_____

Integration Strategy:

_____

Coach's Tip:

Set a ceiling and floor goal for how you can integrate it into your routine. (Chapter 11)

PLAY III: Be Skeptical

Reflect on a recent health or medical piece of information you've recently encountered regarding weight loss or fitness. This can be from social media, news, or another source. Considering the concepts of conventional wisdom, bias, misinformation, disinformation, echo chambers, and cognitive biases.

List one step you can take to critically evaluate and verify the accuracy and reliability of this information.

_____

Coach's Tip:

Write down your thoughts and any actions you plan to take to ensure a more informed and skeptical approach towards health and medical information in the future.

Contemplating Mark Twain's wise words, **"Good decisions come from experience. Experience comes from making bad decisions."**

As you stand at this crossroads in the story, the opportunity for learning beckons. Will you choose the path that may lead to challenging experiences, understanding that even missteps are valuable lessons? Or will you opt for a route that seems safer, where learning comes steadily, but perhaps less dramatically?

Each choice is a step towards health knowledge, shaped by your previous personal experiences and the lessons they bring.

"Choose Your Own Health Adventure"

If you're drawn to **Identify Your Inner Voice and True Purpose**, *let your intuition guide you to page 149 in the Spark Chapter.* This section offers a glimpse of self-discovery, offering methods for identifying your life scorecard and an introduction to your avatar. It also introduces spark igniters, tools designed to stimulate personal growth and self-awareness.

If you're looking to **Elevate your Motivation and Inspiration**, *I dare you to turn to page 287 in the Challenge Chapter.* This section explores unique concepts like the universe test and your quantum coach, providing innovative perspectives on personal growth. You'll also learn about setting realistic challenges that involve establishing floors and ceilings to define and achieve your goals effectively.

If your primary goal is to **Lose Weight and Optimize your Digestion**, *turn to page 55 in the Nourish Chapter.* The recommendations provided in this chapter will help you improve your body composition and jumpstart your metabolism. The concepts that will help you are the Nourish Target, Metabolic Flexibility, Intuitive Eating, EAT Protocol, and the 80/20 Eating Principle.

If you want to learn how to **Increase Strength and Improve your Metabolism**, *run to page 219 in the Move Chapter.* Here, you'll explore the effective 2nd Gear Strategy, delve into the three foundational pillars of movement, review compound and functional movements, and discover the importance of incorporating play into your routine.

For those seeking to **Boost Energy Levels and Overcome Fatigue**, *chill out and to page 119 in the Rest Chapter.* This section will introduce you to the concept of your chronotype and circadian rhythm for optimal sleep. It provides detailed guidance on the RESTED Protocol, designed to optimize your rest and energy and two-minute timeouts, a strategy to rejuvenate and maintain sustained energy throughout your day.

If you want to prioritize **Being Present, Awareness, and Clarity**, *please focus on page 171 in the Connect Chapter.* This section is specifically tailored to enhance your mental fitness and sharpen your focus flashlight, a technique for cultivating mindfulness. You will also explore the happiness gap for true happiness and find your "thrive tribe" to achieve a heightened state of community and support.

CHAPTER 10

CHALLENGE

Be careful of the silent killer. It hides and can strike at any time without warning, and no one is safe, even you. Evoking the suspense of a thriller, the term "silent killer" conjures images of an unseen assailant lurking in the shadows, poised to strike when you least expect it.

This menacing phrase appropriately captures the hidden nature of certain medical conditions that may quietly wreak havoc on your health, often revealing their lethal impact only when it's too late to reverse course. Just like that, you're the latest victim of this silent assassin.

This silent killer is named... "Desserts."

Just playing, the silent killer is actually stress, but did you know that "desserts" spelled backward is "stressed." Sweet irony, isn't it?

Stress and challenge are directly interconnected, as challenges often induce stress, which can either hinder or propel your health, depending on how it's managed. Stress is a commonly misunderstood concept that varies from individual to individual, making it crucial to distill its definition into its simplest form. Such a clarification can revolutionize your understanding of stress and reshape your interaction with it. What overwhelms one person may leave another unaffected or might even be enjoyable to someone else.

With that in mind, my version of stress can be defined as "a response to a situation that a person *perceives* to be overwhelming in that the person does not think or believe they can meet the demands of the situation." My definition emphasizes the role of individual perception and belief systems in shaping the stress response. It suggests that stress is not solely determined by external events but also by how you interpret and respond to those events.

Emergency Alert System

There is a well-known mechanism your body uses to manage stressful situations called the hypothalamic-pituitary-adrenal (HPA) axis. The HPA axis is part of the sympathetic nervous system and has a complex set of interactions among three glands: the hypothalamus, the pituitary gland, and the adrenal glands. This axis plays a critical role in your body's stress response, as well as regulating various bodily functions, including digestion, the immune system, mood, and emotions.

When you perceive a stressor, whether it's a previous painful memory or fear of a current situation, your hypothalamus secretes corticotropin-releasing hormone (CRH), which then prompts the pituitary gland to release adrenocorticotropic hormone (ACTH). ACTH travels through the bloodstream to stimulate the adrenal glands, which then produce adrenaline and cortisol, the primary stress neurotransmitter and hormone.

The release of these necessary hormones prepares the body for a "fight or flight" response by making various physiological adjustments, such as increased heart rate, elevated blood pressure, dilation of air passages in the lungs, increased metabolism, suppressed digestion and immune system, and mobilized energy reserves. We all know what this feels like.

STRESS RESPONSE

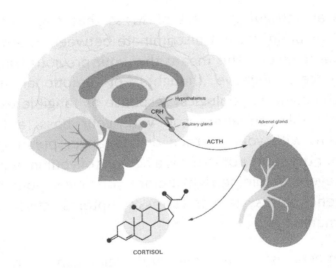

Think of it this way: Think of the HPA axis as a car's emergency alert system. When a potential collision is detected, the system quickly activates various safety features, like alarm signals on your dashboard, automatic brakes, and deployed airbags, to prepare for impact and then resets to normal once the danger has passed. This alert system has various body symptoms you may recognize, such as anxiety, restlessness, fatigue, sleep issues, GI issues, and brain fog.

When this occurs, it shuts off the other part of your "parasympathetic system," which is a component of the autonomic nervous system responsible for promoting states of repair. When activated, the parasympathetic system encourages bodily functions that are essential for relaxation and long-term survival, such as slowing the heart rate and promoting digestion, essentially allowing your body to "rest, relax, digest, and reproduce" when it is not facing immediate threats. This is your cruise control setting.

Allostatic Load

Here's an intriguing aspect of stress that might astonish you. Your brain doesn't discriminate between internal and external stressors. This means that your previous traumatic experiences, negative thoughts, or emotional turmoil elicit the same physiological response as tangible external stressors—like an altercation with your boss, a heated argument with your partner, or a stranger pursuing you. Whether the source of stress is a figment of your imagination or an event unfolding right before your eyes, your body's emergency alert system and stress symptoms activate in the same manner.

If this mechanism is used over and over, it can contribute to a range of serious health issues. Allostatic load is "the wear and tear on the body" that accumulates as you are exposed to repeated or chronic stress. This can result in cardiovascular diseases, gastrointestinal problems, and compromised immune function. Additionally, it can exacerbate mental health conditions such as anxiety and depression, disrupt sleep patterns, and impair cognitive function.

This "silent killer" can insidiously damage the body and mind over time, manifesting in serious health conditions that may not become apparent until they are severe. This is a key mechanism in functional medicine, and I've seen countless patients who have issues with their digestion, metabolism, sleep, and energy because of stress causing constant emergency alarms.

Here's Your Surfboard

Jon Kabat-Zinn, a mindfulness expert, said, "You can't stop the waves, but you can learn to surf." This statement encapsulates a fundamental philosophy of mindfulness and stress management. The "waves" metaphorically represent the inevitable challenges, stressors, and difficulties that we all face in life. Just as one cannot control the ocean, one cannot fully control external circumstances. However, what we do have control over is our reaction to these "waves."

The idea of learning to "surf" suggests that while we may not be able to eliminate stress or challenges, we can acquire skills to navigate them more effectively. Mindfulness teaches us to be present in the moment, to observe our thoughts and feelings without judgment, and to make deliberate choices about how to respond to life's challenges rather than reacting impulsively. This "surfing" skill allows us to ride the waves of life with balance and poise, making it easier to handle stress and adversity.

The Silent Healer

Now that you understand the various health effects of stress, doesn't it make sense to prioritize removing this potential silent killer? If it's contributing to your gut, fatigue, insomnia, and metabolism issues, shouldn't we create a plan to eliminate it?

Not so fast! Conventional wisdom often paints stress as a uniformly negative experience for your health. However, emerging scientific understanding, particularly in the field of hormesis, challenges this notion. Stress, it turns out, isn't entirely the villain it's often made out to be. When encountered in the right doses and contexts, stress is actually beneficial and required for your health.

What Doesn't Kill You Makes You Stronger

We've all heard Nietzsche's famous nineteenth-century quotation, "That which does not kill you makes you stronger." Those wise words have echoed in countless universities and sports locker rooms. To the Stoics, life was about a challenge. "Those who are never tested should be pitied because they don't know what they're capable of," Seneca said. There's also been a recent revision that is worth reminding us, "What doesn't kill you makes you stronger. Except for bears; bears will kill you."

I want to show you how true those words actually are. The term "hormesis" is rooted in the Greek word "hormo," which means to excite or set in motion. It refers to the physiological principle where moderate stress or exposure at low doses triggers a beneficial adaptive response in the body.

A paper in the journal *Aging Research Reviews* elaborates that hormetic stress occupies a "sweet spot": an optimal zone of stress exposure that stimulates the body without overwhelming it. In this zone, stress becomes a catalyst for physiological improvement without veering into harmful territory.

RESILIENCE GRAPH

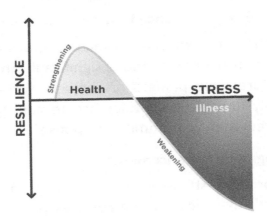

Hormesis isn't a pathway to superhuman abilities; rather, it's an evolutionary survival strategy. Subjecting your body to extreme conditions like intense radiation won't transform you into a superhero like the Incredible Hulk. While certain aspects of you might change color, it would be for reasons you'd rather avoid.

The optimal way to harness the benefits of hormesis isn't through subjecting yourself to extreme, harmful stress but by cultivating a lifestyle that incorporates a balanced array of minor stressors. I call these micro-challenges, and although slightly uncomfortable at times, they serve essential roles in supporting robust biological and neurological functions and fostering physiological resilience. The benefits of micro-challenges include the following:

Physiological Resilience
Micro-challenges will strengthen your physiological systems. For instance, intuitive eating can enhance metabolic flexibility, helping the body efficiently

294 THE ESSENTIAL HEALTH PLAYBOOK

switch between burning carbohydrates and fats for energy.

Increased Tolerance to Greater Stresses

Consistent exposure to mild stressors can build up your resilience to more significant stressors in the future. Cold plunges or showers, for example, not only improve your tolerance to cold but may also strengthen your immune response.

Cognitive Enhancements

Hormetic stress isn't solely physical. Intellectual challenges, like solving complex puzzles or learning a new skill, can stimulate the brain, improving focus and cognitive flexibility.

Dietary Benefits

Studies have shown that hormetic stress from certain phytonutrients can activate protective cellular pathways, leading to potential health benefits like reduced inflammation and increased longevity.

***

Comfortable, Cozy, Stagnant, Entitled

The advancements of modern technology and progressive societal structures have introduced an unprecedented opportunity for a lifestyle almost devoid of stress. The notion that our modern lifestyles may be incongruent with our evolutionary past has been substantiated through various disciplines such as anthropology, biology, and psychology. The difference between our ancestral environment and our current way of life is often referred to as the "evolutionary mismatch."

The struggle for basic biological needs is an evolutionary norm that has shaped numerous adaptations in our physiology, psychology, behavior, and culture. These adaptations have allowed us to improvise, adapt, and overcome harsh environments and challenging times. Until now. We now have everything we need; oxygen, water, food, shelter, and safety.

So, what happens when an individual lacks challenges in their life? The absence of challenges can lead to stagnation, complacency, and a decreased sense of self-worth, ultimately resulting in a variety of physical, mental, and emotional issues. Like a game where taking the tough shots and enduring rigorous training leads to victory, making difficult choices now may set the stage for an effortless win in the game of health.

I've observed the following traits in patients who lack any form of daily challenges:

TRAITS IN PATIENTS WHO LACK ANY FORM OF DAILY CHALLENGES	
Stagnation and lack of personal growth	Without challenges to overcome, you may find yourself trapped in a state of stagnation.
Loss of motivation and ambition	The absence of challenges can lead to a decrease in motivation and ambition. When there are no goals to strive for or obstacles to overcome, you may become disinterested in setting any goals.
Decline in cognitive function	Challenges help to keep the mind sharp and engaged. When you're not faced with any difficulties or problems to solve, your cognitive function may decline over time.
Increased risk of mental health issues	A life devoid of challenges can contribute to the development of mental health issues such as depression and anxiety. Without the sense of accomplishment that comes from overcoming obstacles, you may feel empty, unfulfilled, and experience a decline in self-esteem.
Decreased social connections	Without challenges to tackle, you may find it difficult to relate to others who are actively pursuing their goals and overcoming obstacles. This inability to connect with others on a deeper level can lead to feelings of isolation, loneliness, and a decrease in overall life satisfaction.

Courage, Wisdom, Inspiration, Energy, Purpose, Gratitude

These are the qualities I want my patients to feel and strive toward. Courage over comfort, redefining the concept of "challenge" and incorporating the mantra "get comfortable with being uncomfortable." This method emphasizes the importance of intentionally and consistently creating small, daily, and weekly tasks (micro challenges), alongside setting ambitious long-term goals (macro challenges).

By embracing a tad of discomfort and pushing past your comfort zone, you can witness amazing health benefits, maintain motivation, accelerate accomplishment, and ultimately achieve optimal health. By adopting and integrating my recommendations below, you will not only redefine the meaning of challenge but revolutionize the way you approach your aspirations, fostering sustainable growth and self-improvement.

Macro and Micro Challenges: The Key to Sustained Motivation and Accomplishment

Maintaining motivation and consistently achieving goals can be a daunting task. One effective strategy for overcoming this hurdle is to embrace the concept of micro- and macro-challenges. By integrating my two-tiered system into your playbook, you can foster a sense of accomplishment and inspiration, ultimately leading to greater success in your health, as well as personal and professional pursuits.

Macro-Challenges: Long-Term Goals for Inspiration

Macro-challenges are significant, long-term objectives that require dedication and effort promoting health and personal growth. Key examples include transforming personal health and lifestyle, starting and growing a business, achieving advanced educational goals, mastering a new skill or craft, and making a tangible impact in a community or for a cause. These challenges foster skills like resilience, discipline, and leadership, while inspiring individuals to extend their capabilities and achieve meaningful, life-changing goals.

By setting ambitious macro-challenges, we provide ourselves with a source of inspiration that fuels our motivation and drives us to push beyond our comfort zones. As you work toward these long-term objectives, you learn to overcome obstacles, adapt to change, and cultivate resilience. Furthermore, the achievement of a macro-challenge can be profoundly rewarding, reinforcing your belief in your own capabilities and inspiring you to make proper choices that improve your health.

Micro-Challenges: Daily Motivation Boosters

Micro-challenges are small, achievable tasks that you can complete on a daily basis. They serve as small stepping stones toward your larger goals and help to maintain motivation by providing you with regular opportunities for accomplishment. These small, manageable tasks can be seamlessly integrated into daily routines, offering immediate gratification and a sense of achievement.

For example, starting the day by drinking a large cup of water sets a healthy tone, trying a new prebiotic food, or avoiding eating after 6 PM can significantly impact dietary habits. Walking 5,000 steps, taking a 30-minute walk after dinner, incorporating 10 air squats every 90 minutes at work, going to bed 30 minutes earlier, or cutting electronics thirty minutes before bedtime are simple. Sending an encouraging text to a friend, stretching right before you eat lunch, and organizing your workspace for two minutes, can significantly enhance your level of accomplishment and make the most daunting tasks seem less overwhelming, increasing the likelihood of success.

COURAGE OVER **COMFORT.**

YOU ARE

WHAT YOU DO.
NOT WHAT YOU SAY YOU'LL DO.

Really, More Stress??

The idea of deliberately adding challenges to your daily routine may seem ridiculous, especially if you're already managing all of life's inherent difficulties. I fully understand that you might feel perpetually on the defensive, grappling daily with challenges related to your health, work-life balance, or other personal issues. However, trust me when I say that integrating even a few of the recommendations at the end of this chapter can enhance your coping mechanisms for everyday stressors.

Universe Test

Life inevitably presents challenges, setbacks, obstacles, hurdles, and even tragedies. These adversities test your patience, resolve, and resilience. Over the years, I've employed reframing tools with my patients, designed expressly to empower them. These concepts worked wonders for them. When you're in a defensive position, they will help you better cope with life's complexities.

We can learn to reframe life's hurdles as opportunities for personal growth. Instead of perceiving setbacks as negative experiences, view them as trials set by a "universe test," which aims to assess your resilience, resourcefulness, and emotional composure. This perspective can help you develop the mental tenacity needed to triumph over adversity and accomplish your objectives.

The universe test is a concept that imagines the universe is intentionally and strategically presenting you with challenges so that you can successfully execute your defensive game plan. By viewing life's inevitable setbacks and obstacles as purposefully designed tests from the universe, you can approach difficulties with a proactive and positive attitude. The idea is to recognize each challenge as an opportunity to put your coping strategies and resilience into action. It's a test and you have the answers; it's that simple. Consider it your quantum coach.

Applying the universe test principle in everyday life can be surprisingly easy once you become familiar with the concept and intentionally practice it. By consciously choosing to reframe challenges as opportunities for growth, you can develop a habit of embracing adversity with a positive mindset.

This approach can be applied to every single aspect of your life: health, work, relationships, and personal goals. The key is to consistently remind yourself that setbacks and obstacles are natural components of life's journey and that the universe test is designed to help you hone your resilience, resourcefulness, and emotional composure. As this way of thinking becomes second nature, you will find that you are better equipped to navigate the complexities of daily life with greater confidence, adaptability, and inner strength.

***

Chasing the Impossible

Jason is an extraordinary individual, and you may remember his experience in the foreword. His story exemplifies the transformative power of setting challenges. Together, we crafted a regimen of micro-challenges designed to equip him with the skills and resilience to take on any massive macro-challenge he set for himself.

In 2016, Jason's macro challenge was to row across the Atlantic Ocean, a daring feat requiring extreme mental and physical fortitude. The journey spanned 3,000 miles and was filled with unpredictability—from team members bailing on their mission in the middle of the Atlantic to treacherous weather to equipment malfunctions. Jason accomplished his challenge by completing this adventure in fifty-four days but was very unsettled by his experience. He recognized the mistakes he made and knew he not only could do way better but arrange a team that could actually break the world record.

Jason and I engaged in an extensive conversation about his prior experience and identified areas for improvement in his preparation. Thus began the era of Jason's training micro-challenges. To prepare, we incorporated a series of targeted micro-challenges that honed in on stamina, mental resilience, nutritional strategies, and strategies for tackling some of the most emotionally grueling situations imaginable.

I had him start with simple micro-challenges that included my "intuitive eating" protocol, basic functional movements, quick breathwork exercises, short cold showers, and phytonutrient performance supplements. Once Jason got the hang of these small hormetic stressors, we graduated him with some biohacking strategies that included long fasting phases, personalized food plans, valuable second and fifth-gear training protocols, holotropic breathwork, extreme cold exposure, and completely customized nutraceutical formulas.

Realizing the Possible

So just one year later, in 2017, Jason pushed off with a new team and a new mindset and plan. I'll spare you the amazing details, but yep, you guessed it. Jason and his team rowed the same distance again, this time breaking the world record as the fastest team ever to row across the Atlantic Ocean. The previous macro-challenge had paved the way for this new accomplishment. The micro-challenges we set prepared him to break barriers—both his own and those set by others.

Most recently, in 2021, Jason formed and led a team to row across the Pacific Ocean from San Francisco to Hawaii. The team shattered another world record by completing the journey in nine fewer days than the previous record-holders. His story was so profound that the Oscar-winning producers of *Free Solo* made a documentary about his challenge titled *Chasing.*

The micro-challenges Jason undertook revolutionized his self-perception. They instilled in him the ability to overcome hurdles, adapt to change, and cultivate an exceptional level of resilience. While his exploits might seem extreme, the foundational principles apply universally to you, me, and everyone else. Challenges equal resilience. Resilience results in health.

Jason's story is compelling proof of what can be achieved when you align micro- and macro-challenges. It proves that whatever your own personal "ocean" might be, whether it's losing ten pounds or running a seven-minute mile, with the essential health playbook, you can not only cross your own ocean but maybe even set your personal record while you're at it.

Whether you're aiming to improve your health or achieve a personal goal, the strategy remains the same: start with manageable micro-challenges to build the skill set and confidence needed to tackle the macro-challenges that inspire you.

Micro-Challenges

So, what are these micro-challenges? I've summarized them for you here. These trigger a range of cellular and physiological adaptations that cumulatively contribute to your health and longevity. Below is an elaboration on each of the three categories of micro-challenges I recommend trying:

	MICRO-CHALLENGES	
Physical Micro-Challenges	**Movement:** Different exercise intensities positively stress the body in a controlled manner, leading to improved cardiovascular performance, metabolic efficiency, and muscular strength. Specific types of exercise may engage different adaptive pathways.
	Temperature: Cold baths and hot saunas engage thermoregulatory mechanisms. Saunas can induce heat shock proteins that assist in protein folding and cellular repair, while cold exposure activates anti-inflammatory and immune mechanisms and enhances metabolic rate.
	Breathing exercises: Techniques such as hypoxic training, holotropic breathing, or breath-holding can improve your body's efficiency in oxygen utilization and blood pH and improve your blood chemistry.
Nutritional Micro-Challenges	**Food control:** Fasting or my "intuitive eating" strategy and low-calorie diets can activate autophagy, a cellular clean-up mechanism that can also improve metabolic flexibility.
	Spices and herbs: Turmeric, clove, ginger, garlic, and onion contain various bioactive compounds that have antioxidant, anti-inflammatory, and even anticancer properties.
	Supplements: Compounds like zinc, resveratrol, and ECGC activate various stress-response pathways. For instance, resveratrol has been shown to mimic some of the benefits of caloric restriction.

MICRO-CHALLENGES	
Mental Micro-Challenges	**Mental activity:** Cognitive challenges like reading, puzzle-solving, or playing chess can stimulate neuroplasticity, improving cognitive function over time.
	Demanding performance: Stressors such as public speaking or leading a workshop can activate the "fight or flight" response in a controlled setting, which may improve stress resilience and focus.
	Focused attention: Practices like mental fitness have been shown to improve attention span, emotional well-being, and even immune response.

***

Breath Work: Your Simple Switch

"No matter what you eat, how much you exercise, how skinny or young or strong you are, none of it matters if you're not breathing properly." Those compelling insights come from James Nestor, the author of the best sellingbook, **"Breath."** Allow me to elaborate on why his perspective may indeed be accurate.

A substantial number of individuals, perhaps including yourself, may be unaware of the immediate and profound impact that strategic breathing can have on your physiological state. Breathing is the most fundamental human action. It catalyzes the critical mechanism of oxygen supply, which in turn keeps all the processes in your body going every second of every day.

Doing something as simple as modifying your breathing has a direct and profound impact on your physiology. One could even describe it as the ultimate neurological switch because it can influence your physiology in a matter of seconds.

Breathwork is a practice that has evolved over thousands of years. It holds a unique and pivotal role in regulating your physiology, primarily because it serves as a switch between your "fight, flight, or flee" system and your "rest, relax, digest, reproduce" system, providing a direct means to manually override the autonomic processes and create a state of balance. This is an exceptionally potent strategy in your playbook when you feel overwhelmed or stressed.

Breathwork can be general or specific, practiced on your own or as part of a group program. Broadly speaking, breath work refers to any type of breathing exercise that involves intentionally changing or controlling your breathing pattern, whereas specific breath work programs involve learning particular exercises in a special setting or for a targeted purpose.

Shut Your Mouth!

The nose is for breathing, and the mouth is for eating. Breathing through your mouth is like eating through your nose. Well, not really, but this silly comparison illustrates the importance of nose breathing and may give you a "nose-up" on understanding the proper way to breathe.

Did you realize that your nostrils serve as a built-in thermostat and mood regulator, functioning much like an HVAC system? Your nose is more than just a facial centerpiece; it's the unsung hero that acts as your body's gatekeeper, your mind's personal pharmacist, and the emotional barometer you never knew you needed.

Think of your right nostril as the "go" button. Breathing mainly through this channel revs up your circulation, raises your body temperature, and increases cortisol levels, blood pressure, and heart rate.

On the other hand (or nostril in this case), your left nostril acts as the "stop" button, counterbalancing the actions of its right-sided counterpart. Breathing through the left nostril engages your rest, relax, and digest system, which is responsible for calming you down, lowering blood pressure, cooling the body, and alleviating stress.

Breathing through your nose increases oxygen efficiency. If you primarily breathe through your nose, you're already optimizing your oxygen intake. In fact, nose breathers consume 18 percent more oxygen on average compared to individuals who breathe through their mouths.

CO2: Breath's Exit Ticket

You probably remember learning about carbon dioxide back in fifth-grade science class, so allow me to give you a quick recap. Carbon dioxide (CO_2) is generated as a waste product during cellular respiration. It travels through the bloodstream to the lungs, where it is expelled during exhalation.

The regulation of CO_2 levels is crucial for maintaining your body's pH balance. It essentially acts as a facilitator for oxygen absorption in your muscles. The presence of CO_2 makes it easier for oxygen to be utilized effectively.

If you breathe through your mouth, you're inadvertently expelling CO_2 too rapidly, which hampers the ability of your muscles to make full use of the available oxygen.

Nose breathing, on the other hand, can be compared to a slow, deliberate process that retains CO_2 for an extended period. This retention facilitates greater oxygen absorption, thereby enhancing muscle performance.

Test Your Tolerance

Wouldn't it be interesting to find out how well you breathe or tolerate CO_2? Well, there's a simple test that can reveal this. The CO_2 tolerance test is a test I've been using in my clinic for years to evaluate my patient's breathing patterns and physiology. This quick breath test is a great indicator of your stress and autonomic nervous system. Developed through extensive trials and applications, this test has been proven to be a helpful indicator of a variety of physiological mechanisms and gives strong indicators of anxiety levels and breath mechanics.

The CO_2 tolerance test involves using a timer to measure how long you can slowly exhale through your nose following a deep inhale. Depending on your results, you can glimpse the state of your body's CO_2 tolerance levels. Under twenty seconds reveals you need work, and over forty seconds represents good CO_2 tolerance. Most people are in the middle. Go ahead and try it out to find out your time.

Rise and Relax

There are easy ways to improve your breathing. An effective method that I've created for my patients is called the RISE technique, which is parallel to square breathing, box breathing, or four-by-four breathing. It's a simple and quick breathing technique designed to promote relaxation and mental clarity. Here's how to perform it:

RISE & RELAX

Square Breathing, AKA Box Breathing or 4x4 Breathing, is a simple and quick breathing technique designed to switch your promote relaxation and mental clarity. Here's how to perform it:

1. **Inhale Through the Nose:** Take a slow, deep breath through your nose, counting to four as you inhale. Try to fill your lungs fully by the time you reach the count of four.

2. **Hold the Breath:** Once you've inhaled fully, hold your breath for another count of four.

3. **Exhale Through the Mouth:** Slowly exhale the air through your mouth to a count of four, emptying the lungs completely.

4. **Pause:** After exhaling, hold your breath for another count of four.

5. **Repeat:** Perform this cycle for at least four rounds, or continue until you feel relaxed and centered.

This technique can be practiced anytime, especially if you're feel stressed, anxious, or in need of focus. But you don't have to wait for a tense moment to try this out. Get comfortable with the breathing steps when you're chill, so when stress does hit, you're good to go. You could practice while you're stuck at a red light, skimming through emails, scrolling on your phone, or even right now, as you're reading this.

 REST
(Get Comfortable)

 INHALE
for 4 seconds

 SUSTAIN
(Hold for 4 seconds)

 EXHALE
for 4 seconds

This technique is simple and can be practiced anytime, especially if you're feeling stressed, anxious, or in need of focus. But you don't have to wait for a tense moment to try this out. Get comfortable with the breathing steps when you're chill, so when stress does hit, you're good to go. You could practice while you're stuck at a red light, skimming through emails, scrolling on your phone, or even right now, as you're reading this.

I listen to patients claim they don't have time to practice breathing—which is amusing. We're doing it every second of the day. Simply apply a new cadence to your breathing, and you'll be surprised how much it helps you to switch between your "fight" and "relax" systems. A simple way to apply it is through my RISE steps.

If you're interested in more formal practices, I recommend looking into pranayama, Wim Hof breathwork, diaphragmatic breathing, alternate nostril breathing, Sudarshan Kriya yoga breathwork (SKY), and holotropic breathwork. Each of these has its own unique focus, from altering states of consciousness to healing trauma or enhancing a connection with nature. These specialized techniques are usually led by certified practitioners and may require dedicated training or classes, either in person or online. Many of these methods are supported by scientific studies attesting to their effectiveness.

Kelly's Quantum Coach

During the initial weeks of working with Kelly, a clear pattern quickly emerged that was hard to ignore. Whenever she faced an issue, whether with her kids, partner, or simple tasks at home, her immediate reaction was to retreat into a victim mentality. The cycle was predictable: first, the trigger, followed by an emotional reaction, leading inevitably to blaming her poor health for her issues.

"Kelly, you're defaulting to a reactive, victim mode when you face any challenge," I delicately broached the subject during one of our sessions. "You immediately fall into a victim mindset, which then spirals into anger and frustration. Have you ever stopped to think how this might be affecting your overall health?"

"I don't know," she sighed. "Whenever something bad happens, I can't help but feel overwhelmed. And then, yes, my gut acts up, I feel exhausted, and the only way out seems to be distracting myself by scrolling through my phone or grabbing something to munch on."

"One hundred percent." I nodded, recognizing this common pattern. "You're not just reacting to the situation at hand; you're triggering a physical stress response that worsens your gut symptoms and fatigue. Your coping mechanism—scrolling through your phone or eating snack foods—only serves to dig you deeper into this cycle."

Does this sound familiar?

Are you aware of your emotional triggers?

Do you feel that your energy and digestion are also affected?

The resonance in her eyes told me she understood. "I get it. I just don't know how to fix it," she said, raising her voice in frustration. I grinned inside because I knew she needed a reframe.

I'd been there myself, navigating through the dark time of my life with a similar pattern of behavior. I knew she needed an immediate reframe, a "quick win" to break the cycle and instill a sense of confidence.

"Kelly, I have a simple challenge for you," I suggested. "I'm going to introduce you to your quantum coach. Your new mental fitness trainer will test you every day. Every issue, setback, or obstacle is purposefully provided from the universe." She rolled her eyes.

"You're facing challenges regularly, but the key is to become conscious of how you react to them," I articulated. My goal was to instill an initial spark of awareness in these moments. This foundational awareness would serve as the next steps for the mental fitness training we'd undertake. Yet even this preliminary shift in mindset had the potential to bring about significant changes effortlessly.

"Whenever you find yourself spiraling, pause and thank your quantum coach for the challenge. I'm also giving you a personal micro-challenge. Every morning for the next three days, while you're in the shower, take five square breaths and finish your shower with cold water for two more breaths. That's it. Can you commit to that?"

She looked at me, her eyes reflecting a blend of skepticism and curiosity, but eventually nodded. "I guess it's worth a try."

Her willingness to try this defensive strategy was all that I needed. It was simple, and it took her energy and attention off her perceived daily challenges and redirected it to my challenge. I could not wait for the next meeting to hear how it went.

As anticipated, this modest micro-challenge achievement spurred her to complete another task, cleaning her room, then her kid's rooms, followed by making a protein shake for breakfast and eventually reorganizing her pantry! While these might appear as small wins, they exemplify the cascading positive impact of setting and accomplishing micro-challenges, which can ultimately result in massive health improvements.

The Ultimate Reframe

My experience with Kelly is far from unique. Many of the patients I work with show similar patterns that negatively affect their health and headspace. Identifying these patterns and introducing fun and unique interventions, like the concept of my universe test, quantum coach, and micro-challenges, is a game changer.

I'll be honest, it's far from a quick fix. You can't merely snap your fingers and expect an imaginary coach to solve all your issues. However, adding this concept to your playbook will aid you in reframing any situation, allowing you to better handle the inevitable challenges life throws your way.

As a matter of fact, I've been actively consulting my own quantum coach while navigating the substantial challenge of writing this very book. The frustration of finding the perfect words to share with you has been challenging. My own personal quantum coach has helped me reframe this frustration into meaningful insights and lessons. The lessons I'm gaining from this experience not only enrich my personal journey but will also enable me to offer more effective guidance to myself and my future patients.

Challenge Yourself. Inspire Others. Transform Your Tribe.

I want to share another significant story that encapsulates the extraordinary power of setting personal challenges and how they can reverberate throughout an entire community. This story hits close to home. It's a tale of my wife, Natalia, who decided to mark her fortieth birthday in a way most people wouldn't dare to contemplate. She chose to run forty miles.

What makes this story extraordinary isn't just her individual achievement; it's how her bold goal became a beacon for others. To represent the accumulated journey of her forty years, we invited friends and family to join her in the last third of the run. What unfolded was a spectacle of human potential and unity. More than thirty of our closest friends and family showed up, and some ran the longest distances they'd ever attempted—including our thirteen-year-old, who completed thirteen miles. Even avid runners hit their personal record of twenty miles.

When Natalia crossed the finish line at the forty-mile mark, the atmosphere was electric. Those who joined her were not just applauding her achievement but also basking in their newfound sense of what was possible for themselves. Her challenge was shared around our local town, and she was congratulated by people she'd never met before.

Other local individuals were inspired to set similar lofty goals for their own birthdays, and we witnessed the impact of this challenge reverberate throughout our community. It was a shared victory for our thrive tribe, an epiphany that testified to the domino effect one person's ambition can ignite.

Why do I share this story with you? Because it perfectly illustrates that when you challenge yourself, you're not just elevating your own life. You're sending ripples through your own thrive tribe, inspiring them to also reach for more than they thought possible. It reaffirms the belief that our personal quests for improvement can serve as a lighthouse for others, illuminating pathways to potentials they hadn't dared to envision.

If you've been teetering on the edge of setting your own macro-challenge, I hope Jason's, Kelly's, and Natalia's stories serve as a friendly nudge. Consider taking some small steps not just for yourself but for the untold impact it could have on those around you. Your courage to dream and act could be the catalyst that inspires your community to discover new horizons.

Summary – Don't Limit Your Challenges; Challenge Your Limitations

I've introduced a handful of new ideas in this chapter to better understand stress, including your emergency alert system, allostatic load, and even offered you a surfboard to just ride the waves. Stress is a perceived phenomenon, and you have the power to alter your relationship with it and use it to your advantage.

I also introduced you to your silent healer, and explained what doesn't kill you will make you stronger. By setting micro- and macro-challenges and embracing the tests the universe is handing you every day, you can also reframe your experience to your advantage.

So, if you're challenged by nagging symptoms like fatigue, digestive issues, injury, or any illness that hinders your ability or mobility to participate in regular activities, I encourage you to apply any of these challenge concepts. Treat any setback as an assessment of your resilience, adaptability, and mental fortitude. With this mindset, you can shift your energy from dodging health problems to finding the opportunity to overcome them. I wish I had this wisdom when I was sick, scared, and confused.

Let's look at a few simple challenges that you can add to your playbook. By consistently utilizing these plays, you will find that adopting this reframe mindset becomes increasingly more accessible and natural. Embracing this philosophy will undoubtedly lead to a healthier life and greater resilience, fueling that unique spark inside you.

THE LAZARUS METHOD GAME PLAN

PLAY I: Set one Macro Challenge

Write down one significant, long-term goal that you aspire to achieve in the next year.

Macro-Challenge:

_____

Coach's Tip:

The bigger, the better. Write down anything that comes to mind, and you can add to it later. Aim for the stars.

PLAY II: Set a couple of Micro-Challenges

Below are various examples of micro-challenges that are designed to help you make incremental progress toward your health goals. Select at least two in each category that will help you with your health goals or add your own.

Coach's Tip:

Select one of your health goals from the Spark Chapter Playbook and attach five micro-challenges to it.

NOURISH

1. Drink 1 large cup of water first thing in the AM.
2. Eat 5 colors of vegetables today.
3. Try a new prebiotic food today.
4. Plan & prep your meals for the day.
5. Drink a protein shake for breakfast.
6. Avoid eating after 6 PM for a day.
7. Remove all grains for a day.
8. Find a new healthy dinner recipe.
9. Swap coffee for green tea for a day.
10. Skip dessert and opt for fruit.
11. Prep healthy snacks for the next 48 hours.
12. Organize your supplements for the week.
13. _____
14. _____
15. _____

MOVE

1. Walk 5,000 steps today.
2. Take a 30-minute walk after dinner.
3. Take a walk during a work call.
4. Do 10 air squats every 90 min at work.
5. Put a kettlebell in your garage.
6. Walk or cycle to work.
7. Use a standing desk for an hour.
8. Use the stairs all day instead of the elevator.
9. Complete a 5-minute stretching routine before bed.
10. Perform 10 pushups before bed.
11. Do a 30-second plank between commercials.
12. Place a foam roller next to the TV.
13. _____
14. _____
15. _____

REST

1. Go to bed 30 min earlier than usual.
2. Practice RISE breathing for 2 minutes.
3. Gaze as far as possible for 30 seconds in the afternoon.
4. Make a hydration drink and replay your daily gameplan.
5. Place your feet on the grass, sand or dirt for 5 minutes.
6. Cut all electronics 30 minutes before bedtime.
7. Use a Mindfold during a mental fitness session.
8. Try a progressive muscle relaxation technique before bed.
9. Make a hydration drink and replay your daily gameplan.
10. Listen to ambient music 30 min before sleep.
11. Read for 20 minutes before sleep.
12. Wake up without an alarm.
13. _____
14. _____
15. _____

CONNECT

1. Call a friend or family member you haven't spoken to in a while.
2. Smile at strangers for a day and watch what happens.
3. Resolve a conflict in your personal or professional life.
4. Praise a colleague or friend for their abilities.
5. Write down a blessing you observed today.
6. Send a quick handwritten thank-you note to anyone.
7. Go outside before bed and stargaze for 5 minutes.
8. Try a 1-minute breath technique when you check your email.
9. Offer to help any neighbor with a simple task.
10. Give a genuine compliment to a stranger.
11. Bring full awareness to a mundane chore.
12. Sleep on the ground on purpose for one night.
13. _____
14. _____
15. _____

LEARN

1. Watch a TED Talk on health at lunch.
2. Experiment with any DIY project.
3. Clear your workspace of distractions before you work.
4. Read an article about a subject outside your expertise.
5. Solve a challenging puzzle.
6. Practice a new language for 20 minutes.
7. Star or listen to a new podcaster on a topic of interest.
8. Attend any health webinar or workshop.
9. Pick up a fiction book and read the 1st Chapter.
10. Learn the basics of a new instrument.
11. Read about a historical event.
12. Sketch or doodle on Freeform for 5 minutes.
13. _____
14. _____
15. _____

SPARK

1. List 3 things you are grateful for.
2. Create a vision board.
3. Thank a person you admire.
4. Make a mind map.
5. Write a letter to your future self.
6. Add more detail to your Ikigai.
7. Establish a personal mantra.
8. Write down your strengths and weaknesses.
9. Make a list of people who inspire you.
10. Write down 5 things that make you happy.
11. Take 2 minutes to quickly organize your closet.
12. Text any friend, "Thinking about you & hope you're doing well."
13. _____
14. _____
15. _____

PLAY III: Your Quantum Coach Universe Test

SECTION 1: IDENTIFYING CHALLENGES

1. List any three recent challenges, problems, issues or setbacks you have faced. *Example: Meeting started late, causing me to be behind for my next call and the next meeting.*

2. Describe how these challenges made you feel initially. *Example: Rushed, Impatient, Frustrated*

Challenge # 1: ➡ Made me feel

Challenge # 2: ➡ Made me feel

Challenge # 3: ➡ Made me feel

SECTION 2: REFRAMING CHALLENGES AS UNIVERSE TESTS

3. Now, Reframe these challenges as "Universe Tests," from your Quantum Coach. Write down how each challenge is an opportunity to display your defensive gameplan, resilience, and intentional response. *Example: This is a test to practice patience and I focus on what I can control.*

4. Identify specific reframing strategies you can use for each Universe Test. *Example: It's an opportunity to practice how I can respond and not not react. Remind myself that this is part of life and I'm prepared for it.*

Universe Test # 1: ➡ Reframed Strategy

Universe Test # 2: ➡ Reframed Strategy

Universe Test # 3: ➡ Reframed Strategy

Coach's Tip:

This approach can be applied to every single aspect of your life: health, work, relationships, and personal goals. The key is to consistently remind yourself that setbacks and obstacles are expected components in the game of life.

Echoing the ancient wisdom of Lao Tzu, **"A journey of a thousand miles begins with a single step."**

As this book unfolds, two distinct paths lie before you, each promising its own thousand-mile journey. One offers a step towards clarity and self-understanding, a voyage deep within. The other beckons you towards the vastness of the world, filled with discovery and external adventures.

The choice is yours: which single step will you take to begin this next exciting leg of your health journey?"

"Choose Your Own Health Adventure"

If you're drawn to **Identify Your Inner Voice and True Purpose**, *let your intuition guide you to page 149 in the Spark Chapter.* This section offers a glimpse of self-discovery, offering methods for identifying your life scorecard and an introduction to your avatar. It also introduces spark igniters, tools designed to stimulate personal growth and self-awareness.

If your primary goal is to **Lose Weight and Optimize your Digestion**, *turn to page 55 in the Nourish Chapter.* The recommendations provided in this chapter will help you improve your body composition and jumpstart your metabolism. The concepts that will help you are the Nourish Target, Metabolic Flexibility, Intuitive Eating, EAT Protocol, and the 80/20 Eating Principle.

If you can't wait to **Enhance Brain Function and Mental Clarity**, *navigate to page 255 in the Learn Chapter.* This section is dedicated to helping you diminish brain fog, enter your personal flow zone, and offers insight into achieving a mental makeover. It introduces the principles of neuroplasticity, providing you with tools to sharpen your cognitive abilities and enhance mental acuity.

If you want to learn how to **Increase Strength and Improve your Metabolism**, *run to page 219 in the Move Chapter.* Here, you'll explore the effective 2nd Gear Strategy, delve into the three foundational pillars of movement, review compound and functional movements, and discover the importance of incorporating play into your routine.

For those seeking to **Boost Energy Levels and Overcome Fatigue**, *chill out and to page 119 in the Rest Chapter.* This section will introduce you to the concept of your chronotype and circadian rhythm for optimal sleep. It provides detailed guidance on the RESTED Protocol, designed to optimize your rest and energy and two-minute timeouts, a strategy to rejuvenate and maintain sustained energy throughout your day.

If you want to prioritize **Being Present, Awareness, and Clarity**, *please focus on page 171 in the Connect Chapter.* This section is specifically tailored to enhance your mental fitness and sharpen your focus flashlight, a technique for cultivating mindfulness. You will also explore the happiness gap for true happiness and find your "thrive tribe" to achieve a heightened state of community and support.

CHAPTER 11

YOUR HEALTH PLAYBOOK

1st Half: Game Prep

"Knowing is not enough; we must apply. Willing is not enough; we must do." - Bruce Lee. This famous quote emphasizes the essential gap between knowledge and action. Merely possessing knowledge about what is essential for your health is insufficient; it's the application of this knowledge that truly makes a difference. The transition from intention to action is crucial; it's where real change happens. Without this shift, even the most profound understanding of the seven essential elements remains unproductive, and the willingness to make healthier choices serves no practical purpose.

Owning and understanding this essential health playbook filled with all the winning plays is futile if you lack a strategic game plan to execute them effectively. If you don't try the plays provided at the end of each chapter in this book, I can guarantee they won't be effective. You need to actually perform them to get any benefit.

Without a tailored game plan that takes into account your unique lifestyle, preferences, and challenges, even the most effective health strategies can remain unutilized, much like the winning playbook that is ignored by the head coach.

The key lies in developing a game plan that translates the plays from this playbook into actionable steps tailored to your individual health goals and circumstances. The game plan provided in this chapter acts as a bridge between knowledge and action, ensuring that the valuable insights from the playbook are not just theoretical health concepts but are actively brought to life in a practical, manageable, and sustainable way.

Think about it for a moment: Have you ever found yourself enraptured by an insightful podcast, a thought-provoking documentary, or an inspiring book? Engrossed in each word, you might have felt a moment of understanding, nodding in agreement as you absorbed the astonishing insights and fresh perspectives.

In those moments, the material resonates so deeply that it feels like a revelation, leading you to think, *This is brilliant, that makes perfect sense, and I should do this!* Perhaps the words were so profound that you even paused to jot down notes, with a real intention to incorporate something into your routine or begin taking action in a meaningful way. How effective are the plays provided after each chapter in this book if you don't perform them?

Now think about how often you actually translated those inspiring ideas into action, transforming them into a habit that you sustained over time. If you're like the majority of people, you may have embarked on this journey with enthusiasm but found yourself fading along the way. Remember, action is nothing without intention and intention is nothing without action.

Take Corey, for example. He would often spend his long commutes stuck in traffic, immersed in a health podcast or audiobook. Lost in the brilliance of the interview or story, he would feel a surge of inspiration, only to return home and completely disregard everything he had just learned. Though he never truly applied these recommendations, the act of listening provided a sense of connection to his health goals, even if it was superficial.

Does this scenario sound familiar?

How many times have you tried to make healthy changes, but they didn't last?

I must confess, I've been there. As I revealed earlier in the book, my obsession with learning everything about health has led me to spend hours every day reading, listening, and absorbing knowledge from brilliant minds. Yet, the application of these ideas was where I often stumbled. I might experiment with a new concept for a few days or even weeks, but invariably, it would slowly fizzle away.

The disconnection between understanding and action is not a mere quirk of human nature. There's a logical explanation behind why so many of us struggle with this. It's grounded in the science of establishing a habit, and it's a critical concept for you to overcome your nagging symptoms or reach a level of high performance.

That's why I've dedicated this entire chapter to introducing simple concepts that you can use to integrate your new knowledge from this book today. The crucial aspect is to create a game plan that converts the strategies in the playbook into practical steps customized to your specific health goals and situation.

The game plan outlined in this chapter serves as a crucial link between understanding and action, guaranteeing that the essential elements from the playbook are transformed from mere theoretical health ideas into actionable, realistic, and enduring practices.

Simplicity is Success

In the previous chapters, I presented a wealth of health information, representing the culmination of my years of experience in nutrition, fitness, motivation mindset, and functional medicine. I provided action steps at the end of each chapter to ensure that you can not only easily understand these concepts but also successfully implement them.

Regardless of simplicity, the sheer volume of the information I just presented may cause "paralysis by analysis." As you were reading the previous chapters, you may have been thinking, *How am I supposed to adopt all of these health habits at once?*

I understand that your life is busy, and it would be unreasonable to expect that you could incorporate all of these health ideas into your everyday life without having to compromise other aspects of it.

My approach is to educate and empower, not to demand. I provide reasons, not rules. It's not fair to tell you which habits you should build or which choices you should make. You know what works for your life and circumstances better than I ever could. Instead, I want to equip and empower you with ideas and health strategies so you can make your own choices and do the things you want to do. I'll provide the playbook; you decide which plays will work for you.

This is often where conventional medicine and health coaching programs fall short. They operate under the assumption that they possess the ultimate formula, into which you simply insert yourself, and presto, you get the results you're seeking. Expecting you to conform to a predetermined fixed formula is unreasonable, considering you're a human being, not a calculus equation. The Essential Health Playbook is different.

You Are What You... Repeatedly Do

The holistic method included in this book is successful because it's based on "habit formation through gamification." The foundation of achieving weight loss, boosting energy, improving digestion, or reversing any symptom or illness lies in one fundamental factor: making the right choices. However, altering our daily decision-making is quite hard and might even seem impossible for some.

It's estimated that the average adult makes about 35,000 decisions each day and has somewhere between 60,000 to 70,000 thoughts in one day, with 90 percent of those thoughts being the same as the day before. You may not realize it, but you have fixed rituals and habits, and many of those habits pertain directly to your health.

Understanding how habits are formed, how they can be sustained, and what often derails our best intentions can provide a roadmap for turning those inspiring moments of insight into tangible, long-lasting changes in our lives. This understanding is more than a fleeting spark of inspiration;

it's a tool for building the structures that support our health, allowing us to translate the brilliance of a moment into a lifetime of positive action.

Executing a concept you just learned in this book, a recommendation from a friend, or an idea from that podcast can be a complex process, and success rates can vary widely depending on numerous factors such as the nature of the habit, your level of motivation, support system, and the methods used to implement the change.

A commonly cited model for habit formation is the 21/90 rule, suggesting that it takes 21 days to create a habit and 90 days to turn it into a lifestyle. However, research in this area is mixed, and individual experiences can vary significantly. Other studies suggest that, on average, it takes about 66 days for a new behavior to become automatic. But this can range from 18 to 254 days, depending on the person and the complexity of the habit.

So what's the takeaway here? I want you to establish new healthy habits and change unhealthy habits. Creating new habits is often easier than changing old ones, so we'll start with some things that you're not doing rather than change things you're already doing. Creating new habits can build up your confidence to make healthy changes and can create momentum to change existing habits.

Two Minute Rule

In my clinical experience, the key to success is small changes and incremental improvements, as tiny adjustments can lead to significant long-term progress. I coach my patients to make new habits attractive, easy, and satisfying by using the "Two-Minute Rule."

This concept, coined by James Clear in his fabulous book, *Atomic Habits,* suggests that new habits should be scaled down so that they can be initiated in two minutes or less. This principle focuses on the idea that the initiation of a habit is often more crucial than its complexity.

The Two-Minute Rule for healthy habit formation has proven to be remarkably effective in my coaching programs, and its success is evident across all participants. The premise is simple but powerful: by dedicating just two minutes to a new habit initially, individuals find it much easier to initiate and sustain change. This approach mitigates the feeling of overwhelm often associated with lifestyle adjustments, allowing the individual to focus on consistency rather than intensity.

For example, let's say you want to improve your Nourish score by eating better and hydrating, upgrade your Connect score by incorporating mental fitness into your routine, and power your Move score. This requires some significant changes that can often lead to resistance.

Here's a simple and quick Two-Minute habit approach worth considering:

Mindfulness moments:

Take two minutes each day to practice deep breathing or a brief mental fitness game. This simple and insignificant moment is about establishing the habit.

Water first:

Make it a habit to drink a glass of water as soon as you wake up before any coffee or tea. It's a small step that can encourage better hydration throughout the day.

Healthy snack prep:

Spend two minutes every morning or evening prepping a healthy snack, like putting almonds in a bag or cracking a dozen hard-boiled eggs. This makes it easier to reach for healthier options when you're in need of a quick bite.

Move easily:

Take two minutes at any time during the day to perform a simple movement, such as twenty air squats, a two-minute plank hold, or jumping rope for two minutes. These quick and easy movements cultivate immediate motivation and often lead to much more.

Choose Your Own Plays

You picked up this book for a reason, and perhaps you even chose your own health adventure while reading it. Now you get to select your own health plays. You're the play caller.

If your primary goals are to lose weight and optimize your digestion, you'll want to prioritize the action steps from the Nourish section. If you read this book to increase strength and improve your metabolism, you'll want to prioritize the action steps from the Move section. If you are looking to identify your inner voice and true purpose, the Spark section is first for you.

Got Brain Fog? Start with the tasks in the Learn Chapter. If it's all about boosting energy levels and overcoming fatigue, start with the strategies provided in the Rest Chapter. If your priority is motivation and courage, start with the action items from the Challenge section. If you want to upgrade your awareness and clarity, please focus on the steps in the Connect Chapter.

If you aspire to attain all these health qualities, as I truly hope, then I encourage you to continue reading this chapter. It's packed with essential tools for optimal implementation, presented in a manner that is both engaging and unique!

The Health Game

This essential health playbook provides the strategies and tactics necessary for success. However, having a playbook alone isn't enough. To truly benefit from it, you also need a game to play. Without a game to play, the playbook remains theoretical and unused. It's like having the perfect game plan but never stepping onto the field or court to apply it.

Think about it for a second. Is your daily life that much different than a game?

There are several striking similarities between a sports game and your daily life. Firstly, both require a clear sense of purpose and goals. Just as athletes aim to win a game or achieve specific objectives, you have personal and health goals to strive towards.

Secondly, both involve strategic planning and decision-making. You need to make choices that align with your goals and values, whether it's choosing the right play in a game or making the proper health decisions.

Thirdly, resilience and adaptability are crucial in both contexts. In sports, teams and individuals must overcome obstacles and adapt to changing conditions, and the same holds true for life's challenges.

Finally, teamwork and support are vital in both arenas. Athletes rely on their teammates, coaches, and support staff.

You will need the support of friends, family, mentors, and colleagues. These similarities emphasize the importance of discipline, determination, and a well-defined game plan to succeed both in sports and in the health game.

Changing the Court

Novak Djokovic is one of the greatest tennis players in history. But it wasn't always this way. In the early stages of his career, Novak Djokovic faced multiple challenges. He struggled with health issues, including respiratory problems and asthma, which impacted his endurance. His fitness and dietary habits were also lacking, which hindered his physical readiness for the rigors of professional tennis.

Djokovic also experienced lapses in mental toughness, with occasional struggles in maintaining composure during high-pressure matches, resulting in inconsistent performances. Additionally, he displayed moments of brilliance but lacked the balance and consistency required at the highest level. Despite being a top-ranked player, he had not yet clinched Grand Slam titles due to competition from tennis legends like Roger Federer and Rafael Nadal, intensifying his quest for major tournament victories.

Just like Novak Djokovic faced challenges early in his career, many of us encounter health struggles along our own journeys. We may struggle with issues that affect our metabolism, energy, and endurance, much like Djokovic did with respiratory problems and asthma. Many of us also struggle with our fitness and dietary habits, which often lead to fatigue, brain fog, and digestive issues.

Djokovic realized he needed to address these challenges to reach his full potential. His new training regimen and holistic approach to his game were developed in collaboration with several key individuals, including his longtime coach, Marian Vajda, and other members of his coaching and support team. Together, they developed a new strategic game plan using their own holistic health playbook.

He prioritized physical conditioning, focusing on strength, endurance, and flexibility, making him one of the fittest players on the tour. He also adopted a gluten-free and dairy-free diet as part of his holistic wellness approach, which improved his health and performance. Djokovic honed his mental toughness through meditation and visualization, enabling him to remain composed under pressure.

He strategically adapted his game, emphasizing defensive skills and versatility, which made him a formidable all-court player. Collaborating with a dedicated team of coaches further contributed to his success. His new game plan propelled him to numerous Grand Slam titles and solidified his status as one of tennis's all-time greats. Djokovic's story reminds us that even those who reach great heights face obstacles, and with determination and the right playbook, we, too, can overcome our health challenges to achieve our goals.

The Balls in Your Court

The health game you're playing is no different than Djokovic's. It is always changing and far from predictable. You might be on offense, making all the right decisions with plenty of momentum, and think you're on a winning streak, only to be met with unexpected obstacles. This could be nagging symptoms, fatigue, problems at work, sick kids, traffic, or even larger obstacles such as a recent serious diagnosis, losing a job, or grieving the death of a close friend or family member. These are the moments of defense, the moments that test your ability to pivot, improvise, and adapt and reveal your strength and character.

You may also find yourself on solo missions, like finding your way to a destination after being lost or overcoming the feeling that you're different from everyone around you. Not every aspect of the game is within your control. You'll have periods where it feels like you're benched, unable to influence unfolding events. During these times, the game demands patience and introspection. It offers you a chance to reassess your strategies, learn from your past plays, and prepare for the next match.

As you progress throughout the health game, you gather experience, wisdom, and skills. Smart choices and well-executed plans lead to rewards—be it strength, energy, clarity or achieving your personal goals. But mistakes aren't failures; they're more like errors or penalties that offer lessons. Each wrong play or decision in judgment presents an opportunity to learn, adapt, and enhance your game plan for future challenges.

In the end, this health game is a microcosm of the game of life. Each challenge surmounted, each lesson learned, and each moment of success adds to your personal growth. The ultimate aim isn't merely to "win" but to make decisions that are in alignment with your own personal scoreboard. This allows you to grow and evolve.

***

The Game of Life

The game of life is so universal there have been thousands of years of ancient wisdom that have offered advice on how to play. There are time-honored frameworks and philosophies that were created to establish guidelines, including Ayurveda, Buddhism, Confucianism, Ikigai, Stoicism, and Taoism.

These frameworks not only cultivate an equilibrium in the ever-fluctuating game of life but they are also connected by a universal principle. This principle is not just critical to your health but serves as a pivotal play for integrating the seven essential health elements in your health playbook. By implementing this pivotal play, you can easily distribute your focus across the essential elements—nourish, move, rest, learn, connect, challenge, and spark.

What is the name of this universal principle? *Balance*.

Balance is the state of equilibrium in which all aspects of an individual's physical, mental, and emotional well-being are harmoniously maintained. Balance has also been described as the vital confluence between yin and yang, light and dark, control and surrender, or proactive and reactive.

Balance is about harmonizing one's desire to steer life in a particular direction with the understanding and acceptance that certain aspects are beyond personal control. This balance is not just philosophical but deeply rooted in practical health implications.

When individuals exert excessive control, micromanaging every aspect of their lives, including diet, exercise, sleep, and daily routines, they may inadvertently induce stress and anxiety, counteracting the benefits of their meticulous planning. Conversely, excessive surrender to life's obstacles and uncertainties can lead to a passive approach towards health, where reactive bad decisions may dominate.

Achieving a state of balance is pivotal, where proactive health choices are made with awareness and intention, yet there's a graceful acceptance of life's inherent unpredictability. The art of balancing control with surrender and proactive planning with reactive agility forms the cornerstone of my holistic method of health. Establishing and maintaining balance in your daily habits fosters consistency, paving the way toward achieving elite health. This is the ultimate mission in the essential health playbook.

The winning game plan is...**you**.

The pivotal play is...**balance**.

And the optimal goal is...**consistency.**

Djokovic, Corey, Kelly, Damian, Trevor, Jason, Lucas, Ava, you and I, and everyone else are all striving to discover and maintain balance and consistency in our lives. We all want balance in our social and work time, what we're eating, how we're moving, our sleep patterns, and our headspace. We want to live a healthy life with energy, strength, and purpose and simultaneously savor the pleasures and indulgences life has to offer.

Many people, including myself, are working toward finding and maintaining this balance. This allows us to be proactive and flexible with every twist life gives us. The essential equilibrium is the relationship between being proactive vs. reactive, and in the health game, it is: offense and defense.

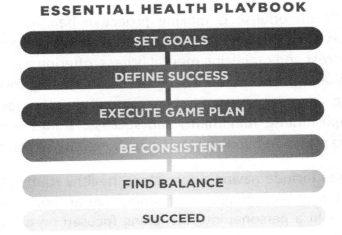

ESSENTIAL HEALTH PLAYBOOK

SET GOALS

DEFINE SUCCESS

EXECUTE GAME PLAN

BE CONSISTENT

FIND BALANCE

SUCCEED

Offense vs. Defense

In a game, offense is simply attempting to score points, and defense is preventing your opponent from scoring. Offense may be controlling the ball in tennis, running a play in football, passing the puck in hockey, or shooting in basketball, typically characterized by speed, agility, momentum, and tactical play.

Defense may be returning the opponent's shots in tennis, blocking shots in basketball, making tackles in football, or intercepting passes in soccer. Defense is typically characterized by discipline, improvisation, teamwork, and strategic play.

Balancing offense and defense involves knowing when to be aggressive and take risks and when to play more cautiously and protect the lead. It requires you to recognize how the game plan is going and to make changes if needed.

Offense

Your life on offense is making proactive healthy choices such as a well-planned food plan, regular movement, proper rest and practicing mental fitness, offering a sense of control and direction. It's based on order, leaning forward, making progress, and creating momentum, described by accomplishment, fulfillment, and success. Things seem to fall into place, and you're moving in an exciting direction.

Examples include having a consistent, healthy routine that's aligned with your goals, being productive at work, making progress in a personal interest, being focused on a project, or being a supportive partner or parent. You're confident, poised, and grateful for having a balance with everything that is important to you.

Defense

Your life on defense is different. This reactive dimension involves developing resilience and flexibility, allowing you to adjust your game plan in response to changing circumstances. There's chaos; you're on your heels, improvising, and generally in a state of uncertainty and pressure. You've lost your balance, and maintaining consistency becomes difficult.

This looks like your routine being interrupted due to frustrating symptoms or unforeseen issues with your health, dealing with a nagging injury, unexpected travel, dilemmas with friends or coworkers, putting out fires at work, being distracted by the noise in the news or social media, feeling disconnected with your partner or kids, and making bad health decisions.

Your Default Day

Take a moment to think about your typical day. You wake up, go through your morning rituals, and prepare for the day. You may have a very organized plan you need to follow to be productive, or it may be a general idea of the things you'd like to accomplish. It may involve many responsibilities for your family and maintaining your home, and there are requirements and deadlines for work. It may be associated with hobbies or projects or have a strong social basis.

Regardless of your exact routine, what you might not realize is that you're operating with a subconscious game plan driven by ingrained habits. This proactive stance is your offense, the framework within which you strive to manifest productivity and a sense of accomplishment.

Momentum Shifts

Now, let's shift the lens to those unpredictable disruptions that interfere with your routine. These diversions could range from minor nuisances—a persistent headache or an uncooperative printer—to major hindrances like a sick child or an urgent work-related crisis. These disruptions steer you away from your original game plan, requiring you to pivot and adapt. This reactive stance is your defense and seeps into your days whether you like it or not.

Reflect on this—can you remember a single day when everything proceeded exactly as you anticipated? No unexpected changes, no work crises, no barking from the dog, no smog, no social or family drama, and no health challenges? A day when everything was perfect?

Certainly not, as the concept of perfect days is a fallacy. We occasionally need to change our plans, make small tweaks, or make significant shifts in our decisions. The momentum shifts of our days, oscillating between offense and defense, is a continuous, recurring theme in the game of life.

What I've gathered from decades of working with patients is that this shift between offense and defense is inevitable; it's a universal human experience. Yet, many are shocked or disheartened when they find themselves shifting gears into a defensive mode. I've observed patients externalizing blame, extreme stress, and pointing fingers at others or at circumstances, even when these are far beyond their locus of control. This is a loss of balance.

I can personally attest to this; the decade following my life-altering accident was marked by a similar mindset. This reactive posture had a direct impact on my health, and I've seen it reverberate similarly in the lives of my patients, often causing them to ignore their goals, abandon their new healthy habits, and lapse back into unproductive patterns. In my professional experience, this derailment often occurs because of an absence of—or failure to execute—their game plan.

So, if you know that defensive scenarios are not a matter of "if" but "when," doesn't it make sense to have a plan in place? The best defense is a good offense. If you develop such a game plan, you will experience greater consistency in maintaining your healthy habits and life balance. The conscious development of both offensive and defensive strategies is the play for balance.

Your Game Plan

Every player needs a playbook and a game plan. They have objectives to guide their decisions and make necessary changes if needed. They are detailed and structured strategies that outline specific actions, tactics, and goals to be followed in order to maximize their chances of success and overcome challenges in a game or competitive situation.

Life is no different. Each one of us requires a strategic health playbook—our "game plan" to establish our habits and integrate our health goals. This helps us forge ahead when our game plan is effective and enables us to improvise, adapt, and adjust our strategy when our game plan falls short.

Balancing offense and defense in this context means taking a proactive approach to your day, your health, and your personal life while staying open to new possibilities and adjusting your approach as necessary. It involves finding the right balance between being in control and letting go, being prepared and flexible. This facilitates balance and consistency and is a total game changer when applied correctly.

PREPARE YOUR OFFENSE

Let's create your own offensive and defensive health game plan. Below is how I've taught my patients to use the PREPARE routine for their health goals. It involves finding the right balance between being in control and letting go, being prepared and flexible.

PRESENCE: **The Pre-Game Huddle**	Every morning, you have two choices: Continue to sleep with your dreams or wake up and accomplish them. Start your day with a moment of silence before plugging into the Matrix. No phone, work, computer, or TV for at least ten minutes. Aim for thirty minutes if possible. The idea is to take a moment to take inventory of yourself by asking three questions. How did I sleep? How do I feel? Are the decisions I made the previous day in alignment with my goals? This is the perfect time to practice mental fitness, train your mind, and write a daily health intention.
REINFORCE: **The Playbook**	Reinforce functions as your offensive and defensive playbook. By regularly reaffirming your goals, you're mentally rehearsing your offensive health goals and the steps needed to achieve them. Affirmations also provide you with the defensive mindset needed to proactively tackle challenges and opportunities. Use encouraging words, thoughts, or mantras that affirm and reinforce your daily intentions. This is your commitment to direct your energy where you want it to flow for the day.

PREPARE YOUR OFFENSE

ENVISION: **Scouting the Field**	Envision allows you to "scout the field" by imagining the path to your goals and foreseeing possible obstacles. By visualizing, you're preparing yourself to make progress by creating a mental image of your offensive health decisions succeeding. This prepares you for the game ahead, increasing your chances of accomplishment. Visualize yourself performing these intentions throughout your day. Envision also allows you to visualize how you're going to respond to inevitable setbacks. Watch yourself in different unplanned situations, and you'll be amazed at how easily you can execute your defense strategy.
REINFORCE: **The Playbook**	No game is won without proper conditioning. Movement ensures that you are physically prepared to execute your offensive plays. Starting your day with physical activity kick-starts your body and mind, creating momentum that is a key element in living life on offense. Prioritize moving however you enjoy. This can be in the gym, yoga, running, biking, walking, hiking, or stretching. This will activate vital hormones and signals in the brain required for optimal performance.

PREPARE YOUR OFFENSE

ABSORB: Updating the Playbook	Constantly learning and acquiring new skills is essential to stay ahead in the game. Reading can be viewed as the "video review" or "playbook update" that fine-tunes your offensive strategy. It's an opportunity to enhance your knowledge and adapt your tactics, ensuring that you're making continuous progress toward your goals. Set a floor goal to spend at least four minutes reading a book that inspires you or on a topic that interests you. Don't read the news or read for work. This is a time to cultivate the spark inside you and nurture other interests.
REFLECT: The Game Film Analysis	The act of reflecting and journaling provides an opportunity to review the "game film" of your life. It offers a moment to reflect on what plays are working, what's exciting, and how you can improve your strategy moving forward. Journaling is a powerful method to clear all the thoughts, ideas, concerns, and emotions we all experience daily. This is your opportunity to do a "data dump" or "cognitive cleanse." It will help you become more present in your daily life. Journaling has no fixed rules; it can be writing, art, or self-talk, requiring only your willingness to engage with your own thoughts at your own pace.

This routine embodies the essence of living an examined and intentional life. Each component serves to set up a strong game plan for your day, enabling you to take proactive action toward your health. (Make sure to check out the Essential Health Toolkit which includes a PREPARE cheat sheet).

Floors and Ceilings

"You do not rise to the level of your goals. You fall to the level of your systems." James Clear wrote this in his book *Atomic Habits*. This means that if you are having trouble changing your habits, the problem is not with you but with your method.

The concept of setting a "ceiling" and "floor" for a specific health goal is a powerful and effective strategy for success in the Lazarus Method. The "ceiling" goal symbolizes the ultimate, most challenging version of what you hope to achieve. The "floor" goal represents a minimal, non-negotiable task that can be easily accomplished.

A ceiling goal is an ambitious, optimal achievement in relation to a specific health goal. While reaching this goal can be difficult, it provides a clear target to aim for. Ceilings are what you're aiming for when you're on offense. However, focusing solely on ceiling goals and not realizing when to pivot to your floor goals often results in disappointment, anxiety and frustration, leading you to give up on your goals completely.

A floor goal serves as a consistent, low-effort task that gives you a sense of accomplishment, confidence, and success, even if it's relatively small. Use floor goals when you find yourself on defense. The crucial point is that it helps to maintain momentum and avoid the feelings of failure that might occur if only high-level ceiling goals were set.

By pairing a floor goal with a ceiling goal, you can make consistent, achievable progress while keeping sight of your ultimate target. The accomplishment of a floor goal can provide the encouragement and motivation to work towards the ceiling goal.

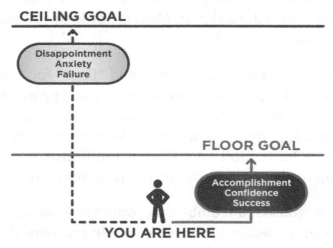

FLOOR & CEILING GOALS

SET YOUR DEFENSE WITH FLOORS

This defense game plan not only aids in maintaining your health goals but also proves extremely beneficial when unpredictable circumstances arise, which they most inevitably will. They provide an opportunity to maintain consistency in your healthy routines without requiring substantial effort or time.

Consider scenarios such as traveling or having that unusually busy day that disrupts your regular health routines. You might not be able to follow your PREPARE routine, apply your EAT plan correctly, move appropriately, or get proper sleep. Setting a simple floor intention that day will allow you to sustain your healthy routines amidst changing or challenging circumstances.

The key is that even though these tasks are less demanding than your ceiling goals, they still contribute to your overall health and maintain the momentum of your wellness journey. Let's dive into more details and examples of Move, Nourish, and Rest to illustrate the power and flexibility of this concept.

Move: Boost Strength	**Ceiling:** Apply all movement pillars six days per week for 30 minutes using three compound movements and hit 3rd and 4th gear for 15 minutes twice per week. **Floor:** Do twenty air squats and ten push-ups per day, anywhere and at any time, which is a more manageable task, but still contributes towards the overall goal.
Nourish: Lean Up	**Ceiling:** Apply all steps in the EAT plan, remove all sugar, gluten, seed oils, fried foods, and desserts, and only eat fresh, organic vegetables. Eat (.8 grams/per lb of body weight) of clean protein between noon and 6 pm for two weeks. **Floor:** Apply two steps in the EAT plan and avoid the red foods in the Nourish Target for a couple of days. Next time you eat at a restaurant, substitute fries with a salad if ordering a burger. These small but meaningful changes help steer dietary habits in the right direction.

SET YOUR DEFENSE WITH FLOORS	
Rest: Reduce Fatigue	**Ceiling:** Sleep for eight hours every night for two weeks by applying all the steps in the RESTED and TIMEOUT protocols and take all foundational supplements. **Floor:** Apply two steps in the RESTED protocol and head to bed just fifteen minutes earlier than usual. This can feel more realistic and less intimidating, and over time, these fifteen minutes can be gradually increased until you reach your ideal sleep duration.
Nourish: Improve Digestion	**Ceiling:** Consume only the green foods in the Nourish Target, follow the fullness formula and hydration pillars, and take digestive enzymes, berberine, L-Glutamine, DGL, and 60 billion CFU's of probiotics daily for three weeks. **Floor:** Avoid the red foods in the Nourish Target, apply one component in the fullness formula, drink two glasses of water, and take a probiotic every day for three days.

Over the years, I've seen a remarkable pattern unfold among individuals who adopt my floor and ceiling game plan. Almost always, these determined individuals not only meet their floor health goals but also consistently strive to surpass them. They push their own boundaries, elevate their own standards, and ultimately raise their own bar. This is where balance is achieved, and consistency is strengthened.

Kelly's Comeback: Changing Uniforms, Changing Lives

Kelly's story was classic. She was always on defense from the moment she woke up. She would wake up exhausted, grab a coffee, and scroll her phone as long as she could before she had to get her young kids ready for school. As soon as they were gone, she'd muster up the little energy she had to clean the dishes and house and would sit down periodically to rest while she inevitably scrolled her phone. She'd do her best to walk in the late morning but often found herself behind and abandoning exercise completely.

I explained the game of life to her and revealed how she was playing her game. "Imagine life as a soccer game. You're one of the players on the field, but it seems like you're limping onto the field wearing the wrong uniform without any of the necessary gear—no cleats, no shin guards, nothing."

She looked intrigued but puzzled, so I continued.

"See, the uniform and cleats represent the basic tools and strategies you need to restore your health and life. We now know what your functional medicine imbalances are and how to fix them, but you need a game plan that works for you. Right now, you're missing some essential equipment. How can you expect to perform well when you're not adequately prepared?"

Her eyes widened as if a light bulb had just switched on. I went on to elaborate.

"Not only are you improperly dressed for the game, but you also lack a game plan. You're running haphazardly around the field, reacting to wherever the ball is kicked rather than proactively positioning yourself to seize opportunities or defend against challenges. This represents your reactionary approach to your health and life. Instead of having a plan to reverse your weight gain, fatigue, or bloating - you're merely reacting to external circumstances, spreading yourself too thin, and draining your energy."

I could see her nodding with tears again, connecting the dots.

"After just five minutes of frenzied, aimless chasing, you find yourself giving up, arms folded, scowling, and disillusioned. You've essentially sidelined yourself. No longer an active player, you have become a spectator in your own life, a victim of circumstances, rather than an empowered individual capable of change."

I could tell it was a moment of revelation for her. I planted an important seed of hope and said with complete confidence, "The good news is, the game isn't over. It's only the second quarter. You can call a timeout. You can change your uniform, put on your cleats, and re-enter the game with a renewed strategy."

"The key to turning things around is to evaluate your scorecard, define your goals and success, set your floors and ceilings, use PREPARE for your offense, focus on progress, and get a little better every day. With the right coaching, tools, and mindset, you will shift from being a hopeless player on the field to becoming a star player."

We sat in a moment of shared silence, allowing my explanation to sink in. Kelly finally spoke, her voice tinged with a newfound determination, "I'm soo ready to change my uniform and my game plan."

And so began Kelly's transformative journey, one in which she took proactive steps using the strategies listed in this playbook. It wasn't going to be an overnight change, but the first step had been taken, and sometimes that's the most significant part of the journey.

Kelly was a testament to human potential and perseverance, reminding us that when we consistently show up and give our best, even if it's only a small step, we're capable of achieving great things.

You, too, can harness this magic, your inner spark, to go beyond what you thought was possible. So, set your game plan, target your ceiling on offense, shift to your floor on defense, and watch as you surpass your own expectations!

2nd Half: Keeping Score

You've established your values, defined personal success, set your health goals, and created your game plan. You've applied the PREPARE strategy and know how to apply your offensive and defensive strategies. So how do you know how you're doing?

In every game, there are those who triumph and those who fall short. This is often determined by the final tally - be it points or goals. The ultimate aim is to accumulate a higher score (or lower for golf) than your competitor. Bravo, you're now bestowed with the title of the victor. Here is your trophy.

Not so fast. Before you start giving yourself high fives, there's a twist. The points are not uniform; they vary from person to person. The techniques and actions that score for one player might not work the same for you. With such a discrepancy in scoring, how can we determine who comes out on top?

Many might contend that the winner is the person who is most attractive, physically fit, wealthy, joyful, and widely adored, while the rest are deemed less fortunate. Second place, it seems, is just the first among the defeated. This is the game that we all play, whether we realize it or not. But there's a better game to play.

Consider this: *What if you implemented your very own unique scorecard?*

You can create a personal tally that reflects your own perception of success, a ledger that keeps track of your individual achievements, each point being a reflection of the decisions you make every day. Every day, we often find ourselves at the crossroads of decisions, questioning which path to pursue.

- *Should I order this or that from the menu?*
- *Will I tell my partner how I feel or just keep it to myself?*
- *Should I slow my scroll and get back to work?*
- *Should I buy this snack for my kids, or is there a better option?*
- *Should I wake up or sleep for 15 more minutes?*
- *Should I wear this outfit, or will I be judged?*
- *Do I head to the gym or just go tomorrow?*
- *Should I head to bed or watch one last episode?*
- *Do I take this supplement or not worry about it?*
- *Should I have another drink or stop now?*

Balancing Act: Internal and External Scorecards

Life pushes us to evaluate our choices constantly, and the metric we use to gauge success in these instances significantly impacts our overall health and happiness. I explain this concept as your "Internal Scorecard" and your "External Scorecard."

Internal Scorecard

The internal scorecard is a reflection of one's deepest-held values and beliefs, serving as a barometer for how authentically and consistently these values are applied in daily life. It's a personal metric, often unseen by others, that gauges success based on individual standards of integrity, purpose, and fulfillment. This internal assessment focuses on healthy choices, self-improvement, personal growth, and inner satisfaction rather than external validation.

The internal scorecard is about introspective evaluation. It is the measurement of success based on your true values, beliefs, intentions, personal aspirations, and the authenticity of your spark.

Examples include opting for a healthier lifestyle, prioritizing meaningful conversations, showing vulnerability, investing time and energy in supportive relationships, making purchasing decisions based on your values, or pursuing a career or hobby aligned with your values.

These are just a few of the thousands of decisions that we all make all the time. It revolves around self-improvement, growth, and alignment with your current goals. This scorecard asks:

- *Am I making quality health decisions?*
- *Am I becoming the person I wish to be?*
- *Am I making progress towards my personal goals?*
- *Am I living true to myself and values?*

External Scorecard

In contrast, the external scorecard is governed by societal norms and expectations, measuring success by how well an individual conforms to these collective standards. It often manifests in the pursuit of recognition, status, and material success, influenced by cultural benchmarks like financial status, appearance, possessions, career achievements, or social popularity.

Examples include where you live, what you're wearing, your vehicle, your social circle, how many followers you have, and maybe even your kid's school or sports teams. The list goes on and on. Success here is defined by others' approval and by cultural benchmarks. While the external scorecard is more visible and socially reinforced, it may not always align with one's personal values, leading to a potential conflict between societal approval and personal authenticity. It prompts us to ask:

- *Do people like or respect me?*
- *Am I financially successful?*
- *Will people judge me?*
- *Am I fitting in?*

Personal Health Score

Balancing these two scorecards is a nuanced and ongoing process, requiring individuals to navigate between external expectations and their own internal values to achieve holistic health.

When the Internal scorecard is well understood and placed at the forefront of your decision-making process, the external scorecard no longer appears as a perplexing maze but rather as a map with clear paths. You become able to sift through the inevitable pressures, select what aligns with your true self, and discard what does not.

External validation still holds value, but it ceases to be the sole determinant of your choices and actions. Your health goals become your game plan, allowing you to navigate the outside pressures with a newfound sense of ease and confidence.

In this process of self-realization, the external scorecard transforms from a distracting tyrant dictating your actions into a tool to use at your discretion. You can see all the distractions and outside expectations from a new perspective. You may choose to agree to some while defying others because you now have a clear gauge of what aligns with your internal scorecard. You realize that just because someone else is winning doesn't mean you're losing. And just because someone else is losing doesn't mean you're winning.

Personal Score

Do you ever wish life came with a personal dashboard, a control panel that displayed your personal performance metrics just like a game does? A game's scoring system is simple. It's numerical, objective, and offers immediate feedback. Goals scored, points accumulated, rebounds made, penalties committed—each action either elevates or diminishes your performance, clear as day.

But when it comes to the game of health, how do you keep score? Of course, modern technology provides us with an array of wearable devices capable of tracking your sleep, steps, vitals, HRV, and even your ketone and blood sugar levels. These devices give us insight into our physical health and provide invaluable feedback on our lifestyle choices.

But is there a method to track our personal performance beyond the realm of data? A way to gauge our alignment with our values and aspirations? How do we measure the daily decisions that don't influence our blood sugar but might steer the course of our lives?

The Four Quarters Strategy for Personal Health Score

If you rely on the power of your internal scorecard, you'll have a method to track, evaluate, and enhance your performance in tangible ways. There are some universal strategies in the essential playbook to help you design your personalized performance metrics.

Have you ever had a day when you felt you were on defense the entire day? A day where everything seemed to go wrong from the moment you woke up? I think we've all had those days. The Four Quarters Strategy can be viewed as a health game plan strategy, considering the handful of obstacles, surprises, and momentum shifts that each day presents. Here's how the rule reinterprets life's daily journey:

	REINTERPRETS LIFE'S DAILY JOURNEY	
Morning (First Quarter)	Think of this as the start of your game. It's your offensive game plan where you use the PREPARE method and set your initial intentions, goals, and basic strategy. Even if you encounter unexpected challenges or setbacks, remember that there's a whole game ahead with plenty of opportunities to turn things around. **Action Steps:** Use the PREPARE Playbook **Score:** Rate yourself from 0-10 in your health choices and performance for the morning using your internal scorecard.
Midday (Second Quarter)	This is the phase when you still have good energy and can take a quick moment to recall your initial moves and adjust your strategy as needed. No matter how the game starts, you have the chance to pivot, change your plans, or introduce new ideas. You can ask for help from other team members, just like calling for backup in a game, to overcome the obstacles you face. **Action Steps:** Use the TIMEOUT Challenge **Score:** Rate yourself from 0-10 in your health choices and performance for the 1st half using your internal scorecard.

	REINTERPRETS LIFE'S DAILY JOURNEY
Afternoon (Third Quarter)	Now, you're in the thick of the game. You might be completely energized from offensive success, or your energy might be low from all the tiny changes you made. Despite any hiccups or unforeseen circumstances that have occurred, the afternoon is your opportunity to remind yourself of your daily intentions and the health goals you've established and are working toward. **Action Steps:** Use the RISE & RELAX Plan **Score:** Rate yourself from 0-10 in your health choices and performance for the third quarter using your internal scorecard.
Evening (Fourth Quarter)	This is the end of the daily game. If you're an early chronotype, your energy may be low, but it's also your opportunity to reflect on your internal scorecard and the day's wins and losses. It's time to begin to rest, recharge, and reflect on the day. Every game, every day, ends, but the lessons learned are invaluable for future plays. This is a great time to prepare the game plan for the next day. **Action Steps:** Use a Gratitude Journal, and the RESTED Protocol **Score:** Rate yourself from 0-10 in your health choices and performance for the entire day using your internal scorecard.

The Four Quarters Strategy, like a well-played game of offense and defense, emphasizes resilience, adaptability, strategic thinking, and collaboration. Every quarter of the day is a new round, a fresh chance to respond to challenges, make meaningful decisions, and adapt your game plan as necessary. Even the wrong moves or poor decisions become opportunities to learn and improve your game plan.

Progress, Not Perfection

This chapter provided a game plan and scoring system based on your values, health goals, and personal definition of success. The power of this playbook is that it offers a realistic, practical, and proven strategy to achieve health. It's based on my "progress, not perfection" philosophy which emphasizes gradual improvement and setting realistic goals, shifting the focus from seeking unattainable perfection to appreciating consistent, incremental progress.

It's about balance, consistency, and habit formation through gamification. It's incredible how fast you can reverse nagging health symptoms by applying these proven guidelines. It's also remarkable how fully integrating the essential health elements into your everyday routine can lead to a profound health transformation and a major upgrade in every aspect of your life.

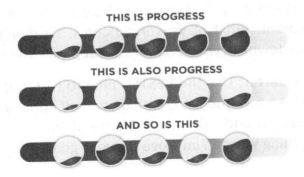

THINK PROGRESS,
NOT PERFECTION.

THIS IS PROGRESS

THIS IS ALSO PROGRESS

AND SO IS THIS

Let's say your current health goal is to lose body fat and gain muscle. This is what a potential game plan may look like.

1st Quarter: Set your offense strategy using the PREPARE plan.

Wake up and check in with yourself before connecting to anything that distracts you from your goal. Remind yourself of your goal: lose fat, and gain muscle. This will allow you to be clear of the goal and visualize yourself making the correct choices that day but allow for flexibility if something comes up. Set a hard daily challenge if you're up for it. (Example: Hit 15,000 steps today)

Execute your nourish and move game plan with clarity and excitement by using the Nourish Target, EAT Plan, Movement Pyramid, and 2nd Gear Strategy. Your Offense Plan (ceiling goal) is to follow these guidelines as planned.

Your Defense Plan (floor goal) is not to eat any red food in the Nourish Target, apply at least 1 in the EAT Plan, and move any way you can for at least 20 minutes. Simple.

2nd Quarter: Take a moment in the day to assess what quarter you're in and to check in with your game plan. Apply the TIMEOUT plan and adjust if necessary.

3rd Quarter: Reflect on your choices that day without judgment. What plays worked and what didn't? Write them down anywhere. Learn and apply for the next day.

4th Quarter: Use the RESTED plan to rest and recover and take a moment to remind yourself about your goal to lose fat and gain muscle. Write down one win and one thing you can improve for your goal.

This is a simple and basic game plan that does not take a lot of time. It allows you to make progress toward your health goals. It's about balance, consistency, and habit formation through gamification. It's incredible how fast you can reverse nagging health symptoms by applying these proven guidelines. You can even start by simply integrating a few of the plays at the end of the previous chapters.

It becomes exciting when you can apply other plays provided in the essential health playbook. Integrating the essential health elements into your everyday routine can lead to a profound health transformation and a major upgrade in every aspect of your life. If you want more guidance, the Essential Health Toolkit and our coaching programs provide a detailed game plan worksheet designed for each individual, and the health results are immediate.

CHAPTER 12

GAME TIME

In Chapter 2, I offered you an option. You were presented with a simple choice. Are you going to take the red pill, use the reactive, conventional approach, take a pill for every ill, and just get by to survive, or are you going to select the blue pill, use the Lazarus Method in the Essential Health Playbook, reach your full potential, and strive to thrive?

If you're reading this, I congratulate you. You chose wisely. The blue pill you selected allowed us to take a meaningful journey together as we reviewed a game plan for the functional, proactive approach for elite health and performance. You have a playbook, and a method you can use to achieve your health goals.

Take a moment and think back about all the health concepts, strategies, and tools we covered together in the previous chapters. The "2nd Gear Strategy" emphasized the importance of Zone 2 training for enhancing mitochondrial function and improving metabolic health, adaptable even for busy schedules.

In tandem, the "80/20 Eating Principle" offered a flexible approach to diet, accommodating life's fluctuations while maintaining nutritional balance. Complementing this, the

"EAT Approach" allows for personalized diet management, focusing on aspects like meal timing, quantity, and type. We also discussed the "Flow State," which enhances concentration and creativity, thereby reducing stress.

The "Focus Flashlight" concept taught you to direct and stabilize your attention, much like holding a flashlight, to foster greater awareness and mental control. The "Four Quarters Rule" breaks down your day into strategic phases, enhancing adaptability and self-reflection.

In parallel, "Metabolic Flexibility" underlines the body's ability to efficiently switch between energy sources, essential for sustained energy and better blood sugar control. "Mental Fitness" is physical training but for the mind, focusing on present-moment awareness to handle life's challenges with greater clarity.

The "Nature Pyramid" provided a structured way to connect with nature, benefiting both your health and perspective. The "PREPARE Protocol" established a comprehensive daily routine encompassing self-reflection, intention setting, mental preparation, physical energization, personal development, and introspection.

The "Quantum Coach" concept reframes life's challenges as opportunities for personal growth and resilience building. Alongside, the "RESTED Protocol" offers a step-by-step guide to achieving rejuvenating sleep, which is critical for optimal energy. The book also introduced the "Thrive Tribe," a supportive health community for shared learning and encouragement in health goals.

I introduced you to the "Ultimate Wonderdrug," underscoring its extensive benefits from mood enhancement to longevity, an essential factor for holistic health and performance, and shared a new way to assess your choices using your own "Internal Scorecard." These were just a few of the key plays to help you beat fatigue, boost strength, fix your gut, and achieve elite health.

My Spark is To Empower You

At the beginning, I conveyed my mission in writing this book. It was to offer more than cutting-edge health concepts, diet plans, personal training plans, meditation guidance, personalized supplements, and functional medicine protocols. I wanted it to be different. I wanted it to be the book that was handed to me when I was confused about my health and looking for answers.

I wanted to connect with you on a profoundly personal level. I wanted my words to resonate within you, sparking a fire of motivation that manifests in tangible improvements to your health. It was my sincerest hope that the meaningful conversations we'd had, page by page, would inspire you to embrace a new way of approaching your health so you'd be inspired and excited to take your first step.

Now that we're nearing the end of our journey, I realize your head may be spinning from all the health information. That is normal and well... expected. In fact, it's not only expected; it's part of the process. Being healthy in our modern world can be challenging without a playbook, a game plan, and a coach. But it shouldn't be. Let me assure you once you begin implementing the concepts from each chapter at your pace, you will see how easy and effective it can be.

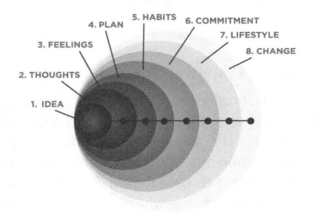

**CHANGE TAKES TIME,
ENJOY THE PROCESS.**

1. IDEA
2. THOUGHTS
3. FEELINGS
4. PLAN
5. HABITS
6. COMMITMENT
7. LIFESTYLE
8. CHANGE

Moving into a New Playing Field

Here's a part of the playbook that you might not like to read, but it's essential. You're responsible for making some simple changes. Like a player on the sidelines poised to enter the game with a new playbook, you are on the brink of a health journey. This journey will shift you from your present lifestyle to a state of being defined by health, happiness, strength, resilience, and balance.

This yearning for transformation is universal and ingrained within your being, urging you to improve and evolve. I've witnessed it myself, observed in my patients and I know that you can do the same. When it comes to your health, accept the things you can't change, have the confidence to change the things you can change, and have the knowledge to know the difference. Read that again.

It is important to understand that every change, no matter how insignificant it may seem, triggers a ripple effect of possibilities, reshaping your reality in unforeseen ways. Even tiny lifestyle changes amplify your confidence and optimism, unlocking a world of untapped potential and enticing you to step outside your comfort zone.

First, let's address the obvious fact: *Change is a challenge.* All of us resist change to a certain extent, and that resistance often leads to paralysis. I personally resisted change for years and I witness resistance every day with patients in my practice.

Change often seems elusive, hovering just out of reach despite our sincere desire for it. You might experience sporadic bursts of motivation that fizzle out just as quickly, leading to unfulfilled attempts to health. It can feel disheartening, perhaps even leading to a sense of failure. I've experienced this, as have many of my patients, and my hope is that the strategies outlined in this book will assist you in managing it.

However, it's essential to examine these experiences to understand what truly drives change and growth. Is it merely willpower, or do factors such as previous programming, social conditioning, environment, trauma, or socioeconomic disparities play pivotal roles? If health transformation were purely logical, wouldn't you just seek quality information that automatically leads to growth-oriented actions? The answer is likely no.

In the grand journey of life, it's important to note that we change through four significant paths.

First, when pain or discomfort sears through your existence, pushing you to the brink, you change because you absolutely must. It becomes a path of salvation, a way to salvage the fragments of your shattered self. **It's when you hurt enough that you have to.**

Secondly, when knowledge seeps into your mind, igniting sparks of wisdom, you transform out of sheer desire, fueled by the newfound enlightenment. **It's when you learn enough that you want to.**

Thirdly, when you've been endowed with enough resources, opportunities, or love, you finally transform because you have the means to do so. The abundance you receive paves the way for your evolution. **It's when you receive enough that you're able to.**

Lastly, when you bear witness to such magnitude of greatness or beauty, it inspires you to transform. The universe reveals such awe-inspiring spectacles that it stirs the soul and provokes change. **It's when you witness enough that you are inspired to.**

Which one of these do you resonate with?

The initial catalyst for my health transformation was the first path mentioned above. The pain seared through my existence, pushing me to the brink, and I had to make a change. As I grew older and accumulated valuable insights and wisdom on my health journey, I started to realize the profound impact of the other paths. Amazing changes will occur when you gather knowledge, receive resources, and witness others make transformations.

My mission in writing this book is to offer you the power of paths two, three, and four: **learn enough that you want to, receive enough that you're able to, and witness enough that you are inspired to.**

Quieting your mind, being curious, and tuning into your internal scorecard is key. It demands stillness, a gentle journey inward where you navigate past distractions and listen to your inner voice. It's not about making drastic changes overnight; it's about acknowledging and honoring your authenticity. Life is a dynamic journey, and each decision either brings you closer to your true self or pushes you further into inauthenticity.

Starting this health journey is an act of courage and commitment. Disconnect from distractions, become present, and take stock of yourself. This proactive approach can help you meet your true self, your spark, without waiting for external solutions.

Captain Badass Dad

Remember Captain Dad Bod, aka Corey? Stress, quick fixes of fast food and cocktails, and his sedentary lifestyle led him down a dangerous path quickly. He knew conventional medicine would only make matters worse with pills, so he passed on the red pill and hesitantly chose the blue pill.

"You have the look of someone who's seen this before," Corey said, gesturing to his physique.

"I've seen some amazing transformations," I replied, "and you can be one of them." In my practice, I've encountered countless middle-aged men who, almost without realizing it, have allowed their health to deteriorate. I knew exactly what to do.

Corey and I discussed his symptoms, lab results, and goals. Once he saw his personal dashboard, he was clear on his weaknesses and vulnerabilities. We reviewed the Lazarus Method game plan integrating offense and defense, setting his game plan, and pursuing "achievement belts" as milestones in his journey. He was such a sports fanatic that the game of life, personal scoreboard, and four-quarter strategies made perfect sense to him.

"I've never thought about my days like that," he said.

Then, I presented him with his white belt, symbolizing a clean slate and the beginning of his transformation.

"You're kidding, right?" Corey chuckled as I handed it over.

"I'm serious, brother," I replied. "This is your journey, and every step deserves recognition. Plus, it'll make the whole experience more engaging and fun."

Corey wore a skeptical expression but agreed to play along. "All right, Sensei. What's the first mission?"

We reviewed his white belt tasks, and he replied, "That's it? That's simple!"

Two weeks passed, and Corey came back eager for our meetings. At each meeting, he'd update me on his progress and the little missions he'd completed to earn his next belt.

"Slept seven hours a night for a whole week!" he'd exclaim, or "Haven't touched fast food for a month!"

"That's amazing, considering how you started. You've definitely earned the green belt," I'd respond. "Ready for the next challenge?" I would give him knuckles, smiling from ear to ear. I was stoked because I was watching inspiration right before my eyes.

"Hit me!" he'd yell with his deep, powerful voice.

His work was also improving. His coworkers, who once pitied Corey's perpetual tiredness, now sought his advice on how they, too, could achieve such a turnaround. And on the weekends, on the golf course, Corey had gone from trailing behind his friends to outdriving them—all the while playfully rubbing it in. He never missed an opportunity to talk sh*t.

The belts became a game for him, a visual tracker for his progress. His family got involved, asking him every week what color belt he was on, turning it into a collective journey.

"Even my kids are into this," he told me during one session. "They keep asking, 'Dad, when are you getting your purple belt?'"

"And what do you tell them?"

"That I'm making progress every day! I'm on offense, drinking less, following your personal food plan, doing your mental fitness, and even starting to lift weights every day. I even have abs under this dad bod. I'm going for that purple belt!"

"Honestly, I thought that the scorecard and four-quarters plan was kind of a joke at first," he then admitted. "But they helped me break down my program into smaller, manageable tasks. I always had something to aim for, and it was a blast!"

"Corey, you've come so far, not just in executing your game plan, but in fundamentally changing your life. What's the biggest change?"

"My dad bod completely evaporated, and it feels like I've unlocked a part of myself I didn't know existed. And to think I almost passed on this program."

When Corey reached the twelve-week mark, the atmosphere in our meeting was charged with anticipation. We reviewed his journey and discussed the improvement in his lab results and his final Health Dashboard. The numbers would speak volumes.

The results were a medical and personal triumph. Corey lost thirty-four pounds, and his body fat percentage plummeted from 38 percent to 24 percent. It wasn't just a superficial transformation; his internal health metrics had seen a drastic improvement too. His blood pressure, once a lurking concern, normalized.

The inflammatory markers, often the silent heralds of chronic diseases, returned to normal ranges. His A1C levels—a critical indicator of long-term blood sugar control—fell from a pre-diabetic 6.4 percent to a much healthier 5.8 percent. Astonishingly, his liver metrics indicated a near-miraculous self-healing, alluding to a detoxified system and better metabolic control.

But this wasn't just about numbers on a scale or a lab report. Corey's achievements extended far beyond that. His sleep quality had drastically improved, allowing him to wake up refreshed and focused each day. His dietary habits underwent a fundamental change—gone were the fast foods and sugary temptations, replaced by a balanced, nutrient-dense food plan.

He had his own movement routine, not as a chore but as an enjoyable daily ritual. This resulted in not just a physical transformation but a psychological one as well. He radiated a newfound calm and confidence, as if years of burdensome stress had been lifted off his shoulders.

The auditory symbol of Corey's transformation was his laugh—a sound that had shifted from weary and forced to one that emanated from the deepest wellsprings of genuine joy. It was the laugh of a man who had come to appreciate his body, to experience life unrestricted by physical or emotional constraints. It was the sound of true health, as radiant and infectious as his newfound vitality.

And these changes didn't go unnoticed. Corey's family, friends, and co-workers were spellbound witnesses to his transformation. No longer the panting dad huffing and puffing at soccer games, he was now the exuberant, athletic figurehead in community activities. Whether it was playing sports with his kids or racing up flights of stairs, Corey did it with a zest that was palpable, often breaking into a massive grin that said it all.

Kelly's MVP season

And Kelly? Well, wait until you hear about Kelly's second-half comeback. Remember her and my pep talk about her uniform and lack of a game plan? Our next meeting was memorable, to say the least. She walked into my office with a curious smirk.

"Kelly, what's up? How are you feeling?" I asked her.

"I can't even describe it. I just feel...terrible," she said.

"Terrible? What the heck happened??" I questioned.

"Well, I did everything you recommended and..."

"And what?" I replied anxiously.

Kelly paused, her eyes narrowing as if to arrange her thoughts. She stared at me for what felt like thirty seconds, and then all of a sudden, the biggest grin appeared, and she laughed like I hadn't heard her before.

"Total game changer!" she beamed. "I totally followed your food plan to a T, and it's crazy what happens when you eat real food. I haven't missed one single day of your personal training plan. I'm training my mind, setting my intentions, and, most importantly, hitting my floor goals when I'm on defense. It's like I've become a whole new player!"

"A whole new player?" I was so relieved she was messing with me. "You mean a whole new person!"

"It's like I've been lifted out of a fog," she explained. "I've lost twelve pounds, and my bloating is virtually non-existent. I used to feel so drained in the afternoon, but now I'm like a supermom throughout the day. I didn't realize how transformative that would be and how quickly. I'm more productive, more present with my family, and genuinely happier."

"Was it the game plan we discussed?" I asked.

Kelly looked contemplative for a moment. "You know, I think the biggest shift has been in my mindset. I've been doing the mental fitness activities you recommended. Now I understand what my game plan looks like, what my goals are, and how my health ties into that.

"Before, I was aimlessly going through the motions—eating mindlessly, skipping exercise, ignoring my body. Now, I have a game plan, and everything I do is aligned with that. My kids, my relationships, and my health—they're all interconnected."

As I sat there listening to her, profound happiness washed over me. I didn't want to interrupt her flow of words; her story was too important, too real. As she continued to speak, my mind wandered back to my own journey—a reflection of sorts. There's an overwhelming joy that comes from transforming a life marked by illness, fear, and despair into one of health, achievement, and prosperity. I couldn't quite put that feeling into words, but at that moment, I didn't have to. I understood it deeply, and I felt an immense sense of relief and happiness for her.

"So, are you ready for more?"

Kelly took a deep breath, her eyes shining with a kind of clarity that can only come from personal revelation. "Are you kidding me? I feel like I've found my spark. I want to keep going every single day!"

So, it wasn't just about changing her "uniform," metaphorically speaking. Kelly transformed into the star player she had always aspired to be, not just on the health and fitness field but in the intricate game of life itself. She often revisits that one eye-opening photograph taken in Hawaii, the one that initially jolted her to confront her reality.

Initially, it was the appearance of her in her bikini that shocked her, but as she progressed through the program, she came to understand that the true source of her unhappiness lay far beneath the surface.

Kelly realized she had been chasing what I introduced in the Connect chapter as the "happiness gap." It's that elusive space between where you are and where you think you should be, often defined by societal metrics or external judgments. She had been operating on an external scorecard driven by cultural definitions of success, beauty, and happiness. It was a scorecard that always made her feel inadequate, no matter how hard she tried to measure up.

However, once she recalibrated her values and priorities in line with her genuine self, the transformation was almost electric. Her motivation didn't just improve; it skyrocketed. What used to feel like uphill battles—maintaining the proper food plan, consistent movement, and mental fitness—suddenly became part of her flow state.

Executing her game plan went from being a series of chores to a fulfilling, even exhilarating, set of daily activities. The goals on her personal scorecard now aligned with her deepest values, providing a profound sense of purpose that made every step in her journey feel not just possible but deeply rewarding.

In making this internal shift, Kelly wasn't just patching up symptoms or chasing transient goals. She was undertaking a complete overhaul of her life philosophy, guided by a new internal scorecard that she crafted for herself. This isn't just about achieving good health or losing weight; it's about embracing a holistic version of success that encapsulates all the essential health elements in the Lazarus Method.

Corey's and Kelly's amazing stories reiterate that it is never too late to take charge of one's health. Everyone, irrespective of their past, can chart their own path toward health and happiness. Their transformative journey started with a mere seed of belief and plenty of self-doubt.

Their transformation transcended mere dietary changes or temporary exercises; it represented a complete paradigm shift in their understanding of health, wellness, and personal potential. They boosted their energy, increased their strength, fixed their gut, and found clarity in their life. It was more than a physical metamorphosis but also an emotional and spiritual awakening. They didn't just become healthier in body; they were enriched in mind and spirit.

The Lazarus Method Community

I have also shared the uplifting stories of Jason, Natalia, Trevor, Ava, and Damian, each detailing their unique experience using this playbook. Thousands of additional individuals have undergone remarkable health transformations, and I wish I could spotlight each unique experience.

Throughout this book, I have introduced a range of intriguing health concepts and provided practical strategies to integrate them into your life, along with various choices for your own health adventure. Recall in Chapter 2, where I presented the metaphor of choosing between two pills.

Are you going to take the pill that leads to the reactive, conventional approach, and just get by to survive?

Or...

Are you going to take the proactive path of energy, strength, resilience, and reach your full potential?

My intention is that, by now, the correct choice should be crystal clear.

If, at the start of this journey, you found yourself leaning towards the red pill rather than the blue, don't worry – it's never too late to alter your course. This moment can be a turning point, a chance for you to embrace the modern, holistic approach laid out in this playbook.

The path you choose from here on is entirely up to you. Every step forward is a step towards transformation, and the direction you take now is a decision I leave in your hands.

~~Final~~ First Game

As we end this memorable journey together, it's my hope that you're now empowered with a wealth of knowledge, insights, and strategies to make the health choices to increase energy, gain strength, improve digestion, enhance mental fitness and champion your health and performance.

Look, let's be honest. If you think this book—or any health book, really—is the magic playbook that fixes everything, you're setting yourself up for disappointment. This book has unique concepts and a method that will upgrade your health, but it's not a magic wand.

Remember, the winning game plan is you, the pivotal play is balance, and the optimal goal is consistency. The real game changer is how you apply it. Reading about health is great, but don't confuse it with actually doing something about it. So, if you find yourself chasing different health books or scrolling on social media hoping to stumble on the ultimate "cheat code" or "life hack," just know this book is a kickstarter, not a finish line. The real action starts when you put it down and actually start living these concepts. Knowledge is power, passion calls the play, and your game plan allows you to apply it.

~~Complacent~~ Contentment

You now have the knowledge and, hopefully, a newfound passion to pull that switch. You may even feel ready to begin "chasing" your dreams. This is a great feeling, as this new energy is a powerful catalyst for positive change. Leverage this energy, but be mindful of the "happiness gap." You don't need to chase anything.

Embrace where you are at this very moment. Being content and grateful with your current circumstances serves as a potent antidote to this cycle of endless "chasing." Contentment allows you to value the present moment, appreciating what you have rather than focusing on what you don't.

Contentment should not be confused with complacency. While complacency involves a lack of desire for improvement, contentment serves as a balanced platform from which to build. It encourages us to appreciate our achievements and the resources we have at our disposal while still maintaining an open mind toward personal growth and improvement.

By operating from a place of contentment, you can work on improving your habits without falling into the draining cycle of perpetual "chasing." If you're examining your life and feeling that your progress isn't up to par, it's important to step back and view the broader perspective. Often, we get caught up in the minutiae of our daily struggles and setbacks, losing sight of the overall journey and the milestones we've already achieved.

By "zooming out" and considering the big picture, we can gain a clearer understanding of where we truly stand. This wider view helps us appreciate the health plays we've successfully integrated and the momentum we've created. It allows us to recognize which health habits we've neglected, without judgment of failure. It's about seeing beyond immediate success and obstacles and acknowledging the long-term evolution of our lives.

The essential health playbook provides you with the emotional bandwidth to engage in incremental improvements without sacrificing your current happiness, creating a virtuous cycle of contentment and growth.

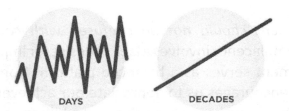

IF YOU'RE LOOKING AT YOUR LIFE AND YOU DON'T THINK YOU'RE MAKING ENOUGH PROGRESS.

ZOOM OUT.

DAYS   DECADES

Unopened Playbook

So, before we part ways, I want you to take one last journey with me. A journey into one of the most promising landscapes you could imagine. A landscape of excitement and potential.

Imagine standing now in the silent and longest aisles of the grandest library you've ever known. The air is rich with the scent of time-weathered pages and the wisdom and whispers of stories past. As you browse through the countless book aisles, you find yourself drawn to a specific volume, bound in familiar aspects of laughter, excitement, pain, triumph, loss, and promise.

It's a captivating-looking book titled, *"Your Life."*

You skim through the first chapters, each brimming with people and characters you love, forgotten about, become distant from, lost, and found. Each page echoes with your voice, your heart, your experiences, your memories, and your entire personal history.

And then, you arrive at the present, the chapter titled *"Now."*

You glimpse forward, and the pages are pristine, untouched, unwritten, waiting for the upcoming adventures in your days yet to come. That's where you stand at this very second. The ending of this book may be near, but your story is far from over. It's time to pick up that pen, embrace the promise of the blank page, and start crafting the next healthy chapter of your life. You're not merely writing a story—you are the story.

As you turn the page on this chapter, may you write your own saga—a life complete with health, charged with vitality, anchored in strength, and filled with purpose, gratitude, and balance. A life where you nourish your body, move with excitement, rest soundly, learn continually, challenge your limits, connect meaningfully, and your spark beams bright, illuminating all of the brilliant opportunities ahead. Start now.

CREATE YOUR PERSONAL HEALTH PLAYBOOK

THE LAZARUS METHOD PROGRAM

My mission in writing this book wasn't just to share health knowledge but to motivate you to improve your health and transform your life. I sincerely hope that by sharing my personal health struggles and the heartfelt stories of my patients, you feel inspired and equipped with a foundational playbook to embark on your own holistic journey toward health.

Sharing my expertise and insights of The Lazarus Method with you has been an honor and a privilege. Writing this book presented its own set of challenges, particularly as I navigated the delicate balance of offering guidance without delving into specific nutritional, supplement, mindfulness, and fitness protocols. While writing may not be my strong point, each health element proved so rich in content that I felt I could write an entire book on each one.

The Essential Health Playbook isn't just a book—it's a roadmap for a transformative lifestyle. It's a proven method that's been honed and refined through countless success stories. I'm confident that, armed with this knowledge, you are fully equipped to embark on your health journey, just like those who have found success before you.

In Chapter 2, I encouraged you to pause, reflect, and consider which essential health element resonates most with you. I even challenged you to give yourself a grade in each element and note which recommendations could be most beneficial for your health journey.

The image below is a great visual representation of how you can assess your strengths and vulnerabilities in each health element. Evaluate yourself on a scale from 0 to 10, where 0 is the lowest and 10 is the highest, for each health element to identify your focus areas in this book and determine your next steps using the Essential Health Toolkit.

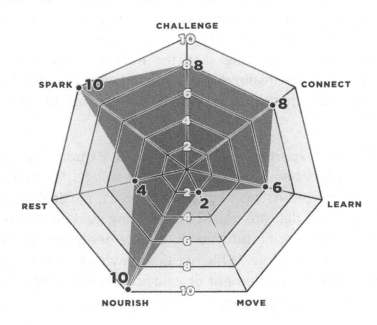

These are the first steps for your game plan. It's important to know where you are and where you want to go. Understanding your current health status is the perfect pre-game strategy before executing your health game plan. Remember, every improvement, no matter how small, is progress. Every step forward, regardless of its size, is a victory.

Personal Invitation

This is where "The Lazarus Method" comes in, not as an imposition but as an invitation. I have offered you an evidence-based method and provided simple plays to practice for each essential health element. I've outlined a collection of valuable tools and offered a proven game plan for holistic health.

However, while these tools and plays may make the journey smoother, it's you who will write the remaining chapters of your story. Your choices, habits, and actions will decide the game's twists and turns, ultimately shaping your journey toward better health. You ultimately decide how your story and the game unfolds.

If you'd like a coach to help create and implement your personalized playbook, know that I'm here to assist. While the strength of the hero is crucial, remember even the strongest of heroes had a wise mentor.

The Lazarus Method programs combine the wisdom of experience with cutting-edge strategies, guiding you not just to reach but exceed your health goals. Through this program, you will receive personalized guidance and become part of a vibrant, supportive community.

We offer a range of health and wellness programs tailored to individual needs, from self-guided approaches to fully personalized coaching. The Train, Master, and Maintain programs provide comprehensive tools, including eBooks, video content, meal planners, mental fitness instruction, game plan worksheets, fitness routines, and access to exclusive events and a supportive community.

Personal Health Mastery

Our Master Program is a transformative health experience strategically tailored to your individual goals and unique physiological makeup. It encompasses comprehensive blood chemistry analysis, microbiome evaluations, as well as genetic and methylation aging assessments. It includes everything you need to personalize the ideal health and performance program specifically for you.

It combines state-of-the-art functional medicine protocols with advanced biotracking technology to precisely measure your metabolism, enabling me to design a personalized playbook and game plan focused on optimal body composition, enhanced energy, and longevity strategies.

The effectiveness of this program lies in its ability to identify your specific strengths and weaknesses in the essential health elements. Participants receive a personalized plan detailing their optimal food plan, exercise schedule, supplement regimen, mental fitness prescription, rest routine, and individual challenges, which empower them to achieve their health objectives immediately.

To learn more, check out our website and take advantage of the complimentary "Essential Health Toolkit," which is the perfect companion to "The Essential Health Playbook." It provides you with simple implementation strategies to use right away and start seeing results immediately. Our online platform also has a wealth of complimentary resources tailored to your individual needs.

Start by taking our quiz—it's a tool designed to help you identify the areas where you need the most support. As you explore the platform, take advantage of the resources we offer. This is your opportunity to dive deeper into the concepts I introduced in this book.

I'm excited to see how your journey unfolds, how you conquer challenges, and how you celebrate victories. Please share your wins and successes with us on social media. The path to optimal health and performance is yours for the taking, and I'm here and ready to guide you every step of the way.

Review Request

Thank You for Reading, The Essential Health Playbook!

In the journey towards better health and wellness, every step counts, and your decision to read "The Health Playbook" is greatly appreciated. Your commitment to exploring new playbooks to health and performance is not just a personal triumph but a valuable contribution to a broader conversation about holistic health.

My mission has always been to offer education and inspiration through my unique approach. Your feedback is a crucial part of this mission. It's your experiences, insights, and perspectives that help shape and refine the tools and strategies presented in this book.

Your Opinion Matters

Your thoughts are more than just feedback—they are the guiding lights for future editions of this book and the development of new ones. Your input is invaluable in making sure that the content remains relevant, practical, and transformative.

Share Your Thoughts

Please consider taking a couple of minutes to leave a review on Amazon. Your review doesn't just help me; it helps others who are on a similar journey to find and utilize this resource. Share what you loved, what resonated with you, and even areas where you see room for improvement.

Here's how you can leave a review:

Scan this barcode and share your thoughts, experiences, and feedback.

About the Author

Dr. Ryan Lazarus has been a patient as long as he's been a doctor. At age 18, he faced a near-death experience in a devastating sports accident that crushed his organs. For years, he grappled with life-altering health issues, including Type 1 diabetes, digestive failure, and immune problems, each day presenting a new battle to be fought. He's navigated through a maze of trauma, illness, confusion, setbacks, and despair, often questioning the purpose and meaning behind chronic illness and suffering.

Enduring years of hardship and struggle, he not only developed resilience but also a deep-seated passion for helping others. Dr. Lazarus's journey of overcoming pain through self-guided exploration in functional medicine, nutrition, and fitness led him to devise a unique, holistic health strategy. This approach, born from his personal experiences and the gaps in traditional healthcare, integrates functional medicine, personalized nutrition, fitness routines, sleep and stress strategies, supplement prescriptions, and mindset optimization.

Through trial and error, research into various healing paradigms, and relentless determination, he gradually crafted a method that works for everyone. As he began to utilize this tailored system with each of his patients, he was astounded by its replicable success across a diverse range of cases. This became the genesis of The Lazarus Method, an integrative approach to health.

As the founder & clinical director of the Lazarus Method, a pioneering health program, he imparts his essential health elements, drawing from his extensive credentials as a board-certified functional medicine practitioner, nutrition specialist, and personal trainer. Holding a master's in nutrition and a bachelor's in exercise science, his unique approach is based on habit formation through gamification, which has transformed the lives of thousands of patients.

Dr. Lazarus resides in the small town of Danville, California, where he lives with his wife Natalia and their two children, Cienna, aged 14, and Easton, aged 12. Completing their family tribe is Charlie, their 10-year-old Golden Retriever who shares the family's love for travel and the outdoors.

An adventurer at heart, Ryan devotes his time and energy to exploring the United States national parks and journeying across international borders. These family expeditions serve as both a learning experience for his children and a source of inspiration for himself. He has a profound love for the beach and the mountains, where he finds a unique sense of tranquility and connection with nature.

Made in the USA
Monee, IL
10 May, 2024